Thrill Killers
A True Story of
Innocence and
Murder Without
Conscience

ii

Dear Reader,

We proudly present the newest addition to our internationally acclaimed true crime series of *Real People/Incredible Stories*. These riveting thrillers spotlight men and women who perform extraordinary deeds against tremendous odds: to fight for justice, track down elusive killers, protect the innocent or exonerate the wrongly accused. Their stories, told in their own voices, reveal the untold drama and anguish behind the headlines of those who face horrific realties and find the resiliency to fight back...

Gripping and terrifying, this true story begins as Amy Shute and Jason Burgeson are saying goodnight outside a Providence club after a night of dancing. Suddenly, ten gaping eyes with evil intent fall on them. In **Thrill Killers: A True Story of Innocence and Murder without Conscience** by Ray Pingatore and Paul Lonardo, five men had been prowling the streets looking for victims. They force the young couple into the backseat of a car and drive them to a remote area - in this chilling *In Cold Blood* like story of innocence and savagery.

The next time you want to read a crackling, suspenseful page-turner, which is also a true account of a real-life hero illustrating the resiliency of the human spirit – look for the New Horizon Press logo.

Sincerely,

Dr. Joan S. Dunphy
Publisher & Editor-in-Chief

Real People/Incredible Stories

Thrill Killers
A True Story of
Innocence and
Murder Without
Conscience

By

Detective Raymond Pingitore, M.S.
and Paul Lonardo

New Horizon Press
Far Hills, NJ

Pingitore, Raymond and Lonardo, Paul. Thrill Killers: A True Story of Innocence and Murder without Conscience.

Cover design: Wendy Bass
Interior Design: Susan Sanderson

Library of Congress Control Number: 2007934016

ISBN 13: 978-0-88282-291-4
ISBN 10: 0-88282-291-8

New Horizon Press books may be purchased in bulk quantities for educational, business, or sales promotional use.
For more information please write to:
New Horizon Press
Special Sales Department
PO Box 669
Far Hills, NJ 07931
1-800-533-7978
Email: nhp@newhorizonpressbooks.com

www.newhorizonpressbooks.com
Manufactured in the USA

Author'r Note

This book is based on the experiences of the authors and reflects their perception of the past, present and future. The personalities, events, actions and conversation portrayed within this story have been taken from memories, interviews, research, court documents, letters, personal papers, press accounts and the memories of some participants.

In an effort to safeguard the privacy of certain people, some locations, individuals' names and identifying characteristics have been changed. Events involving the characters happened as described. Only minor details may have been altered.

Contents

Part 1

Portent of Evil

Introduction

For me, the evening of June 8, 2000 was like any other. I completed another shift and my mind was still at work when I left for the day. That night, even while I was with my daughter, I was monitoring the radio anticipating the next call. I had taken her to skating practice and then for a quick bite to eat at her favorite Chinese restaurant. Even this I couldn't fully enjoy. It seemed I was only truly content when I was working. If I kept my mind occupied with my job, I didn't have time to think about any problems in my own life. It really was like I was living two different lives. One in which I was lost and unhappy, and another, in which I was too busy to think about it. Even as the cases piled up on my desk, there was at least some comfort in knowing that, no matter which file I picked up, there was someone who was worse off than me. I don't know that the misfortunes of others necessarily made me feel any better about my own predicament, but it certainly helped me see that I was not alone and not as disconnected from everyone as I sometimes feel. It also made me think that because I had become as absorbed as I do in my work, solving a criminal case or getting involved in someone else's violent domestic situation, I am actually able to do for others what I could not do for myself in my own private life - establish some kind of control.

However, something had me feel unusually anxious all day. I was unable to concentrate at work. I grabbed a file, read several pages and minutes later could not recall what I had just read. Opening file after file, I found myself reacting the same way. I could not concentrate. What was wrong? I was not tired. No more than usual, anyway. I just had this weird feeling that something bad was about to happen. This was not so unique in my line of work. Still, it was not only work that troubled me. I was worried about those in my personal life, and thought it might have something to do with my wife or daughter. The truth is I'm not sure what set off my anxiety. It could have been a recent comment from my wife, a look she gave me or it could have been work neglected. Maybe it was some kind of vibe that another officer or a suspect gave off that made me ill at ease. Mind you, that was not unusual, either. I felt uneasy a lot around the police station. Many of the cases I worked on were violent ones. Most of the time, I dealt with them and moved on. But whatever it was, that evening I was especially apprehensive, and I couldn't shake the feeling.

I had never heard the name Gregory Floyd, or knew anything about any of the other four young thugs who were prowling the city of Providence that night with guns and homicidal intent. But that was about to change.

Many cities today are peopled with groups of individuals from vastly divergent ethnicities, experiences and lifestyles. Providence is no exception. However, the paths of two very dissimilar groups of young people were about to cross with violent consequences, and while it is arguable that much could have been done to avoid the tragic turn of circumstances that followed, the one thing that I can say with confidence is that it was the choices made by the five young men, which attributed absolutely and singularly to what happened to Amy Shute and Jason Burgeson.

Chapter 1

Making Plans

Jason had begun making plans for the night several days before. All week he had looked forward to the evening, and he was very excited to have gotten his truck back from the repair shop the day before, just in time for his date with Amy. In the few short months he had known her, he could not have been happier. That afternoon, he called Arnold Banker, a friend from high school, and asked him if he wanted to go to a dance club later on. He explained that it was techno night at the club, and Arnold knew that Jason loved the fast-paced dance music. Banker was interested as well. Even though it was only Thursday night, it was the unofficial start of the weekend and the city was usually jumping with activity and people.

And girls.

Besides, Jason was a good friend and Banker liked hanging out with him.

As soon as Banker hung up his call with Jason, he phoned Stephen Cone and asked him if he wanted to meet Jason in Providence that night for what was sure to be a good time and some laughs. The three young men had gone to high school together. They were only two years removed from Apponequet, but with all the changes that can happen during college and later in life, they understood that there was no way of knowing just how close any of them might remain with each other. This was an opportunity they thought might not come again. So the plans were solidified. Banker got back in touch with Jason and arrangements were made to meet at a major intersection downtown at 9:45 P.M.

It turned out to be a reunion of sorts, because Jason had already spoken with Jennifer, and he was counting on her being there, perhaps even with Cathy. But the girls had a surprise planned for him. They had convinced Natasha to join them, and all three of them were going to a bar together. After going through a brief period where they had not been on the best of speaking terms, they had recently reconciled their friendship and they wanted Jason to see them all together again. They knew their reconciliation was something that would make him very happy. Jason was absolutely delighted in being around all his friends, who likewise enjoyed his fun-loving, free-spirited personality.

Jason had also extended an invitation to his sister, Kellie, to join them in the hope that she would show up to share in the dancing and fun. Although Kellie was six years older than Jason, their closeness was never hindered by the difference in age. As a child, she begged her parents for a little brother to play with. When Jason finally came along, she was elated.

When Kellie and Jason were small, they played together all the time. However, when they grew older and Kellie began dating, Jason had a difficult time sharing his sister's attention with someone else. Kellie's solution was to bring her kid brother with her. Through a good portion of her teenage years, Jason tagged along on all her dates. As a result her curfew was earlier, but she didn't mind because she could not stand to see her brother crying when she walked out the door without him. As might be expected, the package deal did not always go over so well with some of the young men who asked her to go to dinner or the movies. But these were the boys that she broke up with quickly. If they couldn't accept Jason, they were not for her.

As the siblings got older and their lives became busier, Jason was hardly ever home. As a teenager, he was either at school, working or doing something fun. When Kellie visited her parents, she always hoped that Jason would be there. If he was, she was so happy to get to talk to him. They chitchatted about everything that was going on in their lives at the time. And with Jason, it was always something. When he talked about his hopes, ambitions and dreams when he became older, he wanted to do radio and said he would be famous. Kellie laughed and told him that he was crazy, but she knew he could do anything to which he set his mind. Sometimes he asked his sister's advice on a variety of topics, though mostly it was about girls - that all consuming mystery of teenage boys. She was readily available for counsel to him, the way she was there for him when they were younger, protecting him from kids who were mean to him.

There were also many times that she gave advice without him asking for it, and he replied, "Kel, I know." She didn't want him to think she was being a pest; she just wanted to be sure that he was safe all the time because he was so trusting of everyone.

Two days earlier, on Tuesday, June 6, Kellie had driven to her parents' house right after work. As always, as she turned down Southworth Street, she eagerly looked ahead into the driveway to see if Jay's SVU was in the yard. It was, and she became instantly excited about the opportunity to spend some time with her brother. Soon, she was sitting on the bed in Jason's room and talking to him while he was on the computer. They talked mostly about his new girlfriend, Amy, and he told his sister how much he liked her. But Kellie already knew that.

Kellie liked Amy a lot as well. What she liked most of all was how happy Amy made her brother. Amy was very pretty and Jason was very proud to have her as a girlfriend.

One day, when Amy was at the Burgeson's house, Kellie and her husband, Nick Surdis, stopped by after lunch. While she was visiting her family, Jason took Amy for a ride on his four-wheeler that afternoon. They rode around for about an hour in the sand pits near the house, and when they came back they were both covered with mud. But they were laughing and smiling. As Amy looked down at her feet, she joked, "Honey, you wrecked my sneakers. Looks like somebody owes me a new pair." Jason's face immediately lit up and he looked at his sister with a little gleam in his eye. Kellie knew exactly what that glow was about. She had called him *honey*, and it just pleased him so much. "Ok," he told Amy. "I owe you a pair of sneakers." Then they got cleaned up and ready to go out. Before they left, Jason invited Kellie and Nick to get something to eat with them.

"Thanks," Kellie said, "but we just ate."

"Too bad," Jason said. "You can just come to hang out with us if you want." Then Jason mentioned that he was going dancing with Amy and some friends on Thursday night. He said they were planning on going to a club in Providence.

"Kel," Jason said, "you and Nick should come with us."

"Yeah," Kellie agreed, "that would be fun."

"You've got to see me dance. I've gotten really good."

"I can't wait."

The two of them had never been out together at a club, because Jason was only twenty. However, now that the bar they liked had an "eighteen and over night" on Thursdays, she had an opportunity to see him dance in a setting other than a wedding or some other family function. And Kellie was excited about it. When she left to go home she told Jason, "Call me about Thursday night."

"I will."

"Later."

"Later, Kel."

Kellie actually intended on going out with Jason that night, but he never called her. She figured he had changed his plans without notice. Or maybe he had just forgotten. He was young and carefree, and Kellie thought nothing of it at the time. She figured he was probably excited about going out with Amy and showing her off to all of his friends. Kellie could not blame him for that, either. But she later regretted not spending that extra time with her brother, though she had no way of knowing what would occur that evening.

Amy Shute had an ongoing, mutual relationship with Jeffrey Harper. For a period they were boyfriend and girlfriend, but that exclusivity was a thing of the past. From the time they began dating six years prior, things had certainly changed between them, but from the age of fifteen to twenty-one, everything changes. Working her way through college and really being out on her own for the first time, it naturally followed that Amy wanted to see what else the world had to offer. This included dating other boys, which was difficult for Harper, who still had strong feelings for Amy, as she did for him. But he accepted this altered state of affair, choosing to continue an unconditional friendship, which Amy was more than happy to extend back to him. He was hoping that one day when she was ready it would be him she chose to be with. The last thing he wanted was to alienate her, and although he did not know how long it would be before any decision was reached, he knew one thing; she was worth waiting for. So they remained close, speaking just about every day and seeing each other often.

On Thursday, June 8, Harper spoke with Amy at about 5:00 PM, soon after she had returned home from her job as a receptionist.

Amy was three semesters short of earning a psychology degree from the University of Rhode Island. The previous January, she decided to take some time off to work and earn a little extra money so she could complete her education. In April, she learned that she had received sufficient financial aid to return to URI in the fall, and was very excited about going back. Meanwhile, Amy thought she would spend the rest of the summer saving money and having fun.

Amy told Harper about her plans to go out that night with Jason and some of his friends, and she asked Harper to meet up with her at the club. Even though Harper had to be at work very early the next morning, he wanted to see Amy and could not refuse her.

Gregory Floyd and Kenneth Day were already downtown. They had taken the bus from Broad Street, by St. Joseph's Hospital, and rolled into the city by 5:15. Minutes later, they were in very familiar territory along Weybosset Street. The roommates planned to hang out in Providence. They mentioned playing some pool at a café.

Both Day and Floyd had troubled lives, and they were no strangers to run-ins with the law. North Carolina authorities were interested in catching up with Day after he skipped out on pending drug charges there before moving back to Rhode Island. He was practically a fugitive while Floyd was on probation, for which repeated violations of its conditions had recently obliged a district court judge to issue an active court warrant for him. The two were already dancing on the razor's edge of long-term incarceration, and they invited further trouble when Day insisted that Floyd take his gun with them.

Floyd concealed the .40 caliber Smith & Wesson in the small of his back, behind the black leather jacket he wore. As Floyd was both under twenty-one and a felon, he could not legally own a gun. And although this was not the first time that Floyd was carrying firearms when he went into the city, it would be the most notable.

Actually playing pool was the furthest thing from their minds. That became apparent when, as they were chilling in front of the pizzeria, a stranger suddenly approached Day. He was a tall, skinny man who said he was looking to buy crack. Even though Day did not have any drugs to sell, he observed that the guy had quite a bit of cash on him. This interested Day very much. Day told the man to go wait down an alley while he went to get "the stuff," and then told Floyd about his plan to rob the guy. Floyd was all for it. The potential for a lot of easy money appealed to him as well. A strung-out dude alone in an alley was no match for two thugs with a gun. It did not get any easier than that, but when they returned to the alley they found that their quarry got away, disappearing somewhere down the other side of the open-ended alley. They were not about to give up so quickly, however. With the taste of money and a thirst for robbery in their throats, they went looking for the man. Figuring he may have gone to Kennedy Plaza to make a score, they headed down Union Street toward the bus depot.

Around 5:30, Harry Burdick had been dropped off at the bus station in Pawtucket by his girlfriend, Elizabeth Zatkoff. He had some fun of his own in mind with his friends in Providence. Once downtown, he hopped on a trolley that shuttled him to the East Side's fabled Thayer Street, alongside the Rhode Island School of Design and Brown University. There, he met up with a friend with multicolored hair who he knew from the training school, who was hanging out at a convenience store with Harry. The three of them shared a joint, a few beers and some heroin. Another friend, Susana, whom he knew from Traveler's Aid Society when they were both homeless, met up with Harry after he had returned to the Kennedy Plaza bus station several hours later that night. Other friends Kenneth Day and Gregory Floyd approached Harry as he was talking with the girl at the bus terminal.

"I'm gonna get some money tonight," Floyd told Burdick, then brandished the gun he had been concealing, as if to indicate that something a lot heavier would be going down before the night was over. He wanted to know if his burly acquaintance was interested in joining them. "Where are you going?"

Harry said he was waiting for his bus that would take him back to Pawtucket when Floyd told him about the "custy" with the wad of cash that they were looking to jack. A custy was what they called anyone looking to score some drugs for money. They were usually more desperate for a fix, so they were willing to pay a little bit more. And they always carried plenty of cash.

After looking at the silver-barreled, black-handled .40-caliber, Burdick was immediately drawn in. He did not need any further convincing to stick around to be a part of robbing someone.

Elizabeth, upon hearing this exchange and seeing the gun, knew nothing good could come if it. She begged Harry not to go with Floyd, but he did not listen to her.

Soon, the three of them, Floyd, Day and Burdick, had returned to the usual hang out spot on Weybosset Street, by "the wall," hoping that the "custy" would return to the alley near the pizzeria. He never did. But there was plenty of quarry and plenty of night left for these predators. They never entirely gave up on their idea of locating custy, either.

Chapter 2

Meeting in Providence

L akeville, Massachusetts is virtually due east of Providence, less than twenty-five miles as the crow flies. But Arnold Banker and Stephen Cone did not have wings. They were driving together in Banker's car and had to take I-195, with its perennial construction delays, into Providence. Not surprisingly, they were late for their rendezvous with Jason and Amy at the intersection of Westminster and Weybosset, arriving at about 10:15 PM. They were happy to see each other, and from there, Banker followed behind Jason's white SUV into the nearby parking lot of the restaurant on Weybosset.

Jason, Amy, Stephen and Arnold stayed at the restaurant for about an hour, the boys catching up and getting to know Amy as they chatted, ate and watched some patrons playing cards. They left for the bar together, all of them piling into Jason's SUV, Banker in the back seat behind Jason and Cone behind Amy. They left Banker's car behind the restaurant parking lot. The time was around 11:30.

Across town, Floyd, Burdick and Day stepped up their criminal efforts, and now there were five of them on the prowl in the city. Day had used one of the few working pay phones to page Raymond Anderson, who was with his girlfriend, Florence Sander, at her home in Providence. Sander was also the mother of their infant baby.

When Anderson called back, Day asked him to pick them up at the pizzeria to help in their search for a guy who had approached him with a roll of cash and looking to make a buy. Day knew Anderson drove a dented car. He explained that the search would be easier in a car, and from what he had glimpsed there was plenty of money for everybody.

Anderson, who had been smoking pot and arguing with his girlfriend most of that day about his lifestyle and his friends, was happy to get away. He immediately got in touch with his friend, Samuel Sanchez.

Sanchez had been beeping Anderson for a couple hours already, looking to smoke up, but Anderson did not answer his page. He knew what Sanchez wanted, and he did not have any weed to spare for anyone else. Now, Anderson needed him. He was anticipating some kind of trouble going down, and he did not want to be implicated by his car. Besides, if there was plenty of money for four of them, as Day said, then there would be enough to split five ways. He told Sanchez that there were a lot of people downtown, and informed him about the opportunity that Day had encountered to make a good score. Sanchez said he was down for that, and picked Anderson up at 11:00.

Day seemed intent on finding the custy or robbing someone else that night, but when he spotted Anderson in Sanchez's old car and they all jumped inside, the game suddenly changed, even if they were not exactly sure of the rules or how it was going to be played. They would figure that out as they went along.

The gang was all together now. All of them had plenty in common. Already, there was a real sense that what they were about to undertake that night would bring them together in ways that they could only begin to imagine.

They shared a feeling of restlessness and discontent that was more than a product of boredom, and went far beyond the usual rebelliousness of youth. It was repressed anger on the verge of snapping. While they were all still young, between nineteen and twenty-one, they weren't going anywhere. And they were bitter about it. Petty larcenies and auto thefts were becoming stale and lost their appeal. A quick fix and a joy ride later and they were right back in the same place they started. They'd get pinched every now and then, but the bullying respect they sought for their crimes always eluded them. That night, they were asking themselves: Is this as good as it's going to get, chasing dopers around Providence to roll?

The answer would be a resounding no.

In their twisted thoughts, they needed to move on, take a bold step forward and graduate from this one room schoolhouse of crime. College, a traditional family life and 9-5 jobs were not the goals these five had their sights set on. It was murder that was on their minds instead. It was certainly something that would separate them from the pack, and though it may never have been talked about explicitly, there was an implied consent to radically and permanently change their status in the community.

"Where's this guy?" was the first thing Sanchez asked Day. The guy he was referring to was the custy Day was seeking, but the custy was just the means to an end.

"Let's do this," Anderson said as the car pulled away from the curb in front the pizzeria.

Jason and Amy walked into the bar around a quarter to twelve. The young man working the door had gone to high school with Amy and did not charge her or her three companions admission to enter.

Later, Cathy, Jennifer and Natasha spotted Arnold Banker and Stephen Cone. By that point, the girls had been there about an hour when they learned from Banker and Cone that Jason and Amy were on the bottom level of the club. They went outside onto the second floor deck and looked down at all the people around the pool and the bar below. They went looking for Jason, and when he saw them together, his face instantly lit up and he rushed over to give them a group hug. "This is so great," he gushed. "I can't wait for all of us to hang out again."

They were introduced to Amy. Jennifer was the only one who had met Amy previously. Jennifer quickly discovered that night that the tight relationship between Jason and her was not easy for Amy to accept at first. At a party that the three of them had attended together several months before, Jennifer began to notice Amy moving Jason to different areas of the club to dance, leaving her alone. Tonight, however, Amy seemed more at ease with Jennifer, and she seemed to hit it off with Cathy right away, as well. In fact, Amy took her by the hand and gave her a personal tour of the club, showing her the different rooms and where all the bathrooms were located. At one point, Amy spoke to Cathy in confidence and told her that although Jason was not her usual type, she found him so sweet that she couldn't help but care for him.

Amy even asked Cathy if she wanted to go out with Jason and her the following night. Cathy told Amy that she already had plans with her boyfriend of two years, but hoped they'd all be able to get together another time real soon.

As they all danced together, it was like there was no one else in the entire club. But Jeffrey Harper was there, and when he saw Amy he just smiled. Then he got up and hugged her, and for him that made the whole night worthwhile. He and Amy talked briefly, but he had to be at work in a few hours and could not stay much longer. As he watched her dancing with Jason and her new friends he tried to keep up his smile. She seemed to be having such a good time. Though this was not easy for him, he was glad he had come. He would miss Amy just as much at home, but at least this way he got to see her.

They were not the only criminals skulking around Providence at that hour, but the five young men cruising the city in Sammie's dinged-up car were not invisible, either. Their quest to find potential victims that night might best be described as uninhibited. They had pretty much given up on the custy and they had their eyes elsewhere and everywhere. It was a club night in the city, and there were a lot of people out and about to size up. Basically, they were interested in someone who looked like they had some money, preferably a male, but they were not chauvinists. Nevertheless, if the guy was well-dressed, groomed and drove a nice car, he was Mr. Right.

However, they soon discovered that the old car actually inhibited their ability to confront an isolated pedestrian with the ideal victim characteristics. The cumbersome vehicle was difficult to maneuver through the heavy, slow-moving city traffic. They needed to be on the streets. Besides, they needed gas. Sanchez had no money, and no one else was willing to dump what little cash they had into the tank, so they decided to ditch the car.

At about that time Providence Patrolman John Lough was standing outside his cruiser, parked facing the wrong way on Peck Street, a one-way that was perpendicular to Pine Street and directly in front of a mega sports bar where fights and disorderlies were common. Lough was watching the front of the building when he noticed a beige car heading west along Pine Street, toward him. As the car drove past, the officer clearly observed five males, three in the back and two in the front, all of whom stared straight ahead and did not make eye contact with him. Lough's attention was drawn to the old, beat up vehicle, and he thought to himself that it was probably not registered. The driver side quarter was discolored with gray Bondo, the door dented on that side. The vehicle and its five occupants disappeared up the road and did not return.

Police presence was something else that they were hoping to avoid, considering the unlawful intentions they had in mind. No question about it, they had to get that car off the road. Sanchez parked it in the lot behind a pizzeria, and then they set out on foot. All at once, they were back in their element, prowling the shadowy streets of Providence which they knew so well. Under the cover of darkness, as a group, they looked for a victim. They walked together down Weybosset Street, then took a right by the Sixth District Courthouse and headed west on Pine Street toward the sports bar, which was always very busy on the weekends.

Day suddenly noticed a tall man who fit their profile. The man was talking on a cell phone and walking by himself. Day pointed him out to Floyd and suggested he approach the guy with his gun drawn. Floyd balked, insisting that with the five of them the gun wasn't needed. Floyd's will prevailed, and they came within eight feet of the man when suddenly a group of people, who the man seemed to know, appeared out of nowhere. The would-be robbers scattered like frightened pigeons dispersing into the night in all directions.

A block or so away, the group came together once more, winding up in almost the same exact spot where their failed robbery attempt had begun, and they all laughed about it. Headed now toward Davol Square, they set their sights on a Mexican-themed restaurant and bar, but the crowds and police presence there sent the gang out in another direction, across the Point Street Bridge, eastward, toward the waterfront and the bar.

It was during this time that Burdick began to talk in earnest about getting a car and looking for a suitable one to hot wire. But they faced the same dilemma with police presence that they had encountered on the other side of the Providence River, and they had to regroup once again. They decided that their best bet was to head back toward Weybosset and the pizzeria.

When Harper informed Amy that he had to leave so he could get ready for work, she kissed him and thanked him for coming.

"I love you," she told him. "I'm glad we had a good night together."

Harper asked her if she wanted a ride home. She shook her head, telling him that her handbag was in Jason's car and it would be easier just to have him drive her home. Amy told him to drive carefully and asked him if he would call her at around 2:00 or 2:30 to make sure she got home okay and to talk. He said he would, and then they kissed and said goodbye. Harper left the nightclub at about 12:50.

Amy and Jason, and everyone else at the bar, finished dancing as the club closed at 1:00. They left together as the patrons all emptied out at once. Being alongside his new girlfriend and some of his best friends in the same place, Jason was in a more spirited mood than usual. When he saw someone he knew handing out fliers advertising an upcoming rave club, he grabbed a stack of the leaflets. Printed on the front in large colorful lettering was the name of the club. The party was scheduled for Saturday, June 10, in downtown Hartford, Connecticut.

"Hey, I'll help you," Jason said, and began to distribute them to the departing crowd.

A rave is an all-night dance party where DJ's and other performers play techno or electronic dance music. Such events had become increasing popular with young people throughout the country. The availability of recreational drugs, particularly Ecstasy, caused raves to be targeted and criticized by law enforcement officials and parents groups. The parties, which are open to those eighteen and older, usually begin after traditional clubs close and go straight through the night until dawn. No alcohol is available, and the parties themselves are perfectly legal.

"Free fliers!" Jason yelled. "Get your fliers here." He didn't let anyone pass by him without taking one.

In no time, they were all gone.

He kept only a handful, making sure all his friends had one, and saving the rest for himself. It was just Jason being Jason, and everyone laughed. The high school friends gathered outside the club near their cars and continued talking.

Five men noted the late model vehicle, as well as seeing Jason and Amy, and Banker and Cone, standing beside the SUV and a gray car in parking lot of a restaurant named Scott's. But there was a tow truck servicing a vehicle across the street, and at that time it was just another opportunity that passed them by like so many others that night. They had happened to drive by the group of friends at the precise moment they were leaving Tommy's together, just before they all got into Jason's vehicle and headed to the bar. The SUV was part of what attracted the attention of the five criminals then, but now the stakes had been raised and everything seemed right.

On their way back to the pizzeria, the five lurking figures were moving north on South Main Street. Across the street from the Superior Courthouse, and directly in front of a seafood bar, a red sports car pulled up to the curb and stopped. Two women got out of the vehicle to use the ATM on the side of the restaurant. Then, a short man exited from the driver's side and walked over to some nearby bushes to take a leak.

Floyd and his posse watched with increasing interest. This relatively secluded location, away from the area night clubs, together with the nonexistent pedestrian and vehicle traffic, all conspired to make it an ideal situation for a mugging.

They could see that no one was in the car. The keys might still be inside and two women were making cash withdrawals. It couldn't have been any easier for them, and a plan was quickly formulated. Two of them would get the money from the women at the ATM, one would take the wallet off the man urinating in the bushes and the two others would be lookouts.

They went into action quickly. Burdick, who had missed the last bus back to Pawtucket, needed a way to get home, and since Sammie did not want to take him, the opportunity to grab a car as well as cash was too tempting to turn down. "Make sure you get the keys from that guy while you're at it," Burdick instructed the others as he and Floyd approached the two women. Sanchez began walking toward the urinating male while Day and Anderson hung back and watched their backs. To anyone else who might have been witnessing this, it would have been like observing a pack of hyenas surrounding a carcass in the wild.

It was late and dark, which made the women and man nervous as Floyd and the other young men descended upon them.

This time, they got within three feet of their intended robbery targets.

The woman at the ATM was the first to react to their approach. One fumbled to enter her PIN. So as not to frighten her off before the machine dispensed her cash, Floyd bought himself some time by pausing and removing his own bank card, pretending to be waiting in line behind her. After seeing him she became visibly upset and awkward. She began to shake, which may have saved her from losing her money, or worse, as she continued to mess up the sequence of numbers.

Suddenly Day yelled out to warn Floyd and the others that a security officer was watching them.

A man who was working at a nearby office building that night walked outside at approximately 1:19 AM. He had observed the approach of the group of men and, perceiving them to be a threat to the two women attempting to use an ATM just outside the building, decided to intervene.

Floyd did not see the man, but he did not want to risk it. "I'll go use another ATM," he said, loud enough for the women to hear him. He and Burdick then made a hasty retreat. The attempt to jump the man urinating in the bushes was also abandoned, and the five of them quickly dispersed into the night.

After the incident was defused, the man zipped up as he was confronted by the security guard and vigorously shook the man's hand, thanking him for his timing.

Unbeknownst to them, a security camera captured an image of the five men walking away from that area of South Main Street, on Westminster and heading back in the direction of Weybosset and "the wall." It was 1:23 AM.

Meanwhile, Jason and his friends had been talking for about a half hour outside the dance bar, huddled close for extra warmth, as it was rather chilly for a June night. He was not ready to go home, and suggested that they go somewhere else. He mentioned a party that he had heard about, but only if Jennifer was up for it. Cathy and Natasha indicated that they were tired and just wanted to get to bed. Jennifer, who was driving, thought twice about it herself. It had been a long day for them. The three girls had spent a good portion of the day at the beach and the afternoon in Boston with Jennifer's boyfriend, before driving to Providence that night. They were beat. And they still had a long drive back.

"Maybe not this time, Jay," Jennifer said. "Another day."

Jason tried to convince them to stay, but to no avail.

"I suppose I'll just drop Arnold and Stephen off at their car in Scott's parking lot and then take Amy home," he said with feigned resignation.

"Sorry," Jennifer said.

"That's okay," Jason said, suddenly beaming as he gave her a big hug. "I'm glad you all came out. It was so great seeing you."

The girls exchanged their goodbyes with Jason and Amy and the other boys.

"Good night," Jason said. "Drive safe, Jen. Okay?"

"I will," Jennifer said. She and the other girls each took with them a flier that Jason had given them. Then they drove off toward the highway as Jason taxied his two high school friends back downtown. In the parking lot at Weybosset and Westminster, the four of them talked inside Arnold's car for another fifteen minutes or so.

Back outside the pizzeria on Weybosset Street, the gang joined a gathering crowd to watch a disturbance that began to escalate between several Providence Police Officers who were trying to deal with a belligerent woman. They stuck around and watched for awhile, waiting to see if anything more interesting would develop. The situation seemed to cool off as quickly as it had begun, and they all lost interest. There was some talk about calling it a night and just going home. Things had not gone as they would have liked. Perhaps it just wasn't their night.

They might simply have taken the He-Who-Robs-And-Runs-Away-Lives-To-Rob-Another-Day option, but Burdick, who still needed a lift to Pawtucket, changed all that when he went inside the pizzeria to use the bathroom. His pit stop turned out to have a re-energizing effect on the down-on-their-luck criminals. Before Burdick came out, however, the others headed for Sanchez's car, hoping to ditch him. It was not just Sanchez, as evidenced by his refusal all that night to give Burdick a ride home, who harbored a fundamental dislike for the portly kid. Burdick rubbed a lot of people the wrong way, including Floyd, who was not even willing to pitch in a couple of bucks for gas, which was all that was needed for the round trip to Pawtucket. But before all of them could even get inside the car, Burdick suddenly emerged. He came running out of the pizzeria into the parking lot and got into the car with the others. Nobody said anything, but they were not surprised. It was typical; you may not want him around, but he was always there.

That's when Burdick produced a handful of latex gloves. He immediately handed them to Floyd, who took the gloves without asking any questions and stuffed them into his jacket pocket. Floyd knew they had come from the pizza place. He had worn similar pairs when he worked there, in food preparation, among other duties. He also knew what they would be used for now. They all knew. The thrill game was back on.

Once more, the group did not need verbal communication to establish their intent. Handing over the gloves was an unspoken directive. In the car again, with gloves and the gun, their murderous will was reasserted.

With little gas and a loaded gun, their prey would have to be close by. They headed toward the Arcade building at the end of Weybosset Street. It was as if they were of a single mind.

Chapter 3

Worldy Collide

Finally, Amy and Jason stepped out of Arnold's car and bade farewell to the boys. Asked by his friends where he was going, with a wink and a smile, Jason responded that he was going back to Amy's house in Coventry. Amy promptly informed him, "You know that's not going to happen."

Jason laughed and then gave them directions to the onramp for I-195 East. At about 1:45 AM, Arnold Banker sped off with Stephen Cone in his car. Jason was in less of a hurry to go back to Lakeville. He and Amy had such a good time together that night that he did not want it to end.

Amy was sitting on the low wall that ran along the side of the Arcade and separated the building from Scott's parking lot. Jason was standing in front of her. Music from Jason's SUV was playing lowly, thrumming from the speakers though the open car windows. He was a big fan of Pink Floyd, and they could very well have been listening to music by this legendary British progressive rock band.

About to enter his junior year at St. Cloud State University, Jason's heart was in other places after arriving home for the summer a couple weeks prior. His burgeoning relationship with Amy had him thinking about staying closer to home. Amy was bright, energetic and pretty. She was petite, 5'4", 110 lbs. and had a smile that could light up any room with long curly hair and hazel green eyes. Jason was crazy about her.

Now they were opening up to each other. It can only be speculated what they were talking about. Perhaps they discussed the similar interests in dance music or their early experiences with college life. But they were not looking around them, unaware of danger or who might be lurking nearby. As they spoke, watchful eyes fell upon them with evil intent.

"Ooh, ooh!" Day aped. "Look at that, look at that!"

Everyone turned and peered out the left side of the car.

"It's on again," Day said, gesturing toward the couple as they drove past them.

"We could get their truck, too," Burdick was quick to point it out.

This was the second time they had seen Amy and Jason. It was later and quieter, and there were only the two of them to contend with. Plus, with a vehicle like that, they were thinking that the couple probably had some money on them.

Sanchez circled the block and came back around so they could get a third look.

Providence patrolman John Lough was working the uniformed patrol shift in a marked cruiser in that area of the city. At approximately 1:55 AM, he was responding to a call when he observed two people talking next to a white SUV beside the Arcade building on Westminster Street. As he rode past them, it struck him as odd that a lone guy and a girl would be parked in that spot so late at night. He felt they did not belong there.

The police officer continued on to his call.

As the car rolled slowly by the couple again, criminal minds were hard at work, scrutinizing the locale, gauging their risk. The lighting conditions were more than minimal on the street, but it was still plenty dark where their two targets were situated.

More importantly, there was no one else in sight.

The plan was wordlessly put into motion.

Sanchez pulled around the corner and parked by a florist and a bank on the other side of the Arcade.

There was another moment of indecision in a night to be filled with reck-lessness and savagery. They had no plan whatsoever, choosing instead to wait and see what happened and then just react to it. The men sat silently in the crowded car for a moment, not even looking at each other. It was go time, and while everybody wanted the act done, no one seemed willing to do it.

"Well, who's going?" Floyd asked.

Anderson and Day were not about to volunteer.

"You don't need me," Day told Floyd pointedly.

Floyd felt more than just the weight of the gun in his back. He was the one that the group wanted as their leader. He had been chosen, his role firmly established, if not defined. But they would all help achieve the end to which Floyd and his gun were the means. He understood this, and accepted it. He would go. But he would not go alone, so he picked Burdick.

"Harry, let's go." Floyd said. He knew Burdick was the right choice to take on this type of confrontational robbery. He was a practiced strong-armed thief. Besides, he was the one who wanted a car so badly.

"We'll wait here," Sanchez said.

The three others remained in the car, which would serve as the getaway vehicle if something went wrong again. Otherwise, it would become the chase car when Floyd or Burdick pulled out in the SUV.

The two men got out of the car and proceeded up the alley along the side of the Arcade Building on Westminster Street, heading toward Scott's parking lot.

When Officer Lough cleared from his previous call, he drove by Jason and Amy a second time, at about 2:10 AM, noticing that the couple was still outside talking in the same spot. Then, his radio crackled again and he was dispatched to a small club just a couple of blocks away.

As Floyd and Burdick casually walked toward Weybosset Street and their intended targets, somewhere along the way, perhaps their mission solidified in their minds. They began to steel themselves for the robbery, kidnapping and perhaps more brutal acts that lay ahead. A surveillance camera focused on this alleyway could not capture their intentions, however, only their movements as they made their way down the alley leading to the parking lot in front of Scott's restaurant. One of the clearer frames showed the two of them at the time of 2:09:59. Floyd wore a dark leather jacket while Burdick, a pace behind Floyd and off his right shoulder, was wearing a white T-shirt and a baseball cap turned backward on his head.

As they emerged from the alley and turned the corner, they saw the couple sitting on the wall in front of the SUV. Amy and Jason immediately jumped to the ground as Burdick started to go around the wall to head them off while Floyd leaped over it and surrounded them.

"Where's your money?" Floyd asked, focusing on Jason, the gun brandished for him to see, but not pointed at him in any more of a threatening manner than at the moment.

"I don't have any," Jason told him.

"You got any?" Burdick asked Amy, who he menaced with his proximity and a confrontational demeanor that had been honed by numerous street muggings.

"No," Amy answered, following Jason's lead, hoping they would go away and move onto someone else. She had no way of knowing that they had no intention of moving on. After a frustrating night of failed robbery attempts, they were not about to let this opportunity pass.

Just then, a set of headlights appeared headed in their direction and Burdick panicked. He thought it might be the cop who he had seen driving in the area just before Sanchez pulled over. If it was a cop, he certainly would find their little gathering curious. All he had to do was pull over to ask what they were doing and it would be all over.

"Get the fuck in the truck," Burdick said, opening the rear passenger door. As Amy got in, Floyd directed Jason into the back, behind the driver seat. Floyd got behind the wheel of the SUV, Burdick in the passenger seat.

"Let me have the gun," Burdick said, and Floyd handed it to him. The keys were in the ignition. Floyd turned the engine over and barreled out of Scott's parking lot onto Weybosset, heading in the wrong direction up a one-way street. From the alley, he emerged onto Westminster, and as soon as he turned the corner he saw the car. Floyd blew the horn on the SUV and alerted Sanchez, who started his car and followed behind the stolen vehicle with the kidnapped victims plainly visible inside.

Patrolman Lough was cleared of a Bar One call at 2:15 AM. Several moments later, he drove by Scott's restaurant. This time, he noticed that the couple and their vehicle were gone. When he looked up, however, he saw the same white SUV headed east on Weybosset Street, accelerating as it approached the intersection of Westminster. Smith, traveling west on Weybosset, discerned that the vehicle began to slow as it approached the patrol car. The officer also observed that a mustard-colored car was following closely behind the SUV.

As the SUV got closer, Lough could see that a male was driving and another male was in the passenger seat. He made out two silhouettes in the back seat. The driver, appearing very calm and cool to the officer, stuck one hand out of the open window and gave a partial wave.

"Hey," Floyd said as he went by.

Lough got a good look at the driver and both vehicles as they passed. He glimpsed Massachusetts plates on the SUV and Rhode Island tags on the four-door car following it. Inside the sedan were three men.

In his rear view mirror, Officer Lough watched both vehicles take a right on Westminster and continue on toward Memorial Boulevard. It would not occur to him until much later that the car was the same one that he had seen on Pine Street earlier that night, the one with the dented gray door and the five young men inside that had driven by him as he was standing outside his cruiser in front of a bar.

Shortly after Jeff Harper got home around 2 AM, he began calling Amy's house. He continued to place calls every ten minutes or so for the next half hour, then he had to leave for work. Every call he made went unanswered.

Burdick turned around to face Amy and Jason with the gun gripped firmly in one hand.

"Where's your fuckin' money?" he asked, trying his best to intimidate the pair and waving the gun between them.

Amy only had ten dollars. She knew it would not be enough to satisfy the five men. As she removed the money from her purse, Burdick snatched the bill from her hand.

"That's fuckin' it?" Burdick complained. "You got any credit cards? You better hand them over or we'll fuck you up bad."

"Man, just shut up with that shit already" Floyd snapped.

It was this tough-guy attitude which Burdick often displayed that irritated Floyd and made other people want to distance themselves from Burdick, not give him a ride home and try to ditch him when he turned his back.

Visibly frightened and listening to them argue, the couple tried to figure out what their abductors wanted from them while trying not to panic. Seeing the terrified look on their faces, Floyd tried to ease their minds, just as he had attempted to do with the women at the ATM. "Everything's going to be all right," he said. "All we want is money." Only just like the two women earlier, Floyd's ploy did not yield the desired effect. Amy and Jason were still alarmed as the kidnappers tried to make small talk, asking them about the clubs they had been to and where the best rave parties in the area were. The men also brought up ecstasy. Known as the love pill because it makes users want to hug and kiss everybody, ecstasy, or "XTC," is a synthetic, mind-altering hallucinogenic with amphetamine-like properties, and was very popular with young club-goers. But no matter what they talked about, the fact remained that Amy and Jason had no money, and if that was all they wanted, then where were they being taken? And why?

The two vehicles traveled south along Pine Street and continued toward Broad Street.

Providence patrolman Marcus Huffman was on duty on the lower end of the south side of his beat. He was on Pine Street, facing east toward the city, parked the wrong way down the one-way street, at the intersection of Somerset. Suddenly, he heard the squeal of tires coming from the area of Hayward, a street parallel with Pine and Somerset. Huffman looked up and observed a white van taking a left off Hayward onto Somerset, then take a right onto Pine directly in front of him. As the SUV drew nearer, Huffman recognized the male driver as Gregory Floyd, who was well known to him.

The patrolman had been to Floyd's apartment on two occasions in the past, the last time being only a week before. Another male passenger was seated beside Floyd, and two other unidentifiable passengers were in the backseat.

"Hi. What's up Marcus?" Floyd said to the officer as he drove by him.

Two things struck Huffman as odd. The first, that Floyd's tone was strange, as if overstating that everything was cool and that there was no reason to pull him over. Second, Huffman had not known Floyd to drive such a vehicle.

The officer observed that the SUV had Massachusetts plates and that Floyd was being followed by what he thought at the time was a beige car, which looked similar to another model in size and body type. He watched as both vehicles proceeded southwest down Pine, disappearing into the distance toward Broad Street.

For Jason and Amy, it seemed like help was all around, but no one would come to their rescue.

Once on Broad, they drove south for a while. Then, Sanchez began flashing his headlights at Floyd, who eventually slowed to a stop along the side of the road.

Sanchez pulled up beside the SUV. "Where are you going?" he asked, looking around Anderson, who was seated beside him, and up at Floyd.

Day was visible in the back, behind Anderson, though both were making a concerted effort to conceal their faces from the victims, or anyone else.

"I'm not sure," Floyd answered. "I'm just driving."

"I know a place," Sanchez said. "We'll bring them to the spot. Follow me."

The spot he was referring to was basically a make out spot, near the Manton section of Providence. Sanchez had lived in that area for a short period of time, and knew it more as a dump site, for everything from stolen cars to major household appliances, or any other item that had outlived its usefulness.

Sanchez pulled out in front of Floyd, and now the SUV was following the car. Sanchez took Sackett Street to Elmwood Avenue, and then drove north on Route 1 before turning left onto Potters Avenue in Providence's West End. At Cranston Street, a right and then a left on Messer Street took them north to Westminster. After crossing the Route 10/Route 6 overpass, they continued north up Valley Street. Sanchez made a left on Atwells Avenue, which transitioned into Manton Avenue to the west. After a left on Glenbridge to Mancini Drive, Route 6 appeared and then disappeared behind them as they moved north up a desolate, unpaved road.

Sanchez had been driving erratically. The circuitous route certainly must have confused not just Amy and Jason, but Floyd and everyone else following behind in the van.

"Are you going to kill us?" Amy asked nervously.

"No," Floyd responded swiftly. "We're just going to have some fun, that's all. You know, off-roading, spinning the tires."

Chapter 4

A Plea for Mercy

B oth vehicles pulled into a narrow access road leading down to the future site of Buttonhole Golf Course, which, at that moment, consisted of little more than vast open space and a seemingly endless expanse of dirt. Sanchez may have been familiar with this spot, but Floyd was not, and he was following very closely. Then the car's lights went out and it stopped suddenly. Floyd saw the brake lights flare and barely avoided rear-ending the vehicle. He shifted to park and took the keys with him. "Stay here and don't do anything stupid," he warned Amy and Jason as he stepped out of the SUV along with Burdick, who was still holding the gun. Jason and Amy did what they were told as the three occupants of the car exited and all five men converged between the two vehicles to discuss what to do next.

The half moon provided the only light, reflecting off the sandy landscape and casting everything in a ghostly glow. Day thought they had traversed some secret, undiscovered desert in the middle of Providence.

"Do they have any money?" Sanchez asked Floyd.

"No."

There was a long pause. Nobody said anything as they looked from one another to the SUV, where Amy and Jason were peering out at them.

It seemed as if their lack of planning had caught them off guard. They wanted money, maybe a vehicle, but there were two kidnapped victims and it hadn't been determined yet what they were going to do with them.

Or had they?

The men could have driven them to an ATM if it was just money they were after. They could just as easily have gained possession of the SUV while leaving Amy and Jason behind. But they had done neither of those things.

Was this some kind of murderous game of chicken no one wanted to back down from, or had the men wandered down a path of no return that they had all been in silent agreement about entering?

The fact was, as bad as these individuals were, these were unchartered waters for all of them.

Sanchez was the first to voice their intent aloud, when in an almost advisory tone he told them that they needed to kill Amy and Jason. Burdick instantly passed the gun back to Floyd without being prompted. Floyd accepted the weapon as if it had been rehearsed. It was a symbolic gesture that was not lost on any one of them. Day emphasized that the couple would be able to identify them. Then he grinned and looked around at Anderson. "We may as well have some fun with the girl." Anderson nodded in acknowledgment. They both wandered over to the SUV together and leered at Amy.

"She's cute," Anderson said.

"Yeah," Day agreed. "It won't matter what we do now."

"We're too close to those houses," Sanchez said, motioning toward the dark structures in the near distance behind them. "Someone might hear. Let's take them down further. Everyone jump in the truck. I'll drive."

Entering through the door nearest to them, they piled into the SUV. Day hopped into the rear cab compartment while Floyd and Anderson sat in the back, with Amy and Jason between them. Burdick flopped into the passenger seat. Floyd tossed the keys to Sanchez as he settled in behind the wheel. They drove down into the lower portion of the construction site with the headlights out, leaving the car behind.

"We can't let this happen," Amy said softly to Jason, her voice small and panic-stricken. "This can't be happening." Jason held her close, but she continued to tremble in his arms. "It's going to be okay," he told her.

Sanchez brought the SUV to a stop near the bottom of the incline.

"This is as far as we should go," Sanchez said. "There might be a surveillance camera on the building out across that clearing."

Everyone got out of the SUV except Amy and Jason. The discussion once again turned to what should be done with these two.

"I say we smoke them," Sanchez said flat out.

None of the others made a single statement on the couple's behalf to let them live. They lacked not only compassion and sympathy, but the strength and the courage to speak up against murdering two innocent people. And the longer that action was delayed, the more remote the possibility became that Amy and Jason would be spared.

"It's got to be done," Sanchez persisted.

"They saw my face," Day added.

Still, no one came forward and volunteered to become the executioner. That task, actually, had already been thrust upon Floyd, just as the burden to rob, carjack and kidnap the couple had been laid squarely in his lap. He had the gun. He was the leader. He had to do it. They would see to it that he did. Each of them had a role to play. This was his.

In the mean time, the topic of rape was renewed. During this argument, the two major proponents of the notion, Day and Anderson, moved back toward the van together. Day opened one of the doors and reached inside for Amy, who was practically seated on top of Jason. "Come out here, baby," he said.

Amy clung to Jason more tightly, holding back her tears. The look on Day's face frightened her more than any of Burdick's cowboy antics on the drive over.

"No, Amy." Jason said. "Don't go."

"You, shut the fuck up!" Day screeched, his normally high-pitched voice sounding whiny. "Now, come on out here. Come on, girl. Don't be shy. I ain't gonna hurt ya." He pulled Amy out forcefully. Jason followed. Anderson stepped between Jason and Amy, who was crying as Day pressed himself against her. "If you give me some head," Day whispered in her ear, "this could all be over. Nothing will happen to you. I'll let you go." He was rubbing the crotch of his pants and smirking broadly, making a low groan in the back of his throat. "Whatta ya say, wanna hook up? Me and you."

Amy shook her head as tears dropped off her cheeks.

"Yo, I'm going to rape you then, bitch," Day said angrily. He pulled a condom out of his pocket, one of several he had removed from the rear compartment of the SUV. He tore open the pink package and removed the prophylactic inside, letting the wrapper fall to the ground. With his other hand he reached over and grabbed Amy's breasts. She screamed and tried to pull away, but Anderson restrained her and held her in place as Day continued to grope her.

"Leave her alone," Floyd said in that calm, forceful way he had. Day immediately responded to this command. More than any of the others, he knew Floyd's temper. His roommate might appear to be quiet and soft-spoken, and for the most part he was, but he could also be explosive.

"You can all get some after me if you want," Day proposed.

"No, I said. Leave her alone."

Sanchez objected to Floyd's interference. "Let them do what they want," he said. But Day had already backed down, and Anderson quickly followed suit, releasing Amy. She then rushed back into Jason's arms.

"Nobody touches her," Floyd said. "That's not going to happen."

And it didn't.

"Fuck all this, man," Burdick suddenly blurted out. "I'm out of here." He stepped away from the group and then started walking up the slope toward the car.

"Get the fuck back here!" Sanchez yelled, but Burdick did not stop.

"I'll get him," Floyd announced, then told Amy and Jason to get back into the SUV as he got behind the wheel and drove through the darkness after Burdick. The others followed, scampering along behind the vehicle on foot or clinging to the SUV, standing on the running board and holding the roof rack.

At the top of the slope, Sanchez was prepared to run up on Burdick and beat him to death, but Floyd got to him first and managed to convince him to get into the truck. Then they all headed back down again, some of them playing the same game as before, using the car as a Jungle Gym. At one point, Day and Anderson began pushing and shoving one another until both of them ended up falling off the roof.

At the bottom of the incline, the five men exited the van together. Burdick, however, continued to dissociate from the others and this infuriated Sanchez. He wrestled the gun from Floyd and threatened to kill Burdick or any individual who defied the resolve of the group. "Burdick you're a snitch," he accused and punctuated his denouncement by pointing the gun at him, practically asking for consent from the others to shoot him, because he believed Burdick would go to the police.

"We *can't* let them go!" Sanchez screamed.

Meandering bands of clouds drifted across the moon, and in the flittering light, Sanchez looked like a madman. There was a tense moment when the others believed that he was going to shoot Burdick, until once again, Floyd stepped in. He prevented the fragging by vouching for Burdick and effectively assuring Sanchez that the husky white boy would not snitch. Floyd then reclaimed the gun from Sanchez, essentially refocusing everyone's attention back on the issue of what to do about Amy and Jason.

The discussion that ensued on this topic could only have been a further prodding by the others to convince Floyd to do the group's bidding. For their own reasons, whatever those might have been, they all wanted the two people in the van to die. They all wanted to be part of it, including Burdick, his present act rebellion of notwithstanding. Full ratification from the group was the only thing holding Floyd back, not conscience, not compassion, not fear of reprisal from the law.

"Get them out," Sanchez directed Anderson, who walked decisively over to the van and told Amy and Jason to get out. Then, the couple was told to sit down on a strip of grass beside the vehicle. Behind them was a short wall of hay bales that extended out into the darkness in either direction. With the five men in front of them, there was nowhere to go. The terrified couple complied, sitting close and holding one another.

"Let's go through everything," Sanchez said as he approached and illuminated the interior light. Anderson and Day then crawled into the SUV and began to rummage through it, looking for anything of value they could find. Floyd and Burdick joined them. In their final hunt for personal property, Burdick inexplicably tossed a portable CD-player into an area of brush on the other side of the hay bales. That was a decision for which he would later

be harshly scolded by Floyd, because there was not much else to be had. The
young couple did not have much. They didn't need much. They had planned
a night of dancing and laughter with some friends. Now they were watching
five strangers ransacking Jason's van, digging between the seat cushions for
loose change and other items that Jason and Amy would have just ignored.
These men did not see value in the same things they did. The only object of
any interest to the street bandits turned out to be a "Tasmanian Devil" coffee mug that contained an assortment of quarters, dimes and nickels.

"Let me see them rings," Anderson said when he emerged, looking
down at Amy's trembling hands. She surveyed each one and began to remove
them one at a time, and hand them to him without any complaint.

"They're not worth much, but you can have them," she said. Then she
got to the diamond engagement ring that belonged to her mother. "This one
won't come off."

As she tried to wriggle it off, Anderson touched his hand to hers. "Don't
sweat it," he said. Then, after a pause, "You can keep it."

Offered this small courtesy, Amy saw a glimmer of hope. There was good
in everyone, she had always thought. In an effort to appeal further to his sense
of propriety, she asked him to help her and Jason get out of this.

It was suddenly frightening to her that she had to try to convince someone not to harm her.

"I don't want to die," she told him. Then she added, whispering softly so
no one else could hear, "I'm pregnant. Please don't hurt my baby."

The ploy for mercy may have worked on Anderson, or any one of the
others individually, but not for them collectively. Frustrated that their only
successful robbery that night turned up only a few dollars and a few coins,
the debate over killing the couple actually began to heat up.

What they were doing now might best be described as a group pep talk,
an attempt to inspire and galvanize their singular murderous will, and to
prompt their designated hit man to finish the job.

As their abductors spoke openly about this in front of Amy and Jason,
and with increasing intensity, having to shout over one another's voices to be
heard as everyone spoke at once, Floyd removed the latex gloves from his
jacket pocket and began to hand them out.

"We need to get rid of them!" Sanchez pressed, feeling a sudden shift forward, moving them closer toward the fulfillment of their objective.

Perhaps sensing doom, Amy began crying uncontrollably. Jason tried his best to comfort her, but he felt helpless. They grasped each other in a desperate embrace and closed their eyes, perhaps hoping that when they opened them again the whole frightful scene would just vanish.

None of these young hoodlums wanted to back down or show any sign of weakness in front of the others. This was perhaps their only fear, and it ultimately controlled them. Because they were too weak to examine that fear more closely, or overcome it, they allowed it to escalate to the point where it became impossible for the individual holding the gun not to fire it. In essence, then, it was all five of them who had their hands on the murder weapon, ready to squeeze the trigger.

As Floyd raised the gun slowly from his side, Day urged him to shoot the couple as they huddled together on the ground crying.

"They saw my face," Day said again. "We have to kill 'em."

"You don't have to do this," Amy pleaded.

"Just take my truck," Jason told Floyd. "I won't report it stolen. Take it. Go ahead."

Floyd faltered suddenly, his right elbow locking at a high angle, so that the barrel of the gun was directed into the trees over their heads.

While Burdick may have been more or less indifferent, Sanchez was growing impatient with the whole process, even as Anderson joined in, encouraging Floyd to pull the trigger.

"Hurry up," Sanchez said. "What's taking so long? Give me the fuckin' gun. I'll do it."

"THAT'S ENOUGH!" Floyd yelled back at him, raising his voice for the first time all night. Sanchez, whom Floyd had seen around the pizzeria but never met, posed a real threat to his authority. He had been challenging Floyd from the start. This was just the latest attempt by Sanchez to usurp his power, and Floyd could not let that happen. He was not about to relinquish the gun or the power that the group had given him.

While this marked the one and only time these two South Providence neighbors had actually been in each other's company, their power struggle held in its balance the lives of two innocent people. Floyd leveled the .40 caliber semiautomatic, pointing it down at the terrified couple.

Jason shifted backward slightly, angling his body so that Amy was completely shielded. She wrapped her arms firmly around his chest and was not about to let him go, tucking her head between his shoulders.

"Shoot them!"

"They saw my face."

"Please, don't kill us!"

"SHOOT THEM!"

"NO!"

With the sound of the victim's pleas in one ear, and those of Sanchez, Day and Anderson in the other, Floyd reached his left hand across his body and gripped the top of the .40 caliber semiautomatic handgun. He pulled the slide mechanism back on the weapon to jack a round into the chamber, but he was unaware that a bullet was already there. His action inadvertently ejected a live round from the breech. The bullet tumbled toward Jason, landing harmlessly on the lower part of his left leg. Then Floyd squeezed the trigger and the next round exploded from the barrel. The metal-jacket hollow point bullet struck Jason on the top of the head. Amy screamed as his body jumped and lurched, causing the black headband he was wearing to drop down against the bridge of his nose, covering his eyes and making it appear as if he were blindfolded. Floyd then shifted, moving around to the other side of the couple in order to get a better shot, and then he fired a second round into the top of Jason's head. His convulsing stopped instantly as he slumped to one side, fully exposing Amy to the gunman. She was still screaming and holding onto Jason when Floyd pulled the trigger a third and final time. This round tore through Amy's brain and she collapsed onto her left side beneath Jason, still clutching him as she died.

Chapter 5

Total
Silence

The echo of the successive reports dissipated quickly in the open field. All at once the yelling and the screaming stopped. For several moments, there was no sound at all. Floyd stood there, numb, feeling nothing, thinking nothing, as the others drew back on their heels, looking from the bodies to Floyd with a mixture of reverence and exuberance. It was a defining moment in all their lives, because even though Floyd had physically pulled the trigger, they were equally culpable.

They were now killers; their status in the violent, criminal world they occupied suddenly elevated. It was what each of them wanted, yet it was something that they could never have achieved alone, not without each other: not without Floyd's gun and his leadership role; not without Burdick, who needed a car to get home because he was such an annoyance no one wanted to drive him; not without Day, who insisted Floyd take the gun with them that night; not without Anderson, who had called Sanchez for the use of his car; not without Sanchez, who escorted them to the secluded location for the execution and who most urgently instructed Floyd to shoot so that all of their individual efforts that night would not go to waste.

With the moon dropping behind the stand of trees, their victims were mostly concealed in darkness, so the murderers did not have a graphic view of the carnage for which they were responsible. Nor was there any blood spatter to denote the terrible violence. Because Floyd had been standing over them, just a few feet from where they were seated on the ground, and shot at a downward angle into their heads, there were no exit wounds. When they left the couple, shot and bleeding, they may not have known if Amy and Jason were alive or dead, but make no mistake about it, they were as high from these shootings as they had ever been from any drug they had ever taken in their lives.

"Let's go," Sanchez finally said. He got behind the wheel of the truck as the others piled inside.

"Ya do 'em?" Day asked Floyd as they drove back up to the top. "They dead?" he rephrased, after receiving no response.

"I don't know."

Sanchez stopped beside his car. Everyone got out at that point and returned to the vehicle they had arrived in. Not about to leave emptyhanded, on his way out of the SUV, Sanchez reached for the coin-filled coffee mug.

"You ain't getting all of it," Floyd cautioned him.

"I need gas," Sanchez announced.

"So do we. We'll split it."

The two of them began to quickly divvy up the money, which netted them about four dollars each. A total of eighteen dollars, then, was what the lives of Jason and Amy amounted to for the five men who stalked, kidnapped, robbed and killed them. It was of little consequence to them that much of their take was in the form of small change, and that all of it would have to be used for gas because even the vehicle they had stolen was low. In the end, they came away with nothing. And they could not have cared less.

Back behind the wheel of the van, Floyd placed the gun under his seat. Sanchez pulled out first in his car, Day and Anderson in the vehicle with him. Floyd and Burdick followed right behind them.

As they drove out of the construction site, Floyd noticed that a light was on in a house along the nearest border of the property. He could not recall if it had been on when they first arrived.

On the road and directionless once again, Sanchez found an open gas station and pulled in. However, he was not happy with price per gallon, so he took his business elsewhere, driving to the south end of Providence with a stolen vehicle that belonged to one of the two people he helped to murder in tow behind him.

He stopped at an all night gas station. They pulled up to the same pump and Burdick got out of the van with the ten dollars he had taken from Amy and the change Floyd had given him. Sanchez handed him the coins he had and Burdick went up to the attendant's booth, dumping all the money onto the counter. Then he turned and started to walk away.

"Hey, hold on," the attendant said. "How much is here?"

"I don't know. Just put it all in."

At the pumps, Sanchez and Floyd filled their tanks one at a time, each putting in about nine dollars. They did this in silence. There seemed to be no apparent concern about being apprehended, and no discussion about what they just did. It was as if it had been just another typical, uneventful night, but the fact was that the five of them were now linked forever in the heinous murder of two innocent young people. As Floyd finished up and returned the nozzle to the pump, the new killers needed to discuss what they were going to do next. They had a stolen car and a dreadful secret. With the unanimous decision to call it a night, there was at least some apprehension about separating. Burdick was warned pointedly by Sanchez to keep his mouth shut.

"If anyone goes down for this," Sanchez told him, "your whole family is going down. You got it?"

Then he informed Floyd that he and Anderson intended to use the SUV in a robbery the next day, most likely a gas station, and that they would dump the vehicle afterward so the crime could not be traced to them. "Put the truck somewhere safe overnight," Sanchez said, "and tomorrow we'll page you to arrange a drop off place for it."

With all that agreed upon, they got back into the vehicles and drove off, proceeding together to Taylor Street. Floyd gave Day his key to get into their third floor apartment. He also gave him his leather jacket, with the gun now in one of the pockets, to take up to the room with him.

Sanchez then dropped Anderson off before heading home himself, just one street over on Glenham. Floyd left the South Providence neighborhood to take his passenger home to Pawtucket. But first, Burdick wanted to see if he could find Susana downtown, at Traveler's Aid. Floyd accommodated the request, having no apprehensions whatsoever about driving the stolen car back into the city.

He parked the SUV in a nearby alley and walked into Traveler's Aid while Burdick waited in the vehicle. Floyd was a familiar sight there, and everyone who worked there knew him. He entered the building at approximately 3:50 AM, unaware that he was being recorded by a videotape surveillance camera. A better quality interior security camera captured Floyd's movements inside the shelter. He was greeted by the desk attendant and then strolled casually into the community room to see if Susana was there. She was not, so he simply turned around and left. No one knew what had occurred so no one looked at him any differently, despite his newfound notoriety as a double murderer. He was just continuing the life he had always known without skipping a beat.

Back in the van, Floyd told Burdick that she was not inside. They drove in silence all the way to Pawtucket, until Floyd mentioned to Burdick that he had come very close to being killed that night. Burdick realized what Floyd had done for him, and he was thankful, promising his friend that he would not squeal. Floyd did not seem overly troubled either way. After dropping off Burdick, he drove back to South Providence and parked the SUV in a parking lot belonging to the Urban League of Rhode Island (ULRI), just a couple blocks from where he and three of the four other murderers of Amy Shute and Jason Burgeson lived.

The Urban League of Rhode Island, one of over a hundred affiliates of the National Urban League, Inc., is a community-based, nonprofit, tax-exempt organization whose mission ultimately calls for the elimination of racial discrimination and segregation in the state and the achievement of parity for blacks and other minorities in every phase of American life. ULRI attempts to facilitate these goals through a number of advocacy programs which enable minorities and the poor to demonstrate their full potential and exercise their human rights. It is also a member of a network of community-based agencies providing health and human services to those most in need.

Floyd had been a beneficiary of this organization's humanitarian efforts, paying his entire eighty dollars a week apartment rent for an entire year.

As dawn was beginning to break on Friday morning, June 10, Floyd walked from the parking lot to his apartment on Taylor Street, where he found Day still awake. The exact location of his gun was not even a thought on his mind at that point. He never asked about it and made no attempt to hide it or get rid of it. As with everything else Floyd did that night, there was little rationale or thought behind his actions. He continued on that same plane of consciousness when he picked up the phone and got on a chat line and bragged about killing two people.

Over the course of the next few hours, the others may have been as wide awake as Floyd, or still feeling as high from the murders the way he was. However, judging from their demeanor, as well as the answers they gave subsequently, I believe they were all sleeping the sleep of the untroubled. And while they were resting soundly at that time, so too were the parents of Amy Shute and Jason Burgeson. Both were blissfully unaware of the violent end that their children had met. They would awaken the next morning to a much different world than the one they had known before they went to bed a night before.

44

Part II

Innocence Lost

Chapter 6

A View
to a Kill

When Freddie Walker arrived for work at 6:30 AM, it was a near perfect spring morning, bright, clear and warm, despite an early warning forecast of an afternoon thunderstorm. The heavy equipment operator for New Construction ruminated that if the golf course he was helping to shape was opened and ready for business that day, there would be a steady stream of men clothed in plaid and pastel colors leisurely milling around the tree-lined fairways on foot and in motorized carts. He could almost hear the quiet hum of the engines and the sharp contact sound of a golf club and ball meeting, muted by the vast open space. This tranquil tableau made him smile.

As it stood at that moment, however, the Buttonhole Golf Course was still under construction, and had mini mountains of earth still needing to be graded and groomed across the twenty-five acre parcel. In actuality, it was still quite a mess in some places, even though the project was in its final phase, and slated for opening sometime by the end of the summer. Funded by private donations to provide activity and social opportunity to children from inner cities, as well as for seniors and beginning golfers, each of the course's nine par-three holes were designed to range between only 100-200 yards in length. The nonprofit facility, under development by the Rhode Island Golf Association, was being built on the site of former Dyerville State Park, which prior to that had been an abandoned and neglected area which had been used as a landfill and an illegal tire dump. A pedestrian bridge and bike path were also being planned. As part of the Greenway Project, a catalyst for renewal along the Woonasquatucket River, the bike path would link recreational areas, green spaces and destination sites of the surrounding neighborhoods to Waterplace Park in downtown Providence. The path would split at Button-hole; on one side the path would cross the river on a pedestrian bridge and enter the Manton neighborhood. On the other side the path would run along the ridge above the golf course, near the Hartford neighborhood and into Johnston.

If all went well, the images Walker had envisioned in his mind that morn-ing would become a reality as early as mid August. That's why he was there so early this Friday morning, as he was every day since the ground began to thaw after the last frost of spring.

The bulldozer operator already had his first cup of coffee and began greasing the fittings of the machine at about 6:45 AM. It was at about this time that he looked up and spotted something in the distance which caught his eye. From a couple hundred yards away, it was difficult to make out any-thing more than the most distinctive colors. Yellow. Blue.

And red.

The unidentifiable pile he glimpsed was lying on the ground beside a stretch of black silt fencing and hay bales that straddled a shallow coppice which fronted the bank of the Woonasquatucket River. The barrier was in place to protect the water from construction debris and silt runoff. With the EPA breathing down their necks, any environmental violation had the potential to impact the construction schedule. Just beyond this was the partially constructed second green. Now, it was just a ring of dirt in the middle of a circle of grass. He could see that part of the orange plastic safety fence surrounding the struc-ture was down on one side. Despite the standing piles of earth and building material everywhere, Walker made the observation that partying teenagers were likely responsible for the mess. It was not an uncommon problem. The area, though remote, was accessible, an ideal spot for young people to drink or just park. For this reason, the indistinct heap did not give him further pause, and he turned away to continue on with the business at hand of readying his machine for the day's work.

At around 8:00 AM, Elizabeth Zatkoff left her South Attleboro, Massachusetts home with her infant and drove to the neighboring city of Pawtucket, Rhode Island to look for her boyfriend, and the father of her baby, Harry Burdick. They had planned to attend an area playgroup together at 9:00. A playgroup was part of a gathering known as "meetups," where local moms get together with their kids, who play while they talk, share experiences and give support and advice to one another. The groups are specific to a child's age, generally infants and toddlers, and the meetings are usually held in one of the mother's homes.

First, Zatkoff drove to the house where Burdick had been staying. He was not there, so she began driving to some of the places she thought he might be. She rode around for a while, but could not locate him. She did not know what to think. It wasn't like him not to at least call if they had plans to be somewhere and couldn't make it. She was mad at him, but at the same time she was concerned. She had a bad feeling all morning that something was seriously wrong and she could not shake it. Elizabeth had no idea just how bad it was.

When Zatkoff could not wait any longer, she went to the playgroup without him. She enjoyed spending time with the other mothers as much as her child delighted in the interaction with the other boys and girls. She had some close friends in the group, and these meetups were the only way for them to get together. They were something to which she always looked forward to. She was not about to let her boyfriend's lateness interfere with this.

Wherever Burdick was during those hours, he was very much afraid. Afraid to sleep, afraid of the knock on his door, afraid the police were onto him. He was afraid to go out on the street, afraid his associates would come looking for him before he snitched, and afraid of any potential witnesses who might recognize him from the previous night. Burdick was afraid of the blood evidence on the T-shirt he was wearing last night and had thrown away, afraid that the latex glove he had left behind would be discovered and traced back to him.

Zatkoff would not find Burdick until much later. It was after noon when she finally caught up with him. He was outside a market in Pawtucket. He appeared preoccupied, disoriented.

"Where were you?" she asked, shoving him angrily, even though she was relieved to see him.

Burdick's gaze seemed to pass right through her. "If you had been through what I been through you would understand," he said cryptically.

"What the hell are you talking about?"

That's when he told her a story. It was mostly fictional, because it was filled with lies and half truths. The only factual statement he made to her was that two people had been killed the previous night by his friend, Greg. Murders, he told Zatkoff, to which Floyd had confessed his responsibility.

Zatkoff considered this information, trying to gauge the verity of what he just said carefully in her mind before responding. It proved to be too much for her to grasp, and she all but dismissed the possibility out of hand. She tried to reassure Burdick, and herself, that Floyd was probably just lying. She told him not to worry, but Burdick was still pretty shaken up, and she just let it go.

Lunch ended at 12:30, and the contract carpenters and other employees of Buttonhole Golf Course were just getting back to work. The sounds of hammering and the whirring of an electric saw could be heard coming from the club house being built on the southwest corner of the property. The rumble of a diesel engine on the large bull dozer was louder still. The greens superintendent and the assistant groundskeeper were driving around in an electric golf cart, surveying the progress being made on the course. When the supervisor spotted a DOT inspector in his jeep, he stopped and chatted for awhile. On the drive back to the office trailer, both men noticed a pile of what experience could only have led them to believe was a pile of trash. It was resting on the fringe of what would become the fairway along the second hole of the golf course. The supervisor turned and headed in that direction, and as he got closer to the spot the image slowly came into focus. He squinted in disbelief when it first started to take on a familiar human form.

When he realized that what he was looking at was, in fact, a person, he stopped the cart and got out. His assumption that it could only be a drunk or homeless person, leaning over or sleeping, was shattered all at once when he noticed all the blood. He stopped in his tracks and become instantly frightened. He took only a couple of steps closer just to be sure that his eyes were not deceiving him, but remaining a good twenty feet away. From that distance, there was no mistake about it. It was a person. Dead. There were flies buzzing all around the body. Then he noticed something else that took his breath away for a moment. Behind the victim, there appeared to be a second, smaller body.

"Oh, my God," he said softly and stumbled backward. The supervisor bumped into the assistant groundskeeper, who he hadn't realized was standing next to him, giving himself another fright. The two men just stared at each other. They didn't say anything, both in a mutual state of shock, but when their eyes locked it was enough to confirm that they were seeing the same thing. At first thought, the body he saw, he thought, was a mannequin because of the gray color.

The supervisor began motioning frantically with his arms to draw the attention of the nearby dozer operator. The operator was a good hundred and fifty yards away, but he saw distress signal and quickly shut down the machine. Then he hopped down from his tractor and began to hurriedly make his way toward the two course workers and the unknown pile. The operator thought someone may have been injured or was in need of some kind of medical attention. However, as the operator walked past the supervisor's golf cart, the greens superintendent stopped him and told him that there were two bodies lying there. The operator fetched up, observing a person with something across his eyes that appeared to be a blindfold. The dead man's hand, lying across his body, was covered in blood, his blue jacket and green hospital pants stained red. A second bloody body, wearing a yellow sweater and white pants, was obscured behind the first. There were tire tracks near them, and he could see that whatever vehicle made them appeared to have also run right over that portion of the protective fencing which earlier he had noticed was down. The operator put his observation skills to further use when he looked up and spotted a purse that was lying further up along the dirt path that lead directly onto the course from the Johnston side. Whatever the connection might be, the police would make that determination. He knew one thing, however, when work had concluded at 3:30 PM the day before, there was nothing in this area. Now there were two dead bodies.

At 12:46 PM, the supervisor removed his cell phone from the golf cart and dialed 9-1-1. The call went through to the Emergency Dispatch Center, located on Smith Street in North Providence. Raymond B. Reynolds received the call. After taking the basic information provided by the witness, he transferred the call to the Providence Fire Dispatch.

"I got a couple dead bodies here," the supervisor said, his voice faint. "I'm very nervous, so..."

"Where are you now?"

"Buttonhole Golf Course. I'm standing, looking over them."

"Well, what happened to them?"

"I have no idea. I'm in the golf course. I was driving by. I just saw them."

The dispatcher instructed the supervisor not to disturb the scene and to meet the police and rescue vehicle at the main entrance at Mancini Drive.

On the morning of June 9, 2000, my shift started at 8 AM. It was well into the lunch hour when I walked into the communication room to talk with my friend, Patrolman Anthony Sasso. We had just ordered lunch when the phone rang. Sasso answered, and I saw the expression on his face change instantly. It was a look you see cops get when they suddenly turn that switch on and have to prepare themselves to do what they had been trained to do. I knew right away it was something big. Sasso just kind of nodded into the phone a couple of times, then said, "Ok," and hung up quickly. He looked at me and said, "Ping, forget lunch. They just found two bodies at Buttonhole."

Chapter 7

Call to
Duty

A t that moment, there still were only five people who knew exactly what happened at Buttonhole Golf Course the night before. Two sets of parents woke that morning having no knowledge that their children had been murdered. Friends who had been out dancing with the couple the night they were killed had no reason not to believe that the pair had gotten home safely. None of them knew that the lives of these two young people had been taken in exchange for a ride to Pawtucket and some gas money. The only ones who had any understanding at all of how something so horrific could have taken place, incredibly, did not seem to be troubled by the loss of life in the least. Aside from Burdick's fear for his own safety, which was a reasonable enough concern for him to have, considering his actions prior to the slayings and his reputation among the other suspects, there did not seem to be any conscionable afterthought given to the two people whose lives had been taken.

By all accounts, the killers went home afterwards and went to bed. How a person can just lay his head down on a pillow and fall asleep after being a part of something like that is mind-boggling. How could anyone have such a lack of feeling for innocent life?

At 1:07, Lt. Louis Courtemanche of the Providence Fire Department, Emergency Medical Division, responded to the scene. Police from Providence were already present when he arrived, and with the two victims showing no obvious signs of life, the ambulance was turned away. The coroner would take this one, Courtemanche realized.

As soon as the bodies were discovered, Chief Richard Tamburini canceled all leaves and days off for the department detectives, who were called back to duty between 1:15 and 1:30. At 1:20, I was among the first Johnston officers to arrive at the murder scene. Providence Patrolman Paul O' Rourke was the initial respondent to the double homicide, and had the scene secured. Providence Detective Patricia Cornell, Detective Sergeant Steven Bathgate and Sergeant Napoleon "Nappy" Britto of the Providence Police BCI division had begun a preliminary investigation and were moving around carefully inside a section of crime tape surrounding the bodies, an area that measured roughly a hundred feet in diameter.

I got my first look at the victims then, and it was a sight I'll never forget. It was revolting on every level, but what was particularly horrifying to me were their ages. These were just kids.

They were both in a semi-sitting position, slumped on their left sides against a tract of hay bales. In this section of the golf course, construction was just getting underway and there was nothing but ashen brown dirt almost as far as the eye could see. The bodies, however, were resting on a narrow swatch of green grass that bordered a forested plot of trees and shrubs, with the Woonasquatucket River just beyond that. The overhanging branches of spindly trees provided them with little shade or protection from the sun and the elements and the insects.

The male victim, his legs folded in front of him, was practically on top of the second victim, which appeared to be female. His dark blue jacket was prominent, the left side saturated with blood, the staining more apparent on the upper part of his left pant leg, the slacks a lighter gray color. A pool of blood had collected near the bodies, running a short distance through the grass down the slight incline on which they were reposed. His head was resting on top of hers, and he appeared to be 'blindfolded,' indicative of an execution-style murder. However, it was clear to me that the simple black headband had dropped down below his forehead following the impact of a gun blast. Resting on top of the male's left sneaker, in the tangle of shoelaces, just below the cuff of his pant leg, was a live round of ammunition. It almost seemed as if it had been placed there intentionally, perhaps a calling card left by the killer. But that was only speculation at this point, and remained to be determined.

The second victim was pinned beneath him, her back pressed against the hay. Her yellow sweater contrasted sharply with his dark blue jacket. She was wearing a white headband, though her face and much of her petite frame was obscured by his bulk. Her right hand was resting on his right elbow, his right arm draped across her bent right knee, which was nestled between his right hip and arm, as if they were hugging in a final embrace.

The remote possibility of a murder-suicide was instantly eliminated with the absence of a vehicle or a weapon. The victims were fully clothed and there was no visual evidence that a sexual assault had taken place. There was no indication of a struggle of any kind, in fact. It appeared to me that they were very scared at the time they were killed, huddled close together and did not put up a fight, probably trying to convince their murderers to let them live. Just looking at the results of this brutal and horrific crime, I was thinking that whoever was responsible might be hundreds of miles away by now.

Tragedy is tragedy is tragedy, but this case was different. It put a whole new twist on human savagery, as far as I was concerned. If it were possible to observe the way the murderers behaved in the hours immediately after the killings, you would never have known that they had participated in such a brutal double homicide a short time before. They seemed to have no conscience at all. Either that or they would have to be lacking some of the basic genetic material that would make them human. It's very disturbing to think that these killers are somehow included in the same species with the rest of us.

There was some confusion at that time about which department had jurisdiction because the property straddled two municipalities, with unequal portions in both Providence and Johnston. Like the park before it, however, the recreation facility was laid out predominantly in the town of Johnston.

However, there was never any kind of adversarial atmosphere or power struggle between the departments. In fact, just the opposite was true. It was not the kind of thing to squabble over. No town or city wanted to have a major crime occur in its jurisdiction. Having the least amount of crime as possible was something to boast about. You'd prefer to have even petty crimes happen across the town line. I couldn't even begin to estimate the number of times that a stolen car was discovered in that park, and some of our guys, perhaps not particularly in the mood to do paperwork that night, would push the vehicle across the line into Providence. Sometimes Providence would push it back, and this was the good-natured game that went on between the departments for years. So, a murder dump site was the last thing anyone would fight about. Solving those types of cases is always improbable, if not impossible. With this grim discovery, however, finding whoever was responsible was all that either department was interested in, regardless of who had jurisdiction. I knew right away it was ours, but both departments were there, and it had to be determined which agency was going to be the lead so the investigation could begin. As with any murder case, you have to move fast and efficiently. There's about a seventy-two hour window, after which time evidence is lost forever and the trail starts to go cold very rapidly. It's exponential. And that's why it was imperative for command to be established right away. We all knew time was working against us. Every tick of the clock would make it easier for the guilty to think, to flee, or worse, hurt someone else, which is not a farfetched scenario. We also knew the person or persons responsible for these killings would be capable of just about anything.

When Johnston Police Sergeant Jones pulled the land specs and determined what I already knew, the case was officially designated to our department. I became the lead detective.

There were some admittedly mixed emotions on my part. Already, there were television news trucks lining up at the top of slope around the entrance of the golf course construction site. Chief Tamburini and the Johnston Mayor, William Macera, were on the scene, as well. I understood then that everything we did would be under a microscope from that point on. Despite all that, I felt very alone at that point with these two, as of yet, unidentified bodies. At headquarters, when this call came in, there was only myself, Patrolman Sasso, who was working the radio room that day, and Detective Albert A. Faella. Initially, Patrolman Parillo and Detective Faella were on the scene there as well. That was it.

I was still a junior detective, and it was more than a little disconcerting for me. It was a hot afternoon, and very humid, which probably didn't help. But worse, still, dark clouds were gathering on the horizon, and moving like a black wall across the sky. The threat of severe weather, bringing heavy rain and lightning to the area did not bode well for this outdoor crime scene investigation.

Considering the difficult task that lay ahead, I took a breath and tried to steady my voice as I turned to Al Faella. "Al, what the hell do I do now?" I asked him.

In a very calming voice, he said, "Ping, calm down. You can do this."

It turned out to be just the boost of confidence I needed.

He assured me that when something like this happens, most detectives don't answer their pages right away. In this case, however, we got such immediate responses from our guys. That was unusual. Still, I have to admit those were a couple of anxious minutes before the cavalry arrived, so to speak, and everyone reported back to work.

When they did, there was a large contingency of officers representing both departments on the scene. You never saw so many police officers in one place that didn't involve a marching band, a Grand Marshal and politicians waving from an open convertible. But this savage spectacle was the furthest thing from a parade you could ever imagine.

Chapter 8

CSI: Johnston

One of the Johnston detectives that called back was David G. DeTora, who worked in the BCI (Bureau of Criminal Identification) Division as a crime scene investigator. DeTora, known to all almost exclusively by the nickname Sonny, is as colorful a character as you'll ever meet. When he started with BCI in 1985, he was the youngest detective in the department. But that was not why they called him Sonny. At that time, the big show on television was *Miami Vice*. Don Johnson's character, Sonny Crockett, was handsome and charismatic. Sonny Crockett had nothing on our Sonny DeTora in terms of fashion. Sharp looking sports jackets, T-shirt underneath, pastel colors, white boat shoes with no socks; that was Sonny DeTora. But as a crime scene investigator, you'd have to go a lot further than Miami to find a better one.

Sonny left work at noon that afternoon, taking a half day off so he could get some things done around his Johnston home. His ten-year-old son was giving his first public speech at his fifth grade graduation dinner. Sonny wanted the time off so he could attend the dinner with his family later that evening.

Sonny was changing the liner of his swimming pool when he heard the sirens blaring in the distance. Right after that, his pager began to go off. When he called the station, Patrolman Sasso informed him about the double homicide. Sonny stopped what he was doing and immediately returned to headquarters, then responded to the scene with his BCI partner, Detective William Warren.

Sonny could not help but notice the media contingent and private citizens lined up all around the vicinity looking down at them like guppies in a fish bowl. However, he had more than enough experience to know that the only watchful eyes he needed to be concerned with would come later and belonged to defense attorneys, whether hired privately or appointed public defenders, of any would-be defendants. He knew they'd be reviewing every move they made on their tapes very closely, listening for every fart. Since the O.J. Simpson case, it's become an acceptable defense strategy to raise reasonable doubt by finding fault with the collection methods of evidence techs, exaggerating every tiny blunder and creating a perception that evidence has been mishandled.

This double homicide was just one of several cases which the Johnston BCI Division was working on at the time. Murder investigations were nothing new to Sonny, and they were all important so he knew what to expect – a high profile case. However, he knew immediately as I did this presented a wild card to crime scene investigations. The importance of getting this one right was not lost on Sonny. The pressure that his division would be under the next couple of days, which he knew would be considerable, would prove to be unlike anything he had ever experienced before. His caseload could not be used as an excuse. There certainly would not be any sympathy coming his way. He understood that his supervisors would want immediate answers from the evidence that was collected. Given that kind of urgency, with a double homicide of this magnitude, there was a need to prioritize. The other cases he was working on would have to be put on hold for a little while.

Sonny and I were happy about that, since my first task that afternoon was to make sure the crime scene was preserved. Some of the additional personnel were used to help secure the area as well as assist Sonny in gathering evidence. The area also needed to be canvassed for witnesses. There was a residential neighborhood along the perimeter, and three golf course workers were already on their way to Johnston headquarters, where detectives would interview them separately. There were fresh tire tracks as well as other evidence scattered around the crime scene and the bodies had to be identified.

The next thing I did was contact the Medical Examiner's Office, requesting that a representative be sent to the scene to further assist in the collection of evidence, specifically from the victims, and to remove the bodies carefully for the preservation of further evidence.

I conferred with Napoleon Britto, who was not just the top BCI man in Providence. Britto had a well-deserved reputation as one of the more elite crime scene investigators in the region. Unfortunately for me, he also had a dark sense of humor. He basically told me that if these murders hadn't been filmed by the amateur filmmaker who captured John F. Kennedy's assassination on his 8-mm camera, this case would never get solved. This was not something I needed to hear. I really didn't know Britto well enough to determine if he was joking or simply pulling my chain, but I obviously had more pressing mysteries to solve.

At 2:02 PM, two technicians from the state Medical Examiner's Office arrived on the scene. At that point, the forensic aspect of the investigation really took off. Now, the crime scene was jointly processed by Johnston's BCI Division, Providence BCI and the State Medical Examiner's Office. With weather concerns a major factor, getting the scene processed before heavy rainfall was critical. The tradeoff was an increased chance of contamination or other problems in evidence collection. But these guys were the best, and they skillfully worked together that day.

Crime scene investigators, as most people may know from the popular television drama *CSI*, are police officers specially trained in methods of evidence collection, documentation and preservation. They are called to murder sites to apply their special skills, which involve everything from taking photographs and video of the scene to lifting latent footwear impressions and cataloguing all other physical evidence on and around the victims.

Sonny and the other CSI personnel on site worked methodically, starting from the outer perimeter of the crime scene and proceeding inward toward the victims, tagging and photographing every item along the way,

then marking them with individually numbered yellow placards before carefully removing them to further preserve them as evidence.

The most pertinent items recovered at the crime scene, besides the hollow point .40 caliber Smith & Wesson bullet resting on the male's left foot,
included a single latex glove found approximately sixty feet from the bodies
and an empty condom wrapper. The prophylactic package stood out in that
dusty, barren terrain. It was pink and only ten yards from the victims. No less
significant were fresh tire tracks which led away from the immediate area and
ascended a slope leading out of the golf course. Close to these distant tire
marks, ninety feet west of the murder site, a small wallet was located. Also
recovered was a pack of cigarettes, a coffee cup and lid, a box of tissues and
other sundry items that might hold clues to the events of the murder and the
perpetrators. Only investigative intelligence or lab analysis could determine
whether or not they held any evidentiary value.

The most challenging aspect of processing this particular crime scene
was the remoteness of the location. Because there were no permanent structures in the area, it made things especially difficult for Sonny, who had to
make accurate field sketches. These were needed to show the spatial relation
between the various items taken into evidence. Establishing a reference line
or a reference point was nearly impossible. At least two fixed points or objects
are necessary for triangulation, which is a method used to establish the exact
location of crime scene evidence by taking the measurements of their distances between specific and permanent points of reference, such as utility
poles, fire hydrants and sewers. Since no such objects were immediately available at this remote location, the crime scene investigators had to look elsewhere. The clubhouse was several hundred yards away, and was still under
construction. Even the river could not be used, because it was likely to be
diverted in the near future. They ended up using part of the cement foundation of the second tee box. The designated area where golfers would hit their
first shot on the second hole would probably remain a permanent structure
on the course. In the absence of GPS technology, or some other type of satel-
lite-based navigation system, this was all we had.

The two main objectives at this point were retrieving the murder
weapon, along with all spent shell casings, and identifying the bodies. The

medical examiner's office would help determine the latter, but pinpointing the ejected metal jackets and possibly the bullets from fired rounds that may have exited the bodies proved to be exactly like trying to find the proverbial needle in the haystack. The metal detectors were all but useless because the soil content of the former dump site was laden with metal, and our BCI guys couldn't go two inches in any direction without registering a hit. But everyone did the best they could with what they had to work with.

Like the unusually swift response time of our detectives, what might have been even more unlikely was how they all checked their egos at the door when they worked that day. In any police department, self-interest is not something that is ever in short supply. On this case, it was not a factor. There was never any griping or resentment about assignments. Everyone seemed to understand what a treacherous crime this had been. No matter how difficult sorting the clues and evidence was, we had to work together quickly. We knew that everything we did individually over the course of the next twenty-four hours or so would factor greatly into the outcome of the case. From the beginning, there was a sense of urgency. The crime scene investigators were aware that every tiny scrap of evidence needed to be preserved so that whoever was responsible for the murders would be held accountable. We knew we had to catch these killers. To put it another way, there was no way we were going to let whoever did this get away. That's why we all wanted to be sure that nothing was missed and that there was a mountain of physical evidence available so that state attorneys could prosecute the guilty to the fullest extent of the law. While this is always the goal at any crime scene that's being worked by our department or other law enforcement agency, the added emotions of working so closely on a brutal and senseless crime such as this intensified the sense of responsibility we all felt. We didn't want to leave anything to chance or risk the slightest possibility that the killer or killers might slip through the cracks in our judicial system because there was insufficient or corrupted evidence. That would just not be acceptable.

The victims' bodies, which had remained untouched to this point, were meticulously photographed. A closer visual inspection revealed that both of them had been killed by gunshot wounds to the top of their heads, the male sustaining two shots and the female one. Both were killed at the scene.

At about that time, a Massachusetts state driver license was discovered in the male's right front pants pocket. The I.D. denoted twenty-one-year-old Jason Burgeson, his address and that he was from Lakeville, Massachusetts. The inset picture showed a good looking, dark haired male youth who still had some 'baby fat' around his cheeks, matching exactly the appearance of the victim upon whom the license was found. Tucked just inside his left sneaker, outside the sock, was a gold-color money clip containing seventy-eight dollars in cash and a personal check for sixty-five dollars, made out to Jason Burgeson from Amy Shute. It was a bank check, so the signer's address was not readily available.

Captain David aRusso advised Detective Faella to go through the wallet found at the scene as soon as BCI had processed the item. Wearing latex gloves, the investigator observed several plastic consumer and personalized cards, including credit cards and a medical plan card, all bearing the name AMY SHUTE. However, no photo ID was present. One card, a video store membership card, bore the name Jeffrey Harper.

Now, with the personal check made out to Jason, found in his pocket, together with the discovery of the wallet full of personal effects discovered nearby, we were reasonably sure that the female victim was Amy Shute. However, we could not be sure until a family member positively identified her remains. But by 2:30, we had tentatively identified both victims, and that was significant. Going back to check, we were able to retrieve the home address of Amy Shute printed on the top left corner. The next difficult task would be going to the residence and having a relative view the remains at the morgue to determine if they were Amy's. It might appear somewhat insensitive to look at this discovery as a positive one, and with what might outwardly appear to be haste and detachment, but from the perspective of a police investigation, promptly identifying the victims and following up on all possible leads is the most effective way to get results.

Faella notified headquarters and advised communications personnel to follow up on contacting Jeffrey Harper by calling the Registry of Motor Vehicles to obtain an address on him.

At this time, as the bodies of Jason and Amy were separated for the first time since they died in their final embrace, several investigators were moved to tears. It was a moment that touched me as well as I realized that in the last moments of their lives these kids only had each other, and little chance against the savage brutes that condemned them.

Personnel from the Medical Examiner's Office removed the young victims from the scene. When they took Jason, Amy was completely visible. Then, the full extent of this heinous crime was known. She was in partial fetal position, with her right leg extended back and away from the midline. His nose was practically touching her left knee. The lower part of her left pant leg was soaked through with blood, with practically no staining anywhere else except some on her left sleeve. Also visible to us for the first time, just out of reach of the young woman's left hand, on the ground close to her fingers, was a clear stone mounted on a yellow band, which is how police describe a diamond engagement ring. Clearly, she had been concealing it in her clenched fist at the time she was shot. Also of some note was a plastic night club admittance band, white with pink stars, on her right wrist. This gave us some clue as to where the couple may have been the night before.

Shortly after Amy's body was removed, a spent .40 caliber shell casing, which is the ejected portion of a live round, was located on the ground between the silt fencing and a hay bale just behind the victims. Now we had very promising leads to follow up on.

Chapter 9

The Manhunt Begins

At 3:00 PM, all investigating officers returned to the Johnston Police Department for a meeting, a major crime briefing which was addressed by Commander Captain David aRusso. He related all the latest information and up-to-date developments regarding the double homicide. Basically, he wanted to get everyone up to speed and on the same page. Communication is crucial at this stage of an investigation. With so many detectives involved, and with so much information being gathered separately, it's difficult for everyone to keep up with all the changes, whether it involves leads, witnesses, suspects or anything else that can get thrown at you during a murder investigation of this scope.

It also gave all of us a chance to breathe. I took this moment as a brief opportunity to decompress, to collect my thoughts, and to reflect.

Things in my life were already hectic, both personally and on the job. I had been working way too much, and admittedly neglecting the things that were really important. I had been on the department sixteen years at that point, and I wasn't making the kind of money I wanted. Overtime wasn't always available, but when it was I took it. I was also taking classes, working toward getting my BCI certification. I was overextended to say the least.

But the problems in my life paled in comparison to the impact these two murders would have on so many people. When something so terrible happens, it forces you to take some stock in your own life, to step back and ask yourself some difficult questions.

On the drive back from the murder scene, an old song was playing on the radio that got me thinking. Strangely, I began to hear the song frequently on different radio stations throughout, not just the course of the investigation, but later during the trial phases. Maybe it was just something I began to take special notice of for some reason, like when you buy a new car and then you start to see the same exact type of car, color and all, everywhere you go. It was a song I'd always liked, but now it takes on special meaning whenever I hear it.

The song was "Turn! Turn! Turn! (To Everything There Is A Season)", by the Byrds.

"A time to be born, a time to die..."

I'd never really given the words much consideration before. But as it played that afternoon and the refrain was repeated, I found myself pondering its meaning.

The lyrics seemed to suggest that life is in a constant state of flux and you have to adjust accordingly to survive. At least, that's how I saw it. It made me think about the birth of my daughter, a day that I still remember vividly. And I thought about these two murdered kids. I thought how terribly fast things can change from one minute to the next. You can have a complete family one day, and then wake the following morning to tragedy.

My shift normally ended at 4 PM, about this time. I thought about what else I might be doing had this appalling crime never occurred. Sometimes, when I had free time, I would immerse myself in outside interests, which included working on antique vehicles, reading and spending time with my daughter, which usually involved taking her skating. I don't know if you could qualify drinking with other cops as an outside interest, but I did plenty of that as well. I did anything to avoid dealing with the real problem underlying everything else - my rocky marriage. If I put half as much time into solidifying the relationship with my wife as I did on advancing my career, that story might have turned out differently, at least.

But it was my work that really consumed me, figuratively, and quite honestly, almost literally. It's a passion that lay people may not understand. The pressure of trying to solve any case can be overwhelming. Most people don't call the police all that often, but when they do they sometimes expect not only instant resolution to their particular problems, but all the wrongs of the world to be righted along the way as well. There's no room for mistakes. And these calls are daily. The constant stress of all this, coupled with my personal problems, conspired to lead me to make some unhealthy personal choices. All the hours, the cigarettes, the drinking; it was a recipe for self-destruction.

My only sanity break, besides my daughter, came when I picked up a book. It was easier to plug into someone else's life, whether fictional or non-fictional, than it was for me to communicate with people in the real world about my own problems. Life can be strange that way, particularly when you consider that my job was to investigate events and interview people on behalf of others, specifically the residents of Johnston and the state of Rhode Island, who had complaints or problems that needed to addressed, yet at the same time it was a challenge for me to open myself up and ask for help when my world was falling down around me. In reading crime novels by writers such as John Lescroart, John Sandford, Robert Tanenbaum and true crime books by Ann Rule, I'd become involved in crime investigations that always gets solved, where every loose end is neatly tied up, and all in the time that it takes to read a book.

My wife recognized that I was not doing our relationship any good when I was grabbing all the overtime I could, leaving little time for her. It was the "us" that suffered irrevocably. All of us suffered - my wife, our daughter and I.

We were headed down the path of separate lives and it seemed my wife was the only one who knew it. I was in denial. I told her that we could use the money. I even said that I was thinking of my daughter, her future, believing for some reason that having a ghost for a dad was the best thing for her. My child was getting caught up in it all, and I didn't want that. But divorce was a foreign concept in my family. I was still old school enough to consider the dissolution of marriage taboo and immoral, grudgingly holding onto old world ideals that my parents had instilled in me. It seemed to work for them and that bygone era. But life was not that simple anymore. Everything was so complicated. Or maybe it was just my life. I know I didn't have to look far to confirm that all the negative thoughts that were assailing me with increasing frequency lately were not completely a product of my own deficiencies. The job can make you callous. In my opinion, cops on a whole do not start out jaded but it comes with the territory. To think about it metaphorically, maybe after running into enough houses and chasing the boogey man out of other people's closets, the boogey man gets into us. In actuality, what develops is an "us against them" mentality, which is just a way to protect ourselves from the boogey man. Whatever the reason, I clearly observed a much higher divorce rate among cops (whether male or female) than the fifty-percentile typically seen in the civilian population. And for officers who married other officers, these were among the shortest unions of all. I had seen some end before the ink dried on the marriage certificate. And some of the couples who were still together had troubles worse than my own, with serial infidelity and alcohol abuse factoring predominantly into the equation.

I often wondered if perhaps some people were just not meant to be married. And, could it be that any of these people become cops?

I was destined to become just another statistic; a divorced cop.

When I reflect on my obsessive work pattern, it's hard to say if I worked so much because my marriage went sour or if my marriage went sour because I worked so much. Either way, sixteen hour days, four or five times a week was not uncommon. But what good is money when your personal life is a wreck? I didn't know how to fix it, so I just kept working. Some days, no matter what I did, it just was not right, and this constant failure in my private life only made me retreat further from those around me, until all I had was my work. If I lost that, I don't know what I would have done. And then the double murder occurred. Now I was being thrust into a horrific double homicide investigation as the lead detective with all my other pressures, and I just hoped that I could handle it.

And, still, I kept thinking about my daughter. If I could have done better by her, I would have. I realized that things may have gone beyond the point of no return between her mom and me, but I thought that maybe our father-daughter relationship could at least be salvaged, and perhaps this might be the time for that purpose, as the song says. I hoped that was true.

One thing was certain, however, that this was a time to gather stones and find the murderers of these two young people.

At this hour, detectives were assigned investigative tasks and everybody began scrambling around in all different directions. It was chaos. But an organized chaos, like an ant colony whose nest has collapsed and the workers are feverishly rebuilding the tunnels.

Statements from the golf course workers who had discovered the bodies were already being taken. The assistant groundskeeper added to the statement he had given to police at the scene. He told Detective Michael S. Petrucci that there was a gate off Mancini Avenue which gets locked each afternoon when work concludes for the day, but there was also a dirt path on the Johnston side by which vehicles could gain entrance to the course anytime.

Freddie Walker, the heavy equipment operator who first spotted the victims but could not identify them from the distance where he'd been working, informed Detective Carl J. Tirocchi that there had not been any problems with employees or anyone in the area, and had not noticed any persons or strange vehicles in the area the previous day.

In his statement to Detective John Nardolillo, the course superintendent emphasized the fresh tire tracks leading away from the bodies and out of the course along the access road.

Detective Joseph Arcuri, Jr. had been requested to respond to a residence near the murder site to take witness statements from three people who would have been close enough to hear the gunshots. Earlier, they had contacted Johnston Police to tell them about some unusual activities they observed the night before. One of the neighbors had reported hearing what sounded like a gun being fired between 2:00 and 2:30 that morning. Communications directed him to a street that abuts the northern corner of Buttonhole Golf Course.

By 3:45, one of the earwitnesses was accompanied by Detective Arcuri to the Johnston Police Station to give an official statement. Sometime early the previous evening, around 6 PM, she said she heard 'banging outside in the distance which sounded like pops or gun shots.' She added that there was about a minute between the two loud bangs. She stated that she did not see anything, however, no persons or vehicles, after the sounds. She further reported that her dog began behaving strangely at that point, the way it did when people set off fireworks on the Fourth of July, and that the animal was too scared to go outside. The witness also said that her teenage son told her that he had heard two loud bangs in the direction of Providence sometime around 2:30 AM. Arcuri made a house call, and at the conclusion of the interview, the detective advised to have her family respond to headquarters as soon as they are able to provide investigators with their formal statements.

Meanwhile, Detectives Albert Faella and Bernard Pisaturo left headquarters headed for Providence. They had been advised to respond to the locations of various nightclubs in the city to try to determine which one had been giving out white bands with pink stars the night before, like the one found on the wrist of the victim believed to be Amy Shute. This was all part of the preliminary investigation to establish a timeline. If we could track the movements of the victims the night before, it would greatly assist us in establishing solid investigative leads and apprehending possible suspects and persons of interest in the case.

Also around 4:00 that afternoon, Detectives Melvin Steppo and Michael Petrucci left Johnston for Lakeville, Massachusetts. The small Plymouth County town was in the Boston-Cambridge-Quincy metro area, with a population around 10,000. It was similar in size to Johnston, only more rural. It had gotten its name from the chain of broad and magnificent lakes which occupy 4,000 acres of the township.

The detectives were expecting the drive to take about hour or so, but they would first be stopping by the local police department to meet Sergeant Thomas Bavin, who agreed to assist them in responding to the Burgeson household. The contact officer gave them directions to the station, which he described as occupying a rundown post-World War II building that shared space with a senior center. From there, they would drive in separate vehicles to the residence of the Burgeson family to notify them about Jason's murder and to conduct interviews relative to the investigation. The most important detail the family could provide was the information regarding the vehicle Jason had been driving the night before.

It was a long drive, and the two detectives had plenty of time to think about and discuss, not just what they were going to tell the Burgesons, but who was going to deliver the horrible news to the family, whom Bavin described as middle-class, respectable people. We knew that Jason's father and mother lived at the house, and that he had a married sister who resided in nearby Fall River. Mel Steppo was the senior agent, and these kinds of things naturally fall into the lap of the officer with the most experience, not the least, as some might expect. Mel was more than just the senior officer in the vehicle. He was the go-to man in the Johnston Police Department when it came to murder investigations. Regarded as the "old pro," Mel handled all the major crimes in Johnston at that time. When a junior detective wanted to know something about homicide work, Mel's name would come up and he could always be counted on for his understanding and guidance. I know all this firsthand, because Mel and I had been partners, and he taught me a lot. In fact, it would not be an exaggeration for me to say that he taught me most of what I know about this job.

In my opinion, he may not have followed all the rules and regulations to the letter, but he always got results. Mel had his own way of conducting an investigation, and it worked for him. On the job for twenty-eight years then, he would put in four more before retiring, and when he left it would be with the respect and admiration of officers not only from Johnston, but in all neighboring departments, as well as agents on the state and federal law enforcement.

At around 4:30, Elizabeth Zatkoff dropped off Harry Burdick in Pawtucket, where he was currently staying with a friend. She was pressed for time, having to get home to feed their baby. She was already late for the infant's mid-afternoon feeding, and barely noticed her boyfriend's melancholy mood.

Burdick was still nervous and afraid, wondering if the two bodies had been discovered yet, not knowing that they had been. He still distressed over the possibility, and what the police might have put together so far. He worried further that some of the others were talking about it, implicating him. A short while later he called his father in Warwick, to ask if he heard anything on the news about a murder. He said no. It hadn't hit the local media yet.

While Harry Burdick was brooding over these thoughts, in Providence, a man was seated behind the wheel of his bus, but he was not going anywhere.

The twenty-eight year old intercity driver for the Rhode Island Public Transit Authority (RIPTA) was on standby. He would only be on the road that day if another bus broke down, so he divided his time between reading the newspaper and chatting with people he knew. He was halfway through his 3:00-6:00 shift, parked in a queue at the Kennedy Plaza bus depot, when one of the buses in front of him pulled out of its space to go on a run. His friend was driving the bus directly behind the one that had been dispatched. As the friend was about to pull up a spot, the first driver saw a white SUV suddenly pull into the empty space. The driver continued to pull up closer to the SUV slowly, to let the operator know that he needed to pull out so he could get his bus in the spot. It worked. The van pulled away, taking a left onto Dorrance Street and disappearing.

Chapter 10

Notifying the families

A t about the same time the driver saw the SUV drive off, Detectives Tirocchi and Nardolillo, who had been dispatched to the Shute residence were just arriving when they saw someone who was about to get into a car that was parked in the driveway. The detectives pulled in behind the vehicle, boxing it in. The detectives got out and approached the man standing beside the open car door.

"We're detectives with the Johnston Police Department," Nardolillo said.

"Who are you?" Tirocchi asked.

The man identified himself as James Colvin, sometimes called "Jim," the boyfriend of Carol Shute, Amy's mother.

"Do you have any guns in the house?" Tirocchi asked next. The question surprised Colvin, who was just leaving to pick Carol up at work. He shook his head. The detectives fired off questions, giving him a bit of the third degree for the next five minutes or so. When they asked about Amy, wanting to know if he had a picture of her, he began to suspect an accident or something terrible had happened. He knew Amy had not been home that night.

Colvin informed the detectives that Amy had actually been staying with her grandmother. Colvin told them that the grandmother had called that morning to say that Amy had gone out last night and had not returned. He said that Amy worked at a local manufacturing company, and that Carol and Amy's grandmother were aware that the girl had not shown up for work that morning.

His description of Amy and acknowledgment that she had a friend named Jason made the detectives all but certain that the female victim was, in fact, Amy Shute. When asked about Jeffrey Harper, the name on the video card which was found in Amy's possession, Colvin told them that he was Amy's ex-boyfriend. The two detectives stared at one another briefly, seeming to have a silent exchange. Then Tirocchi turned to Colvin and said, "Two bodies were found in the woods."

"What?" Colvin choked on the word.

The detective informed him that the first victim, Jason Burgeson, had been shot to death on a golf course in Johnston, and that a second victim had been discovered with him, and they believe it to be Amy.

"What happened? Where is Amy?"

"We need Carol to identify the body at the coroner's office."

"She's dead?"

"Where is Carol Shute at this time?"

Colvin told them she was working. "I was on my way to pick her up when you arrived." The detectives requested to accompany him, and then they followed him to the plant where Carol worked.

On the drive over to the chemical plant, Detective Nardolillo alerted the department about the possibility of a love triangle between Harper, Amy and Jason, and we, naturally, moved on that quickly. Captain aRusso advised Detective Alan Ross to locate Harper and get a statement from him right away.

Harper instantly became a person of interest in the investigation that was only a couple hours old. It was not something we could have just sat on. He was associated with the victims, and the first thing you do in any violent crime investigation is look inward, at known associates, including friends and family, before you consider a random encounter with a stranger. Statistics unequivocally supported the likelihood that Amy had been killed by someone close to her. Where there is more intimacy, there is usually more violence. Some studies have estimated that up to three million women are physically abused by former or present husbands and boyfriends per year. In 2000, 1,247 women were killed by an intimate partner. On average, more than three women are murdered in this country every day by these men. Whatever Jeffrey Harper's involvement with Amy had been, that personal relationship had now became an interest of the police.

We quickly learned that Harper was employed at a parcel service in Warwick, and Detectives Ross and Arcuri were dispatched to the facility to see what they could learn about him. They met with Harper's immediate supervisor, who informed the detectives that he had worked from 3:52 AM until 8:05 that morning. This fact only increased our curiosity about Harper at that point. All we knew so far was that Jason and Amy had been out on a date the night before, a witness believed he heard a gunshot around 2:30 AM coming from the direction of Buttonhole Golf Course, her ex arrived at work at 3:52 AM, and the couple was not seen again until their bodies were discovered by golf course workers later that day. While Harper's work alibi did not dismiss him as a person of interest in the case, it also was not something to get overly excited about. It did, however, warrant further investigation, and we would certainly be following up on that with a personal interview.

Not far away, in West Warwick, Jim Colvin arrived at Carol Shute's place of employment with Detectives Nardolillo and Tirocchi in tow. Jim was quite late by now, and Carol had been waiting outside, having a cigarette with a co-worker when she saw Jim's car pull in. It was Friday, the end of a long work week, and she didn't even mind that he was late. Her weekend had already started. She didn't notice the car that was following him. When Jim got out of the vehicle and approached her, the two men in the car behind him also stepped outside. This caught her attention.

"Who are your friends?" she asked.

Jim hesitated. "They're Johnston Police detectives."

"What do *they* want?"

He wanted to break the news to Carol himself, but he suddenly found that he did not know what to say.

"It's Amy."

He didn't need to say anything more. The expression on his face told Carol that something was terribly wrong. When Harper had called that morning, asking about Amy not showing up for work, Carol thought it was just Amy being Amy, always late. When Harper called Carol around noon to inform her that Amy had yet to show up for work or return home, she was more upset with her oldest daughter for her irresponsibility. Now, however, she realized that the situation was much more serious than missing work.

"What happened to my Amy?" she asked with her voice quivering.

"You need to sit down."

"WHAT HAPPENED TO AMY, JIM?"

Jim embraced her firmly, making sure he was physically supporting her when he told Carol that Amy had been murdered and they needed to go to the morgue to see her.

"No." Carol shook her head. "It's not true."

"It is, Carol," Jim said. "They found her things. You need to go with them to identify her."

"No. I'm not going anywhere with them. It's not true."

She drove with Jim instead. He followed the detectives to the city morgue. Carol would still be in denial when they arrived. She refused to believe what she was seeing and what she was being told.

From the parcel facility, the Detectives Ross and Arcuri notified Coventry police, and representatives from both agencies responded to the residence of Jeffrey Harper, arriving there around 5:00. The boy's father, related that his son was not presently home. However, during this conversation the phone rang.

"Hey, Dad..."

"You need to come home right away," Mr. Harper said before his son could complete his sentence.

"What? Come home? Why, what's wrong?"

"Jeff, just come home. Okay? You'll see when you get here."

"Yeah. All right. I'll be right there."

"Good. See you in a few minutes."

Unbeknownst to the detectives, Harper was calling from the Shute's Coventry home, where he had been talking to Elizabeth Shute, who was the youngest of Amy's two sisters. She was sixteen. She had just arrived when Harper drove up. He wanted to know if Amy had been there. Neither of them knew anything, or that Carol and Jim were on their way to the morgue.

When Harper arrived home a short time later, the young man told the police that he had been looking for Amy all day and that he was very worried about her. To the experienced detectives, he seemed genuinely concerned and sincere. He was deliberately not provided with any information about Amy possibly being the victim of a homicide, and he gave his account of his activities the previous night. He informed detectives that he had been at the popular night club on India Street in Providence, where he said Amy and Jason had been with some friends of Jason at the end of the night. The detectives leaned towards him discerningly. The friends, Harper told the detectives without being asked, he did not know.

The detectives decided that Jeffrey Harper had told them things they needed to follow up on, and they were ready to conclude the interview. The detectives did not want to push him too far at that point. If he turned out to be an actual suspect, they wanted him to be the last to know. They needed to evaluate what he said and see where it led them. Investigators would be talking with Harper again very soon. They knew where to reach him, and asked if he would come by the Johnston police station at his earliest convenience to give an official statement and he agreed. They thanked Harper and his father and left.

The witness and his grandmother arrived at the Johnston Police Station at around 5:40 PM. Detective Arcuri took a statement from the young man, who said that he heard two loud, echoing blasts, like gunshots, separated by about one minute sometime shortly after 2 AM. He was sure of the time, because he had been watching the rerun of an earlier broadcast of the Howard Stern television show, which started at that hour. He said that his dog ran into his bedroom after the shots, and was very scared. The grandmother informed Arcuri that her grandson got out of bed at that time and woke her up, asking her if she heard the sounds. She responded that she had been asleep and did not hear anything. The witness said that he did not look out of the window at any time, and did not see anything or hear anything more.

Detectives Nardolillo and Tirocchi escorted Carol Shute and Jim Colvin into the Medical Examiner's Office in Providence. They were greeted by a receptionist. The detectives announced who they were, and then they waited for the medical examiner to come out.

It was still so surreal to Carol, but the biting reality of it all was slowly sinking in, leaving her tingling and numb.

"Are you going to be okay?" Jim asked her.

"Yes," she lied. Her legs had begun to shake and all the strength seemed to be draining from her body. When the medical examiner appeared, she was barely aware that her feet were moving her forward. The last thing she remembered was reaching a set of double doors when she suddenly blacked out. She heard herself screaming in anguish as she slumped to the floor. The fainting spell did not linger long, but when she became conscious again she was completely inconsolable. At the same time, she felt sick to her stomach, and a small mop bucket was placed in front of her as she continued to dry heave. Considering her physical and emotional condition, the detectives were not surprised when she deferred the task of identifying Amy's body to Jim. She was far too upset to make the ID herself. Fortunately, Jim was able to step in and perform the sad, but necessary task.

Providence BCI Detectives Patricia Cornell and Napoleon Britto continued to assist the investigation, helping our department stay ahead of the approaching storm. Fortunately, the rain held off all day, but the humidity remained, which was more than a fair trade off as far as these crime scene investigators were concerned. They made castings of the tire tracks near the bodies, using Plaster of Paris to replicate the precise impressions, and then turned them over to our guys, Detectives William Warren and Sonny DeTora. The four crime scene investigators from separate jurisdictions worked together throughout the afternoon. Britto and Sonny had the highest regard for one another, and work even more closely today, now that Sonny has retired from Johnston and is working full-time for the State Medical Examiner's Office, doing everything from clerical work to performing autopsies. He went from *Miami Vice* to *CSI* to *Quincy* all in one career. The department's loss was the state's gain.

At 5:50, the BCI investigators cleared the scene, with all the collected evidence transferred and secured in the Johnston BCI Division evidence room. With the other detectives all out following leads, and his job done for now, Sonny asked Captain aRusso if he could leave for an hour or so to go see his son who would be giving a talk. The Captain, being a family man himself, understood, but instructed Sonny to keep his pager and cell phone on just in case.

Sonny managed to get to the restaurant in time to see his son give his speech. He was even able to have a nice dinner with his family, though it would be short-lived. Before too long, not unexpectedly, his pager went off, and it was Captain aRusso reluctantly advising him to report back to work. On a day like this, in particular, Sonny felt fortunate he was able to get away at all to spend the time he did with his family.

Just before 6:00, Detectives Melvin Steppo and Michael Petrucci, in the company of Sergeant Bavin, arrived at the Burgeson's ranch-style home in a quiet Lakeville neighborhood. They were greeted at the door by Jason's father, Ernest, who ushered them inside after acknowledging the local sergeant. As his wife, Nadine, joined them, the homeowner looked at them worriedly for a moment. Mel Steppo broke the awkward silence by getting the introductions out of the way. Then he asked Mr. Burgeson if his son, Jason, drove his own car and if he knew the girl that he had been out with the previous night. Mr. Burgeson, who had a no-nonsense, blue-collar air about him, drew a heavy sigh. His immediate exasperation was one borne of the fear that his son had gotten into some kind of trouble with the car or the girl. He was certainly not thinking that Jason could have been in any worse place at that moment than a jail cell.

He told the detectives that Jason had gone out between 8 and 9 o'clock the previous night, informing them "He had gone to pick up his girlfriend, Amy, in Rhode Island," and he had not returned yet, which in and of itself, was not a cause for alarm or all that unusual. There had been previous occasions where Jason had stayed out all night and had forgotten to call. This, the Burgesons had been thinking, was one of those instances. At that point, the seasoned detective knew what he had to do, and he realized that it needed to be done quickly. "We have some bad news for you," Steppo said quietly. "Your son has been murdered."

It might seem insensitive, but in actuality, the best way to convey this kind of message is to be blunt, matter-of-fact.

It may have only been a fraction of a moment, but for the detectives it seemed like an eternity. You just never know how a loved one is going to react. Mr. Burgeson processed this weighty information quickly, and all at once he erupted in a fit of anger and rage. It was not something that Steppo and Petrucci had never seen before, but at the same time this man appeared almost docile up until then, quite unassuming and reserved. His violent emotional outburst resulted in numerous holes punched through the living room wall and a handful of bruised knuckles. The three officers tried to restrain him, but he was strong, and driven by a blind fury that was understandable to the other men in the house who were also fathers. Even Nadine Burgeson was trying to calm him down, but to no avail. Sergeant Bavin stepped forward and tried to reason with Mr. Burgeson, telling him that he was destroying his own home and that he was only going to have to repair it. This seemed to work, though it may have been that the distraught father had expended all the physical energy he had rather than anything the detectives did or said. Either way, once he had regained his composure, Steppo and Petrucci were in a better position to extract some useful information, particularly about the vehicle Jason was driving, which was what we needed most in order to push this investigation forward.

At that time, a tearful Nadine Burgeson picked up the telephone to contact Jason's sister, Kellie, who was married and living in nearby Fall River. She had been home from work a short time and had just sat down on the couch to relax when the phone rang. Her husband Nick answered it.

"Kellie, come here," he cried out from the bedroom a moment later.

"KELLIE! COME HERE NOW!" His voice was more frantic.

Kellie didn't know what to think as she got up and rushed to the bedroom, where she discovered her husband with tears in his eyes. "It's your mother," he said, as he handed her the phone.

"What is it, Mom?"

Kellie heard her mother sobbing uncontrollably on the other end of the line, unable to get any words out. Her parents had been watching her dog, so she instinctively thought that something terrible had happened to her pet, and that it had been killed. It never occurred to her that it might be Jason who had been harmed.

"Your brother is dead," Nadine Burgeson suddenly blurted out.

"What?" Kellie said, unsure if she had heard her mother correctly. "What did you say?"

"Murdered, Jason's been shot."

With that clarification came a strange sort of sharp focus. Kellie's mind seemed to drift in slow motion. She heard the words, *shot* and *murdered*, but she could not quite comprehend how those words might apply to her brother. They were foreign words. Words you hear in movies. Agonizing thoughts rushed through her mind. *People like Jason don't get shot in real life.* She couldn't imagine who would want to murder her brother.

He didn't hate anybody or discriminate. He loved people for just being themselves and he had friends of every color, religious faith and sexual preference. It was not uncommon for him to find somebody down on their luck and invite the person over to the house for dinner. He was always waltzing in with somebody new for his family to meet.

Everyone loved him. He had no enemies. It couldn't be true.

"The detectives are here now, Kellie."

Detectives? Kellie thought. *What the hell is going on here?*

"You've got to come home right away."

Home, her mother had said. That was a concept Kellie was familiar with. But she had not lived at the house in Lakeville since she got married. That was where she and Jason grew up and played together and had so much fun. It was where Jason, at the age of only three, first began swimming in the pool underwater with no help from anyone. To the amazement of everyone, he would jump off the diving board in the deep end and swim like a fish all the way to the shallow end without coming up once. Home was the place where she and her brother would perform surgery on their stuffed animals and play baseball in the backyard with the neighborhood kids. It was where Jason was always his big sister's little tag-along and she never minded, and if they were playing baseball and the older boys would call him out after three strikes she would yell at them to give him as many strikes as he needed until he hit the ball.

Suddenly it struck her. Jason had been shot. Murdered. That meant dead. It was a word that made sense. Horrible, dreadful sense.

"OH MY GOD!" Kellie cried out. *"IT WAS TRUE!"*

"I'll be right there," she told her mother, her voice sounding far off and faint in her own ears. Then her legs just gave way and she fell to the floor, screaming. She was shaking so much that Nick had to help her get dressed.

In Lakeville, Mr. Burgeson wanted to know how it happened, where and when, all questions that Detective Steppo could not very well answer. At this stage, there was always a danger of jeopardizing the investigation by releasing too much information, even to the families of the victims. The Burgesons were only told what they needed to know.

Mel kept the focus on obtaining information about the vehicle, and eventually Mr. Burgeson and his wife were able to locate Jason's automobile tax card, which listed everything we needed to know to put out an all-points bulletin (APB), also known as a BOLO, (Be on the Look Out). The color, year, make, model and registration describing Jason's vehicle could now be broadcast to all neighboring law enforcement agencies. Steppo immediately instructed Detective Petrucci to call me and pass along this information, which I took, promptly advising a patrolman to issue the APB on the vehicle. Jason's white SUV with Massachusetts plates, would be broadcast via inter city radio, alerting all area departments to be on the look out for it. It would eventually lead to the first major break in the case, but even so, Steppo's work wasn't finished yet in Lakeville. He wanted to be sure they gathered as many facts as possible to take back with them to Rhode Island.

Detectives Faella and Pisaturo had canvassed numerous Providence nightclubs that afternoon, all with no luck. From the outside, many of them looked liked they had been condemned overnight. Windowless, prewar brick-and-mortar edifices by day, but after the sun goes down, the front doors are unbolted and thick-necked hulks check ID's as long lines of young people wait to enter these dark, crowded caves with dim interior lighting, pulsating music and watered-down drinks. They were abandoned this time of the day, however. It was far too early for them to open, and no one had arrived yet to start getting these places ready for the night ahead, so the detectives were not even able to conduct on-site interviews. Then, at Cornellius, they talked to the club manager, who informed them that purple checkered bands had been issued at his establishment the night before, but related that the Complex, the mega dance club on Pine Street, had been issuing the types of bands they were inquiring about. This facility, as expected, was locked up tight, as well, and no one responded to their inquiry. Soon after reaching this impasse, they received word from headquarters to be on the alert for a white SUV with Massachusetts plates, the vehicle that one of the victims had been driving the previous night. Soon detectives began making a thorough sweep of the parking lots around the city's night spots, but their search did not turn up anything.

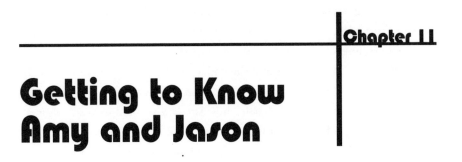

Chapter 11

Getting to Know Amy and Jason

J im entered the back room with Detective Nardolillo and the medical examiner while Detective Tirocchi stayed behind in a waiting area with Carol Shute.

The Coventry man walked tentatively into the prep room; the chilled air instantly raising goose pimples on his arms. An indiscriminate human form lying on a metal table ten yards or so lay in front of him; he hesitated. The body was covered with a clean white sheet so that only the head, resting on a gray rubber block, was exposed. Jim looked around at the two men accompanying him, as if to ask, *do I really have to do this?* Nardolillo nodded in the affirmative and Jim continued forward, moving closer to the body on the table. He still could not recognize the face, which was pallid and slightly bloated. He only knew this was a female because of the long hair, and although it was curly like Amy's, it looked darker than normal because it was wet. As he drew nearer, he could see the sharp creases where the linen had been folded. When Jim got within three paces of the body, he saw the young woman's face and he could not hold back his tears. Despite the discoloration and distention, there was no doubt that it was little Amy lying there beneath the coroner's sheet. With her eyes closed, she looked like she was only sleeping. She was always so full of energy, but when she crashed, it seemed she could fall asleep anywhere. He'd seen her nod off in the back seat of the car on even short trips, with her sisters screaming at each other, the radio blasting. Now, nothing was going to wake her up.

Amy was not his daughter, and she had a good relationship with her dad, but Jim sometimes felt like a father to her. One year in high school, Amy had wanted to go to Cancun with her friends. She had worked hard to save her money but was two hundred dollars short. She asked her mother for the difference, but before Carol could make her decision, Jim gave Amy the money and she never forgot it. He would have done anything for Amy and her sisters. Like a parent, he wanted to protect her, make her comfortable. But there was nothing he could do now. He couldn't take her home to her family. He couldn't make it all better. It was an unbearable realization for Jim Colvin. As he looked down at her and wept, all he could think was that he was glad Carol did not see her this way.

"Mr. Colvin is this Amy Shute?" the detective had to ask, though he already knew what the grieving man's answer was going to be.

"Yes," Jim said, the word barely audible through his loud, involuntary sobs.

The worst possible news for the Shute family was an important factor for our investigation, dramatically increasing the likelihood of apprehending her killers. The positive ID affirmed our belief that Amy Shute was killed alongside Jason Burgeson on Buttonhole Golf Course early that morning. And with Colvin's positive identification, the investigation stepped up.

Soon after I received a call from Detective Petrucci in Lakeville, providing a make on Jason's vehicle, Detective Tirocchi called to inform me that a positive identification of Amy Shute had been made by Jim Colvin, the live-in boyfriend of the victim's mother.

Having these first good breaks in the case may seem like simple good fortune or even blind luck, but it was actually a lot of hard work involving an entire department where manpower was stretched to the max. Johnston is a town of 30,000 with around seventy police officers, including a dozen or so detectives. A case of this magnitude could have been more easily undertaken by a police force with a larger budget and more personnel. For us, it was a real challenge. But we knew we had to respond and quickly, if we were going to catch these savage killers. Everyone did.

Jim and Carol escorted Detectives Nardolillo and Tirocchi to the house in West Warwick, where Amy had been residing with her grandmother.

"Would you mind waiting outside while Carol goes and tells her mother?" Jim asked the detectives when they got out of the vehicles.

"Of course," Nardolillo said.

Several minutes later, the grandmother screamed when her daughter told her that Amy was dead. Her mother's cries sent a fresh wave of grief crashing down on Carol and they fell into each other's arms, wailing in pain.

"Mom, there are detectives outside who need to come in and look in Amy's room," Carol told her after she had time to recover from the initial shock. Jim went outside and brought the detectives into the house. While they were in Amy's room, Carol said she wanted to notify her sister. Jim placed the call for her and informed Carol's sister of the tragic news. "Your mom and Carol are okay," he told her, "but they want you to come here right away."

Then, Jim called home and talked to Elizabeth. He only told her not to leave the house, and that he was on the way to get her. He left, and on the way he stopped to pick up Erin, Amy's youngest sister, who was working at a seafood restaurant.

For Jim, it was only the beginning of what he would be called on to do during this family crisis. He handled some of the most difficult tasks anyone would have to face when burying a child. Carol does not know how she would have made it through it all without him by her side. He was her strength. He carried her.

When Jim returned with the girls, they joined their mother, their grandmother, their aunt and the two detectives. Carol's sister had called the girls' father, and soon he arrived at the West Warwick residence.

The detectives joined the family in the living room after conducting a search of Amy's bedroom. They had been hoping to come across some prominent clue that might lead them to her killer, a proverbial smoking gun. It was certainly a long-shot, but the payoff could be substantial, possibly even leading to an arrest, or at the very least, saving detectives hours of investigative work chasing down false leads.

It was the typical bedroom of a twenty-one year old college girl. Nothing ominous or otherwise significant was recovered. Only a date book type calendar and other assorted papers with Amy's handwriting were removed by the detectives to be taken back to headquarters for further observation and held as potential evidence.

As the investigator turned to Amy's grandmother, she told them that she had been aware of Amy's plans to go out the previous night, though she did not know with whom, informing them that she had last seen her granddaughter at about 6:30 PM, just before her grandmother went out. When she returned home about three hours later, Amy's grandmother said she was already gone. That was all her grandmother knew about the previous night, but she knew a lot more about Amy. What a wonderful and beautiful girl she was. Like Jason, she was as adventurous as she was gregarious. Ever the social butterfly, Amy was not afraid to experience all that life had to offer. And everyone responded to her.

Laugh, and the world laughs with you; weep, and you weep alone. That was Amy's philosophy. She was the queen at her eighth grade dance, but she would always be a princess to her grandmother.

Amy, Carol's eldest daughter, also had been close with her late grandfather, who shared the same birthday with Amy, January 6. Like Amy, he also graduated from Providence's LaSalle Academy. In his era it was an all boy's Catholic high school.

When her grandfather passed away while she was attending LaSalle, Amy became even closer to her nana, moving in with her so the older woman wouldn't have to be alone. In fact, Carol and her girls all lived with her parents for a period of time after she and her husband divorced. Her children were young then, and she was a single mother. In addition to her mother being a loving and supportive grandmother who helped with child care and babysitting, it allowed Carol to save money so she could afford to give her children the best education. For Carol, who was quite religious, that meant Catholic schooling all the way. Amy and her sisters attended West Warwick's St. James School and Notre Dame School, before Amy went on to La Salle

Academy. When Amy first got to the academy she did not know anyone. All her friends went either to public high school or to Bay View Academy, a private girl's school in East Providence. But it didn't take Amy long to adjust and to make new friends. Carol, who wanted to give her girls every opportunity, was elated by her girls' ability to fit in and prosper by their good educations.

Carol and the girls were living with her, and their grandmother was glad. She got to spend a lot of time with Amy, Erin and Elizabeth as a result. The trying moments of such a close living arrangement were superseded by the endearing times they made together. These are memories Carol's mother will always cherish.

Amy's grandmother loved movie musicals, and her three granddaughters were often right by her side watching everything from *Gigi* to *Grease*, from *Meet Me in St. Louis* to *My Fair Lady*. Their absolute favorite, though, was *The Sound of Music*. The girls not only knew who Gene Kelly, Ginger Rogers and Fred Astaire were, they could recite the lyrics from a number of popular musicals by rote. It was something that came in handy when the sisters would get separated in a department store or supermarket. They devised a system for locating one another by singing the theme from *Oklahoma!*

They would all take turns singing verses, then they would laugh, and so would Carol, who appreciated their good humor even though everyone in the store just stared at them.

As Amy's grandmother sat talking to the detectives, memories flooded her mind. One particular which came to mind was the time they all went on vacation together to the White Mountains of New Hampshire. They visited Clark's Trading Post, which is a one-stop Disney World, of sorts, at least New England-style. There are roadside attractions galore, and this place has it all: museums, a family circus, trained bear shows, a two and a half mile train ride on an antique diesel-engine steam locomotive. And of course, one of the best stocked souvenir shops in the entire White Mountains, where you could buy anything from maple syrup to moccasins. All this was set against a backdrop of early Americana: throwback era buildings and store fronts, rustic cabins, vintage cars. They even had one of those photography studios where families dress up in turn-of-the-twentieth-century clothes and take old-looking photographs. How many homes in New England don't have a picture like that on their wall, or tucked away somewhere in a keepsake drawer or a photo album?

Detectives interviewed Amy's natural father, who felt the same way Amy's grandmother did – that the police were investigating a death, a case number, not a person. It was far from the truth, but just like we could not walk in their shoes, they could not walk in ours.

Amy's sister Erin informed them that Amy occasionally visited various Providence night spots. The detective's eyes widened and noted this. Carol, her mother and ex-husband all saw it. Erin, however, was unsure which particular clubs her sister frequented. This information may have been valuable, given the fact that, as of yet, we did not have any real suspects, and aside from Amy's ex-boyfriend, no one who might even be a person of interest. Since this was after the case we had to consider that the killer, or killers, may very well have been someone who was acquainted with or otherwise infatuated with Amy.

Erin added that her older sister met Jason a few months previous on the Internet, on a website that features links to a variety of rave-related topics and interests, everything from dating to disco balls. Erin further related that she, too, had spoken with Amy's ex-boyfriend earlier that day. She said he mentioned that he had seen Amy out at a club the previous night in Providence with Jason and some other people from Massachusetts. He also revealed to her that he had offered to take Amy home, but she declined, telling him she would get a ride from Jason. The boyfriend, she related, then told her that Amy had asked him to call her at home around 2:00 or 2:30 AM. This confirmed what Harper had told investigators himself.

Amy's grandmother verified hearing the phone ringing on at least two occasions at that hour of the morning, though she did not answer either time.

Before they left, Carol provided detectives with a list of the type of jewelry that Amy usually wore, which included her LaSalle Academy High School class ring, a ruby ring, an Irish clatter ring with two hands folded over each other and a shrimp ring, all of them gold-banded. We could use the list to compare them with the items found on Amy, and then perhaps locate any missing jewelry that may have been taken from her and sold to local pawn shops. It was another odds-defying attempt. If this were a football game, it would be the equivalent of a Hail Mary pass. But we were moving the chains down field, and the clock was ticking.

Meanwhile, forty miles northeast, Detectives Steppo and Petrucci continued their conversation with the Burgesons. Since the technician from the State Medical Examiner's Office had already confirmed that they would be using Jason's driver's license as a form of positively identifying his remains, the family was not asked to visit the morgue to view Jason.

Nadine Burgeson confirmed for Detectives Steppo and Petrucci that her son and Amy had been dating the last couple of months. She also informed them that there were occasions when Jason would not return home some nights, but when he did he always called in the morning to let his parents know he was okay. They both intimated that Jason was having some sort of problem with Amy's former boyfriend, whose name they did not know, and the specific problems of which they were unable to elaborate. It turned out this boyfriend had already been unofficially eliminated as a suspect, at least as far as I was concerned. I still thought, however, that he could be helpful to the investigation, having been in close contact with Amy until her death and having been in her presence the night she was killed.

Jason's sister, Kellie, and her husband, Nick, arrived then and the emotional level of the meeting flared instantly as the concerned sibling peppered the detectives with questions while trying to console her mother. Kellie, herself, was overwhelmed with anguish, but she managed to confirm much of what her parents had already revealed to investigators, foremost that Jason had been dating Amy for perhaps three months or so. She also alluded to a vague problem with Amy's former boyfriend, whose name she could not recall either. She said that Jason did not frequent Providence night spots very often. She cried when she told police that Jason had asked her to go with him to the club the night before with Amy and his friends.

She gave detectives the name of Jennifer Laurence, one of Jason's closest friends, who had been out with her brother and Amy the night they were killed. Steppo then asked her to call the young woman at home, which she promptly did. Jennifer could not be reached, however, so Kellie left a message on the answering machine.

Steppo concluded the notification/interview with the Burgeson by advising them to contact headquarters with any information that might aid the police investigation. It was close to 7:00 when the detectives left Lakeville.

The Burgeson family was alone for the first time, with the awareness that Jason was not among them and never would be again, remained in silence while enveloped in a cocoon of shock.

"They'll never find out whoever did this," Kellie said at one point. "The guy is probably in Mexico by now."

"Don't say that!" Ernest Burgeson yelled out.

Kellie recoiled at the sharp sound of her father's voice. She realized that hope was the only thing they had, even if it was just the faith that the police would find out who did this unspeakable act. She knew that if she extinguished that dim light, they would be completely in the dark.

Jennifer Laurence was a nursing assistant, and working at the time Kellie called. When her mother got home, she called her daughter at the nursing home to relay the frantic message that Jason's sister had left on the answering machine: "This is an emergency. I need Jen to call me as soon as possible."

Jennifer immediately returned the call. The only thing she heard Kellie say was, "Jay's dead!" Everything after that got blocked out. Jennifer lost control of her emotions and she began crying, unaware that her hysterics were alarming to some of the patients. Her co-workers were forced to take her outside, to get some fresh air and wait for her parents to pick her up. Going straight to the Burgeson residence, she was surprised by the presence of the Lakeville police, who were there to assist in the homicide investigation.

Not aware when she arrived that Jason had been murdered, she just assumed he had been involved in an accident of some kind, either with his van or his four-wheeler. But when she found out that Jason had been shot to death, she took out a cigarette and lit it trying to calm down. Her parents, who were with her, did not know she smoked, but she could not keep her nicotine addiction a secret from them any longer, and began to smoke one right after another. The officers asked for her help getting into Jason's computer and determining the identities of the individuals who had sent Jason e-mails in recent days, as well as assisting us in establishing a timeline of the victim's movements the night before.

Shaking, Jennifer took them over to it. A piece of paper that was taped to Jason's monitor read, "Work like you don't need money, love like you have never been hurt and dance like there's no one watching." It was the philosophy of someone who lived every day as though it might be the last. The irony was not lost on Jennifer as she began to cry.

Among the unread messages she found in Jason's electronic mailbox was the one that she had sent to him early that morning. She had awakened at 7 AM and felt compelled to write Jason a letter, telling him that she had a good time the night before and hoped they could all get together to hang out again soon. Her tears increased when she realized that her note was never even read, and that Jason was already dead when she sent it.

Jennifer and Jason had been the best of friends. It did not matter that for a while they had been boyfriend and girlfriend. They had plenty of interests in common drawing them together. They lived less than a mile from one another, and she had gone through grade school with Jason, from kindergarten to Apponequet Regional High. It was during their junior year that they started to become friendly. They belonged to the same peer leader group, SHAPE, which participated in various community service activities. They participated in the school drama club, took drama classes and acted in plays together. They dated on and off for a couple of months, but it was not until after graduation in 1998 that their relationship solidified. Jason called Jennifer when he got up in the morning and asked her if she wanted to come along with him on some errands and often she would go. They did practically everything together and shared many of the same social interests, especially when it came to music and dancing. They checked out all the new techno clubs, and Jennifer had her own aspirations of becoming a DJ one day.

Over time they developed almost a brother-sister type of bond. Not long ago, in fact, Jason had taken her aside and said, "Jen, I understand now why you don't see me as a boyfriend. We're just awesome friends. I can see it now. I'm so happy to have you as a friend. You're just like a sister."

Jennifer consoled Kellie like a sister that day. She knew how much Kellie loved her brother, even though they were so different in personality from each other. Jason was laid back and easygoing, and was the type who never sweated the small stuff in life. He was a free spirit. He was always doing things that his sister never dreamed of doing, like leaving the house with little money or going on road trips and not being the least concerned about where he would sleep. For him, it was all part of life's adventure, where risk and discovery went hand-in-hand.

They both missed Jason when he ventured out to Minnesota's St. Cloud State University in the fall of 1998 to continue his education. He was an extremely bright young man with a lot of promise. He had a passion for the arts. He had performed in numerous plays and had received awards for his talent in journalism and creative writing.

Jason was president of his class his freshman year at college. He hoped to become a disc jockey after graduation. He loved music and people. As a DJ, he was already a natural. He had his own show on his college radio station, which was broadcast to listeners far beyond the school campus. He was so entertaining and comfortable on air that the station manager placed him in the 6 AM - 9 AM commuter time slot, which was the most highly listened to spot all day. Jason also enjoyed reading novels, snow skiing, traveling and spending time with his friends and family. He was passionate about everything that he did and everyone he cared about. He lived every moment to the fullest and was always on the go. It seemed like he never rested. It was as if he knew he did not have a lot of time and he just wanted to cram everything into what little time he had.

Josephine Bell, a friend of both Jennifer Laurence and Jason, has said that anytime someone told Jason that they'll do something "next time," his response would always be, "there might not be a next time."

Bell, who was a year ahead of Jason in high school, recalled the day that she and Jason were bouncing around on a trampoline in her backyard. Suddenly, Jason suggested they attend a concert on the water that night, even though they had school the next day. It was impulsive and rebellious, but Bell agreed. Jason drove, and she never felt safer with anyone. At the concert, they listened to the bands, and as the crowds got thicker he took hold of her hand and hardly let it go all night. However, he never made her feel like he was her date, but rather a brother, looking after her and keeping her safe. The way she felt that day was how she always felt around Jason, like he was her guardian. When they talked on the phone, he always told her that he loved her before he hung up. Bell always said, "I love you," back. It was something they both meant, but not like lovers. It was a deeper bond.

"I think he made everyone feel that way," Bell said. "No one ever felt jealous. He was everyone's friend. We were all lucky to have known him."

Chapter 12

Catching
a Killer

A round 7:15 PM, Gregory Floyd called Pamela Crawford, his seventeen year old girlfriend, and asked her if he could borrow five dollars. She had been dating the nineteen year old for about a year. Pamela told him she didn't have any money, but said that she could get some from an older man who worked the parking lot adjacent to a pizza place in Providence. Pamela had known the lot attendant for three years, about as long as she had known Floyd.

They were two among many who were most at home in this section of the city, known as "the wall" because of the low concrete retainer and planter that fronted a length of the street beside the pizza place. But "the wall" was much more than just a physical border that featured a raised garden of trees and shrubbery. It was a gathering place of lost souls. Its location was key, situated in what some consider the heart of the city, which others would argue is Providence's underbelly. Floyd was a fixture there. He had once worked at the pizzeria, but he was not an employee at this time. He did, however, occasionally barter for food with the owner. Floyd cleaned dishes, unloaded delivery trucks or performed any variety of odd jobs for a free meal.

The pizza place shared its littered sidewalk with a café, where you could play pool, drink beer and on a Saturday night get into a fight with someone who had a knife or a gun, you never knew.

There was a donut shop that was also part and parcel of this provincial street culture, a destination that would never be mentioned in the Providence Department of Art, Culture and Tourism brochures.

Police presence there was a constant. Like "the wall" itself, the pizza place was more than what it appeared to be; a late night hangout for restless teens and twenty-something's to carouse and eat pizza after the clubs closed in Providence. It was a place frequented primarily by runaways, unwanted people and children, unloved, unsupervised, who had to look out for themselves on the streets, and who would do whatever they needed to survive, including stealing and selling drugs or their bodies. They were not completely alone, however. Besides each other, there was a network of social services available to them in the city.

Amos House supports Rhode Island's working poor, unemployed and disenfranchised, many of whom are children, by providing transitional shelter space and permanent housing to seventy-five people a night. Their dining hall is capable of serving 900 meals on their busiest days. They also offer a wide range of services including crisis intervention, emergency assistance and health care. Traveler's Aid Society (TAS) is another nearby homeless shelter and advocacy resource center in Providence. Just off Weybosset Street, it was right around the corner from "the wall." Both of these charitable organizations sustained many individuals in their times of need.

According to a 2005 study conducted by the National Alliance to End Homelessness, some 6,866 Rhode Islanders were reported to be without a fixed, regular, or adequate place to live. In fact, the smallest state in the union claimed the second highest percentage of homeless per capita, trailing only Nevada, where sixty-eight out of every 1,000 people are homeless. The numbers are alarming and misleading at the same time. Most of the time, adult homelessness is a temporary situation, lasting a couple of weeks to a couple of months ninety percent of the time. Social welfare programs are able to provide temporary shelter in many of these instances, which often include families. The chronic homeless are a perpetual problem that is more complex and difficult to solve. All of these numbers increase dramatically when children are included.

Besides the homeless and destitute, street criminals also take full advantage of Providence's inner city hospitality, especially the donated hot and cold lunches at Amos House and the free coffee at TAS. Having been homeless for a period of time himself, this was Gregory Floyd's world. Here, at least, he was somebody.

At about 7:45 PM, Floyd picked Pamela up at her home, a second floor apartment on Atwells Avenue in Providence. She was surprised when she saw that Floyd was driving a white SUV. She was doubly surprised when she saw a young Hispanic girl in the passenger seat. She instantly recognized the pudgy nose and pouty lips of the seventeen year old that dated Floyd previously. Pamela didn't acknowledge her as she got into the back seat. She pushed herself all the way forward, positioning herself between the two of them and deliberately brushing her shoulder against Floyd.

"Where'd you get the truck from?" she asked him, more in the way of conversation than any actual interest.

"It's my cousin's."

Floyd didn't mention his cousin by name and she didn't ask as he headed downtown, turning up the volume on the radio.

This was not the first time that Floyd had been out and about in the truck that day. That afternoon, he was seen by numerous people as he drove around Weybosset Street. At least one of them witnessed him dancing beside the white SUV that was parked on the street outside the cafe with hip-hop music blasting from the speakers. Some of the regulars who frequented that area wondered where Floyd had gotten the vehicle. Anyone who knew him realized that it did not belong to him. Now, as dusk was descending on Providence, Floyd drove back to his usual haunts down city.

At 7:50 PM, Detectives Petrucci and Steppo returned to headquarters and briefed me on the details of their interview with the Burgesons. We were interrupted when a call came in for Detective Petrucci. It was Jennifer Laurence. She was still extremely upset after learning about Jason's death and speaking with the Lakeville police. Jennifer recounted her evening with Jason and Amy, and provided Petrucci with contact information on her friends, who were all together the night before. She also let him know about two other high school friends, who spent a majority of the night with Amy and Jason, and were actually alone with the couple before everyone met at the Providence night club, and then again after the girls disbanded from the group and went home separately. These people were important since they had the potential to provide information to help us fill in our timeline and perhaps impart some useful clues that might lead to an arrest. Interviews with all of these young people became an instant priority.

Around 8 PM, Raymond Anderson was attending the high school commencement ceremony of his girlfriend, Florence Sander. The couple knew each other for about two years and were new parents of a four-month old baby, though they did not live together. Sander was graduating from the Metropolitan Regional Career and Technical Center. "The MET," as it is commonly referred, is a unique, state-funded network of six small public high schools spread across three campuses around Providence. When the school first opened in the fall of 1996, serving nearly fifty ninth graders, it immediately set itself apart from traditional schools through its internship program. A second hallmark of the school is its personalized curricula, with no more than 120 students at each location. The students, parents and MET advisors collaborate to design a learning plan which meets each child's unique needs, interests and passions. Together, the tailored curricula allows students to apply their academic learning toward specific careers and placement into corresponding internships within the community.

The co-founder of the MET recognized the slender man standing in the audience of the old Shepard Building in downtown Providence. He and the principal and assistant principal respectively of the award-winning Thayer High School in New Hampshire, came to Rhode Island in 1993 to help improve education in the state. Together, they came up with the motto for their new school, 'One Student at a Time.' Now, the co-founder couldn't help but look at this young man leaning against the back wall of the auditorium as a personal failure on his part. He was one that got away. Anderson had been a former student at the MET before he dropped out the previous academic year to enroll at Hope High School, where he also left before completing the twelfth grade. Although he was nineteen now, had he stuck it out and finished his studies at the MET, he would have been part of the innovative school's first graduating class. All forty-seven graduates, including Sander, had been accepted to various colleges.

After the exercises, Anderson and Sander conversed, making some small talk, mostly about the baby. Then, Anderson's friend gave them all a ride to Anderson's Marlborough Avenue apartment.

By 8:00 PM, Floyd was on Weybosset Street again. He drove the SUV into the parking lot near the pizzeria. As Pamela got out of the vehicle, so did the other girl. Floyd remained inside. Pamela returned moments later with ten dollars she borrowed from the lot attendant. She handed the sawbuck to Floyd, who took it and went into the pizzeria to exchange it for two fives, giving one to Crawford to give back to the lot attendant. When Pamela Crawford got back into the SUV, the other girl was nowhere to be seen, so she got into the passenger seat. Floyd drove off.

At 8:23 PM, Providence police and fire dispatchers, who not long before had responded to the electronic teletype from Johnston, informing the neighboring city to be on the lookout for Jason Burgeson's vehicle, broadcast the information over the Providence Police radio for all on-duty officers to hear. One of these was Patrolman Stephen J. Gencarella, who was working his South Providence post in Car 14.

The twenty-eight-year-old had been on the job for about three years. By his own admission, he was, in a larger sense, an introvert. His quiet, reserved comportment however, was misleading, and occasionally mistaken for arrogance. The truth was when it came to police work no one could claim that he was introverted. On the job, I viewed him as aggressive but fair. The first couple of years, he bounced around different areas of the city before he landed a patrol unit in South Providence, which for any young Providence cop who wanted to get involved, see a lot of action and really learn what police work was all about, this was the place to be. For officers who were less enthusiastic, this was a beat to avoid. The assignment fit perfectly with

Gencarella's character. It was not a skeleton crew of volunteers, by any means. Only the best cops were considered for work there by the top brass. It wasn't just the element of danger posed by the high crime rate and the prevalence of drugs and guns in those neighborhoods that required something extra from the officers who patrolled the mean streets of Providence. Cops in this district had to be observant, have an ability to interact with the residents and be able to think on their feet at all times. When Gencarella was first given the opportunity to work there, he jumped at it. He showed his commanding officers that he was more than capable and quickly earned a car post in Washington Park. He'd been in South Providence ever since.

At the moment that the Johnston broadcast went out on the night of June 9th, Gencarella was on routine patrol in his district. He immediately turned up the volume and pulled over to jot the information down.

The patrolman had already gotten into the habit of memorizing the hot sheets of the most recently stolen cars. Writing them down is not enough, because so many cars pass by so quickly. By the time you check the list and look up it's too late. Experience had already taught him that the older automobiles were probably long gone and never to be seen in one piece again, anyway. Vehicle theft always ranks high on the national crime indexes year after year, and it is no different in Providence, so for Gencarella it was a worthwhile investment of ten minutes before the start of each shift to commit to memory as many of these makes, models and license plates as he could. He had learned very early in his career to rely on this skill, crediting a former partner for this practice and then applying it by constantly scanning license plates. Gencarella was actually working for his partner that night, so the Massachusetts plate number was still fresh in his mind when he spotted the vehicle a few minutes later, not knowing at the time that it was wanted in connection with the double homicide in Johnston.

He was driving through the area between Classical and Central High Schools, along Cranston Street at 8:34 PM. The white SUV, traveling in the opposite direction, jumped out at him initially. When he looked down at the tags and realized it was the stolen vehicle that had just been reported, the license plate seemed to get bigger and bigger before his eyes, until it took up his whole field of vision. He knew instinctively that he had to take the vehicle right then and there, and he reacted immediately. What happened next was perhaps more surreal, and seemed to take place in slow motion for the three-year officer.

The SUV's driver had stopped for the light at Fricker Street, and Gencarella saw that there was a car directly behind it. Without a moment's hesitation, he pulled his cruiser in front of the SUV, nose to nose, effectively blocking it in so that it could not escape. Gencarella purposely left his flashers off. He did not want to do anything that might incite the driver. He did not even want to take an extra moment to call for backup, relying entirely on the element of surprise to subdue the operator of the stolen vehicle. A few seconds later, Gencarella then jumped out of the patrol car with his gun drawn and ready. In a low crouch he made his way around to the driver side door of the boxed in SUV. The patrolman was moving swiftly, running, in fact, but it did not seem that way to him. He pointed his gun directly at the startled driver, Gregory Floyd. The officer did not want to give Floyd any time whatsoever to think or react. Then, Gencarella saw a second passenger, Pamela, and he let out a war cry that further froze both occupants of the vehicle as he pulled the door open, reached inside and turned off the ignition. With the same motion, he grabbed the male driver by the shirt collar and pulled him out of the truck.

Floyd was ruggedly built, and was a more imposing figure than a 5'11" 200 lb. frame might otherwise suggest. Gencarella could not determine whether or not Floyd made any real attempt to flee or fight back, his own adrenaline pumping hard and moving so fast that Floyd may not even have known he'd been apprehended by the police until after he had been thrown up against the vehicle and handcuffed.

"What's this all about, officer?" Floyd asked. "What's happening?"

"Where'd you get the truck?"

"I took it off a kid downtown."

In the next instant, Gencarella placed Floyd in the back of the cruiser. An officer who was on patrol nearby saw what was happening and pulled up to assist.

"What's going on?" the officer asked.

"Take her into custody," Gencarella advised him, pointing toward the woman inside the truck. "Put her in your car." He wanted to be sure the two suspects were separated so they could not formulate the same cover story.

The officer did as he was instructed as Gencarella called into the Sergeant on duty, Al Zonfrilli, who was the next officer to arrive on the scene. The first thing he did was instruct the patrolmen to turn off their radios so that the two individuals in custody could not hear the police transmissions. The less they knew, the better it was for the investigation. Providence understood this wasn't their case, and they did not want to do anything that might jeopardize our murder probe.

Soon, Cranston and Fricker Streets were swarming with both Providence and Johnston police. For Gencarella, it was a little like watching the cavalry arrive. As soon as the stolen vehicle report came across the radio, he knew it was important, but only then did it dawn on him that this vehicle, and perhaps the two suspects, had been involved in the double murder in Johnston. Gencarella went back on patrol to finish his 3-11 PM shift. And while the true significance of the stop he had made and the individuals apprehended would not become apparent until sometime later, several commendations, including the City Council Award and the American Legion Award, later would recognize Gencarella for his diligence and preemptive response that night and serve as a permanent reminder for his contribution to the Shute-Burgeson homicide case.

At 8:55 I responded to the scene, accompanied by Patrol Sergeant Timothy Picard and Detectives Faella, Warren and Steppo.

It was quickly confirmed that the vehicle in question was, indeed, the one that belonged to Jason Burgeson. Detective Faella and I took Crawford into custody. I figured she was the weakest link, whatever her involvement, and that she would divulge some important information. At that point, I didn't even want to talk to Floyd until we got him in the station. I wanted to be sure that everything was documented and legal when he did speak. If we could avoid furnishing him with an opportunity to say he was coerced or intimidated or claim that he wasn't advised of his rights, it would work in our favor. Sergeant Picard transported Floyd to headquarters. Detective Warren photographed the van and stayed with it, along with Detective Steppo, until the tow truck arrived at 9:20 to bring the van to the Johnston Police Department, where the vehicle would be garaged and processed further by the BCI Division. Another important piece of evidence in this convoluted puzzle was now in place, and we pressed on.

Chapter 13

And the Wall Came Tumbling Down

As the two suspects were placed in holding cells, the Johnston Police Station was buzzing with the news of their apprehension. I took a moment to call the Burgesons to notify them that Jason's SUV had been found and that the suspect driving it, along with a female companion, had been taken into custody. They were grateful, but understandably stunned and outraged to learn that the person who may have killed Jason would just be driving around so nonchalantly in his car. I promised to keep them notified of further developments.

Captain aRusso placed a similar call to the Shute family, relaying the news of Floyd's capture to Jim Colvin.

Detective Petrucci, who had just gotten off the phone with Arnold Banker and Stephen Cone, two friends who had been with Jason and Amy the previous night, stopped me to let me know that both young men had given him preliminary statements that were consistent with each other as well as the one given by Jason's friend Jennifer Laurence. Furthermore, he informed me that he would follow up on these conversations by arranging to have them come by the station to provide written statements. To be honest, I barely heard him. My focus was on the suspects we had in custody. It was such a fortunate occurrence, to take nothing away from Officer Gencarella, but I didn't want to blow this opportunity. We had one chance to do this thing right. Fortunately, there was no time to be nervous or to second guess myself. I had to follow my instincts. Fortunately, I had a professional and competent command staff, as well as a solid core of experienced detectives working alongside me, to set me on the right path.

Floyd and Crawford were placed in separate interview rooms for questioning. It was show time. Petrucci joined me in the room with Floyd, who sat across a bare wooden table from us. I advised him of his Constitutional Rights, both verbal and written. He indicated that he understood his rights, signing and initialing each one specified on a Rights Form, which also identified him as a suspect in the murder of two people. A few moments later, to our surprise, he agreed to speak freely and willfully with us regarding our investigation of the double homicide.

"Just tell us what you know," I said. "That's all you have to do. Okay?"

"Yes, sir."

What I found unusual about Floyd from the start was how polite he was. He seemed the perfect gentleman. Everything was, 'Yes, sir,' 'No, sir.' He spoke very softly as well, and many times we had to ask him to speak louder so we could hear him.

The suspect appeared outwardly untroubled, and seemingly unaware of why he was even there. His familiarity with the police may have been why he was so at ease with the situation in which he now found himself, but his dark complexion and eyes gave nothing away. When I asked Floyd was how he came into possession of the SUV that he had been operating he responded "I bought it from someone downtown."

"From who?" I pressed

"This Hispanic girl."

"What's the name of this Hispanic girl you bought the van from?"

"Pauline Parza."

"Pauline Parza? You bought the van from her?"

"Yes, sir."

"How did that come about?"

"She came up to me down city and asked me if I wanted to buy it for three hundred dollars. I told her to meet me in Providence on Sunday and I'd give her the money. She let me keep it to drive to be sure I liked it."

I thought for sure that once we started to ask more pointed interrogatories, there would be telltale fluctuations in his voice or obvious changes in demeanor, but there were neither. He answered all our questions calmly.

When asked to provide additional information on Parza, however, such as her address and telephone number, Floyd was unable. He said he didn't know. It became quickly apparent to both Detective Petrucci and me that he was not being truthful with us. I had asked him to tell us what he knew, but instead he was telling us what he wanted us to believe.

At 9:30 PM, Detectives Warren and DeTora began photographing the van inside and out. They were very careful. The SUV was filthy, and under the harsh florescent lights, the dark smears made by hands and fingers all over the vehicle were hauntingly obvious. On the white paint, in particular, it showed up clearly. They were pressed into the door panels, the hood and even the roof. It looked as if the SUV had been pushed here by a mob. Certainly, some of the impressions lifted would be sufficient for identification purposes, which could then be used to compare with suspects, in custody now or in the future, and determine if there was a match. There were bound to be latent prints inside the van, as well.

As the two detectives went through the interior, removing and meticulously inventorying every item, they came across a black and white pocketbook in the rear compartment. It contained a checkbook belonging to Amy Shute as well as a paycheck made out to her from her place of employment. With each personal effect that the two men uncovered, the individuality of the victims became more pronounced to the investigators. They found out where Jason and Amy worked, shopped, the music they liked, some things they didn't even know about each other. The more they learned about Amy and Jason, the more difficult it became emotionally. It was the same for all the detectives, including myself. And it was only the beginning. But we had a job to do. The detectives continued to carefully remove, tag and place all the items in the evidence room.

Pamela was being questioned by Detectives Faella and Tirocchi. She related the extent of her relationship with Floyd, divulged her activities the previous night and why she had been in the van with Floyd. She had problems of her own, but it was apparent that she had no involvement in either the murders or in the procurement of Jason's vehicle, and she was subsequently released. She did, however, provide some very useful information, including her statement about where Floyd actually resided in Providence. Floyd had given us the same street address, but said he had been staying on the second floor, while Pamela told us he lived on the third floor but used the second only as a place to store some of his belongings. The impact of this inadvertent disclosure would later reveal Floyd's attempt to divert us from his actual living space and any evidence contained there. It was one of numerous examples which might appear to have been just lucky breaks, but were actually the results of an investigation that benefited from the timely and coordinated means by which information was gathered and disseminated. This would be key to answering important questions.

At 9:45 PM, Jeff Harper arrived at headquarters to provide further detail to his previous statement. He sat down with Detective Nardolillo, who was one of our most thorough investigators. Even though Floyd was in custody and instantly became our prime suspect, Nardolillo conducted the interview with Jeff to gather additional information that might be useful and to test our conclusion that this young man played no role in the double homicide. We still had to follow up the possibility that although Harper might not have had any direct involvement with Floyd or the murders, he might have contracted Floyd to hurt or kill Amy and Jason. However, it did not take long for the detective to dispel this notion outright.

Harper wanted to do whatever he could to help, and when he used the term *missing person* to describe Amy's situation, Nardolillo knew he had to say something. Harper still did not know that she had been killed. The way he seemed to feel about her, Nardolillo expected that he hadn't even entertained the notion that she had been harmed. He didn't want to believe that she had run off somewhere with Jason either, and that she just hadn't told anyone, but this seemed the most likely scenario. The last thought in his head was that the girl he still loved was dead.

However, Nardolillo couldn't let him go on believing anymore that she was alive. It would have been cruel to allow him to continue looking for her, especially now when we knew she had been killed and had a suspect in custody. Besides, the media would soon be running with the story, if they were not already, and the detective didn't want Jeff to find out that way. He tried to break the news as delicately as possible, but Harper did not take it well. He completely broke down. Nardolillo couldn't help thinking like a cop as he watched the young man crying, but the reaction he was witnessing only reaffirmed for him what had already been concluded. There are crocodile tears and transparent and insincere displays of affection that any experienced detective can spot right away. This young man was truly devastated. He could see that Harper really loved Amy, and that he hadn't known anything about her death until that moment.

Before dismissing the witness, Nardolillo asked him to view several items found in the rear storage area of the Jason's van to ascertain if he recognized any of them as Amy's property. Harper lost control of his emotions again when he saw the furry black and white handbag that his former girlfriend had been carrying with her at the club, as well as a backpack that he knew belonged to her. Concerned that the depth of the young man's grief would inhibit his ability to operate his vehicle safely, the detective asked him if he needed a ride home. Harper assured Nardolillo that he was okay, and that he would drive slowly.

As Harper pulled out of the station's parking lot, the investigator who had seen it all watched, thinking he had never seen anyone so distraught. The twenty-four-year-old continued to grieve over Amy's death. For a long time afterward, in fact, when he did show up for work, it was reported that he often broke down and started crying. Tragically, nearly two years later, Harper died of a brain aneurysm. Some would say that his profound grief and inability to let go of Amy, even in death, contributed to his own demise. And that might very well be true.

At around 10 PM, Elizabeth Zatkoff and Harry Burdick were on the couch watching the end of the TV show, *GREED*. When the news came on next, it opened with a breaking report of two bodies that were found dead on a golf course that was under construction on the Providence/Johnston line. Burdick sat up stunned and watched the coverage as if he were seeing the images for the first time. The report of the grisly discovery compelled Burdick to act on his own at that moment, even if it was out of self-preservation. It was something he hadn't done earlier that fateful morning, when such action would have been of such significance that it would have spared two lives.

"I guess Greg was telling the truth about killing those two people," he said for Zatkoff's benefit, then he got up and began frantically searching for his sneakers. He found one and slipped it on without lacing it.

"Where are you going?"

"I have to go tell the police what I know."

"Are you crazy?"

"Just help me find my other shoe," he said from his hands and knees as he looked under the couch.

Zatkoff didn't trust the police. She was afraid for him. She thought they would be under such pressure from the public to find the killer that they would arrest him on the spot if he went there now. So she insisted that he telephone them instead.

At about the same time, the local Lakeville news filed a report on the Johnston double murder which involved a native son. The Burgeson family watched intently. They were hoping that there might be some kind of new information available, because even though I was trying to keep them up to date as much as I could, there was some things I could not reveal, and the media has ways of getting facts before anyone else.

The murders were the lead story on every channel, local and national. Kellie Surdis, for reasons she did not fully understand, watched newscast after newscast showing the image of her brother's body, covered by a white sheet on a gurney, being placed into the back of an ambulance. She listened over and over to the interviews of the golf course workers who found the bodies of Jason and Amy. It kept getting stuck in her mind how, when the victims were first observed, they had been mistaken for trash that someone had dumped there overnight. It broke her heart knowing that someone would think of her baby brother, who she played baseball with and football with, who she and her family proudly watched in school plays, as trash.

In the main interview room at the police station, Detective Petrucci and I were trying to find some shred of truth in Gregory Floyd's statement. After going around in circles for three-quarters of an hour and getting nowhere with Floyd, who continued to insist that a Hispanic woman sold him the truck, I was beginning to lose my patience, and I was dying for a cigarette. Floyd's respectful demeanor was what finally set me off, aggravating me to the point where I finally jumped out of my chair and yelled, "Knock the fucking shit off or I'm going to drill you through the fucking wall!" I thought he was playing me and I wanted him to drop the act. But it was not an act. I didn't know anything about Floyd at this point. In some respects, he was a walking contradiction. That was something we would all learn more about in due time.

Floyd displayed no discernible reaction to my outburst. He remained passive and just stared blankly at me. "Maybe we should take a break," I said. "This guy doesn't want to tell us anything."

Detective Petrucci immediately waved off my suggestion. "We're almost done now," he said sedately. "Let's go ahead and straighten this thing out so we can all go home."

I had always been an effective interviewer, with a lot of success getting suspects to confess, but I let Thornton have this one. I sat back and exhaled, trying to calm down, as he stepped in and tried a different approach. Cooler heads usually prevail. Not exactly the old good-cop-bad-cop routine, but I knew what Petrucci was up to. He didn't want to stop the interview prematurely. We had Floyd talking, even though it was mostly all lies. There was a way to get him to confess; all murderers want to talk about what they did. We just had to figure out how to coax the truth out of him before he decided to stop speaking to us altogether.

Petrucci, perceiving certain vulnerabilities in Floyd, made an attempt to appeal to whatever sense of decency this street criminal may have possessed. The detective understood that because the murders were so recent, the trauma of the incident would still be fresh in Floyd's mind, and Petrucci wanted to impress on him the moral horror of such a crime, so he began to repeatedly beseech Floyd to reach into his inner soul and do the right thing, which was to confess *everything* he knew.

This was when a second major break in the case occurred. At 10:05 PM, the phone rang at the Johnston Police Station. Communications took the call from a male requesting to speak with a sergeant or a lieutenant. The call then was transferred to Sergeant John Sinotte, who identified himself to the caller.

"I have some information about what happened last night," the voice on the other end of the line said. The individual was obviously very nervous, and Sinotte realized right away that this was not a crank.

"Now, what exactly are you referring to when you say, 'what happened last night?'"

"The two bodies that were found."

A chill went up the sergeant's spine and his heart rate suddenly increased, his air passages opened up, adrenaline, endorphins and other chemicals suffused his brain. His body reacted to the potential witness the same way it would to the introduction of a glaring clue or smoking gun in any case in which he was involved. He knew this call was something big.

"What's your name, son?" Sinotte asked.

"This is an anonymous call. I can't say."

What the man did tell Sinotte was that he had seen the news report about the deaths and that last night he had been in the company of a male named Greg who said that he had killed a guy and a girl. The Sergeant's body responded to this bit of information like a Geiger counter to a high dose of radiation. The Greg that the caller had named as the murderer had to be Greg Floyd. Sinotte understood how imperative it was to bring the witness in for questioning as soon as possible.

Sinotte said, "Why don't you come down to the Johnston Police Department to tell us about it."

The caller became more frantic at this point. He told the Sergeant that he had an infant son and he didn't want to get in trouble for something he didn't do. He "just wanted to report what he heard."

"I can understand that," Sinotte replied. "I just need you to tell me everything that you know about these murders."

"I don't know anything about them, except what I saw on the news. And what Greg told me."

"Right. Everything you know about these murders from what Greg told you. But if we're going to talk, I need to know who I'm talking to, don't I?"

Sinotte did exactly what he was trained to do. He attempted to build a confidence level with the caller, enough to get the unknown male to identify himself. It worked. Finally, the caller said his name was Harry Burdick, born January 5, 1979, and living in Pawtucket. Sinotte quickly jotted the information down on a small notepad in front of him.

"Mr. Burdick, how about if I arrange to have one of our officers come by your house and pick you up?"

"NO!" Burdick objected vehemently. "Greg might find out. He said if I spoke to anyone about what he did, he'd kill me. No way. You can't come by here."

"Okay, okay," Sinotte said agreeably. Burdick obviously did not know that Floyd had been picked up, and the Sergeant realized that if the witness knew that the suspect was here being questioned, he'd never come in. Burdick was afraid that he would be detained as soon as he set foot in the station, and he did not want the public display of a police escort, which would scream *RAT* to the entire neighborhood.

Sinotte managed to convince Burdick to agree to meet with investigators at a neutral site in Johnston to talk about what he knew, on the condition that he would not be arrested. Sinotte assured him that if he was just a witness providing information about a crime, he would not be arrested. Then, he told Burdick to stay on the line, and put the caller on hold.

At this point, around 10:15, Sinotte turned the caller over to Detective Alan Ross, to make the arrangements and determine a meeting place. They settled on the parking lot of a department store, just down the road from the police station, in a half hour. The detective concluded the call with Harry Burdick, wondering if he was going to show up.

114

Chapter 14

Unraveling
the Truth

D etective Petrucci's technique seemed to be having some effect on Floyd. He might have begun softening, if not cracking. We never got the chance to find out because Detective Alan Ross interrupted our interview. I got called out, while Petrucci remained with Floyd. Initially, I was just grateful for the reprieve from the interrogation. I was reaching for a cigarette when he told me about Burdick's call and the meeting. Like Sergeant Sinotte, I felt as if I had been injected with a shot of adrenaline. The possibility that we were going to meet with the individual who called and provided an important link in the investigation made me super hyped.

"Do whatever it takes to get the guy here," I advised Ross, who nodded as I quickly returned to the interview room and faced Floyd again. "I don't believe you were being very truthful with us," I began, standing over the table and looking down at the suspect. "Besides the holes in your statement that are big enough to drive a truck through, we have someone coming in who said you did it; you killed them." It was all I could do to keep a smile from my face. "There's a witness."

Floyd shook his head slowly. "Can't be," he said. "There were no witnesses."

At this point, I started thinking someone up there is on my side. I don't even think Floyd knew what he said, but it was very incriminating.

"Well, Greg, a person called to tell us that a guy named Greg was responsible for killing Amy Shute and Jason Burgeson. And that person is voluntarily on his way here right now to give a statement to us. You were in the victim's vehicle, and you're facing some serious charges. This is no bluff. Do you know someone by the name Harry Burdick? Well, he's going to fuck you good. If there were others involved with you in this, now's the time to come clean, or you'll be facing these charges alone."

Suddenly, Floyd's demeanor and facial expression noticeably changed. Until that point, his hard features and stern countenance made him appear to be twice as old as he actually was. His mask of stoicism slipped enough to reveal the teenager beneath. He knew he couldn't continue to feed us information that he knew could not be corroborated by witness accounts.

"All right," Floyd began. "I'll tell you the truth."

The suspect proceeded to acknowledge that he had, in fact, been involved in the shootings, but denied being the person who fired the fatal shots. Floyd implicated a man whom he only knew by the name Sammie, as the murderer. He stated that he did not know where Sammie lived, but only that he drove a tan colored car with a loud muffler. He also incriminated three other individuals, Ray, Kenny and Harry. He knew where Raymond lived but did not know about the others. He said they were all walking around down city looking to rob someone and get a car, before Sammie decided on victimizing Jason and Amy, who were sitting outside The Arcade sometime after midnight.

The Arcade is a building in Providence with the noted distinction of being the oldest indoor shopping mall in the country. It was built entirely of granite in 1828, when the city's population numbered only 14,000. The 216-foot structure, which fronts on both Westminster and Weybosset Streets, was originally owned by two separate groups whose architects argued over the building's design. This resulted in a structure with mismatched entrances: The Weybosset Street entrance is topped off by a stepped parapet, while the Westminster Street side is topped by a pediment. The Arcade's twelve massive twenty-one foot granite columns, which were quarried in Johnston and dragged to the construction site by a team of thirty oxen, were the largest monolithic columns in the country at the time, weighing in at thirteen tons a piece.

Its storied history aside, Floyd indicated that all five of them were in Sammie's car when they spotted the two victims outside the building, standing near a white truck. He related that Sammie and another male, unknown at this time, ordered the victims into the truck at gunpoint, while he and the others remained in Sammie's car, and then began to follow the SUV. Floyd explained that he did not know where Sammie was leading them until they pulled into a construction site he believed was somewhere in Providence.

At this time, Detective Petrucci interrupted Floyd's narrative and stepped out of the room to notify the other detectives in the squad room that we were dealing with carjacking and kidnapping as well as a double homicide. It changed everything. This was a whole new aspect now, with the potential for the filing of federal charges and the involvement of several government law enforcement agencies.

Floyd continued his confession, giving us his account of what happened when they arrived at this remote location.

"After Sammie led us to the construction site, there was a dispute whether to rape Amy. I disagreed with this, and seemed to be the only one who did, so there was an argument and Sammie wanted to shoot me. While we were arguing, Sammie all of a sudden aims at Jason and shoots him and then Amy in the top of the head, then states, 'that's how you do it.' Sammie then gave me the gun. He said, 'make sure he's dead.' Amy was laid over and Jason was slumped forward, and I knew they were very much dead. I was scared and Sammie kept saying, 'do it, or else.' I told him they were already dead, but I shot Jason after Sammie did."

Now Floyd was telling us that he pulled the trigger, responsible for shooting Jason a second time himself. His story was changing during the same version, even as he was telling it to us.

He went on to say that after the shootings, they drove both vehicles to a gas station in Providence and put nine dollars of gas in each, using all the money that had been taken from the victims.

"Why were you in possession of Jason's SUV tonight?" I asked him.

"Sammie told me to take it."

At 10:45 PM, Detectives Ross, Pisaturo and Arcuri were dispatched to the department store parking lot to meet with Harry Burdick, who was already there with his girlfriend. Zatkoff was so upset and nervous for Burdick that she removed a ring he had given her and told him they were through. He was moved to tears by her display; Burdick's emotional state perhaps rendered all the more sensitive to Zatkoff's discontent because he knew that things were about to get a lot worse for him.

Burdick was sitting on the hood of Zatkoff's car, while she sat inside with the radio playing, when the detectives arrived. Burdick approached them as they pulled up in an unmarked vehicle. He identified himself, but he was not carrying any form of identification on him. Their collective first impression of the witness and possible suspect was that he recognized detectives easily, leading them to believe that he had spoken to the police in the past.

As Burdick spoke to the detectives, he displayed all kinds of signs of being nervous. He was talking fast, defensively, his voice somewhat high-pitched. He shed tears at times.

He told them that he was hanging downtown when a man he knew as Greg approached him and asked if he knew where he could get a car. Burdick said he told his acquaintance that he did not, and then a while later he saw Greg driving a white SUV.

"Greg asked me if I wanted a ride home and I said yes," Burdick went on to say. "While he was driving, I asked him where he got the car. All he said was that it was his. Then he showed me a black handgun with a silver top and told me that he killed a guy and a girl. He said that if I told anyone, he would kill me, too. I didn't believe him; then when I saw it on the news tonight I realized that Greg had been telling the truth and I felt I had to tell the police."

At that time, Detective Pisaturo presented Burdick with a photo package that he had prepared before leaving the station. Like a pictorial version of an old-fashioned police lineup, where a witness would view a grouping of men through a wall of one-way glass to identify a suspect, the package contained pictures of six males. Burdick was asked to pick out anyone with whom he was acquainted or familiar. He immediately identified Floyd, the second picture in the book, and once again began to cry.

Detectives felt these were the tears of a coward, rather than the product of any kind of sympathy for the two lives that were taken. They were sure he had been lying, so Detective Ross began pressing Burdick for information about the bodies and the location, hoping to trip him up. It proved easier than he anticipated, as Burdick added that before he'd been taken home, Floyd drove them both to Buttonhole Golf Course, where he viewed the bodies. Burdick had now placed himself at the murder scene as well inside the vehicle of one of the victims. The reluctant witness, however, adamantly denied having any involvement in the shootings himself. He told the detectives that this was when Floyd flashed the gun and said he would kill him if he told anyone. He concluded his dialogue by restating that when he saw the news report of the killings on television, he felt he just had to tell the police, even though he was afraid of both Floyd and being falsely implicated in the crime.

Detective Ross, nodded, pacifying Burdick, but not buying anything he was telling them. Like Floyd, Burdick's story was changing on the fly. Ross requested that Burdick accompany them to the Johnston Police Department to provide a formal statement, and he agreed. Not that he had a choice at that point.

At 11:00 PM, Raymond Anderson and a friend decided to go out, leaving Anderson's girlfriend behind with the baby, and not saying where they were headed.

"Where do you think you're going?" Sander asked Anderson.

"Chillin'," he said with a big, toothy smile. "Just going to do some chillin'."

"Yeah, you do that," she screamed as they walked out the door. "Just don't bother coming back tonight." Sander slammed the door shut behind them. She had heard the father of her child use the expression *chillin'* so often it had become a running joke. She knew he was going to be drinking beer, smoking weed and more likely than not getting into some kind of trouble. Anderson's comings and goings had long been a sore point with Sander, especially as of late. The couple had a major argument earlier that day about his friends and his lifestyle of hanging out on the streets. While they did not have as steady of a relationship as she would have liked for the sake of their baby, she at least was trying to do all she could to better herself for the child's future by graduating from high school. Anderson, on the other hand, did not seem to take the responsibility of fatherhood very seriously, continuing to run around with his friends, all of whom would only get him into more trouble. In fact, they quarreled most of the previous day about that very subject. Still fuming, she turned and locked the door.

The gesture proved to be more symbolic than practical. Raymond Anderson would not be coming back that night.

At 11:20 PM, as Burdick was spinning his web of lies in the presence of Detectives Ross, Pisaturo and Arcuri, Floyd was being videotaped by Detectives Petrucci, Nardolillo and me. At the same time, Detective Carl Tirocchi spoke with Elizabeth Zatkoff. She revealed that Burdick was presently residing in Pawtucket. She told the detective that this was not Burdick's permanent address. A girl with whom he was acquainted, lived on the third floor and let him stay there sometimes. Zatkoff said that Burdick would stay with her on occasion, but he was not allowed in her house at that time. He had recently pleaded no contest to violating a no-contact order following a domestic abuse incident and a disorderly conduct charge.

Burdick, however, did not need any help from Zatkoff to impeach him; he was doing a fine job of implicating himself, as well as his co-conspirators, including Floyd, with each word that came out of his mouth.

Floyd was being less than forthright himself, but he did mention Harry Burdick by name, placing him at the scene of the murders, and at least now we had a solid reason to hold a second suspect in the double homicide investigation.

During this interview, taped with Floyd's knowledge and consent, he also implicated two others, Raymond and Sammie, as he did in his previous statement. He could not provide their last names, however. This time, there was no mention of Kenny. There were four of them, in this version, prowling the streets of Providence looking for someone to rob or a car to steal, or both. Once again, it was Sammie, he said, who was the driving force behind the crimes that night. He reported that it was Sammie's car, Sammie's gun, Sammie and Raymond who plotted the robbery and auto theft, Sammie and Burdick who carjacked and kidnapped Amy and Jason, Raymond who ordered them out of the vehicle and onto their knees, Raymond who took money and jewelry from Amy,

Raymond who wanted to rape Amy, Sammie and Raymond who suggested killing Amy and Jason, Sammie who shot them both.

For his part, Floyd said that he tried to talk Sammie out of killing the couple. It was because of this, he said, that Sammie wanted to kill him. "Sammie thinks I'm going to snitch and everything. I, in turn, walk up the hill. Sammie comes up and gets me and brings me back down, has me get down with them, sit down with them, kneel down with them."

During this time, Floyd said of Harry, "He was there, but he was just doing, whatever. He wasn't even paying it no mind, was just standing there. He, he keeps smiling, whatever."

He claimed that Raymond vouched for him, essentially saving his life, and Sammie allowed him to get to his feet. He said an argument ensued about whether or not to kill the kneeling victims, and as he was walking away he turned around and saw Sammie fire three shots. He could not determine if Amy and Jason were dead when they left.

After fleeing the scene and using the eighteen dollars in cash and coins taken from the victims to put gas in both vehicles, Floyd said, "Sammie told me to take the truck. I told him that I didn't want to, that I wanted nothing to do with it. He said, 'You're taking the truck.' He already got my ID, my, you know, my name and everything like that. We ended up fighting and everything. I took the truck, dropped Harry off in Pawtucket, went back down and went to my house. Raymond came down the street with Sammie. We were talking. That's when Sammie said, 'I'll page you tomorrow because we need the truck to do something.'"

"What did he mean by 'do something' tomorrow?" Detective Nardolillo asked.

"Raymond indicated to rob a gas station."

"And did that ever take place?"

"No."

At exactly midnight, the videotaped portion of our interview was completed, but we continued to talk to Floyd. It was officially June 10. The second day of our double murder investigation was just over ten hours old, and already we believed we had two of the perpetrators in custody with at least one other on the radar. We were not about to slow down our pace or lose the momentum we seemed to be gaining.

Chapter 15

Big Wheel Keep On Turning

Since Floyd had indicated that he knew where Raymond lived, we decided to put him to the test. We would drive with him to the residence to have him point it out to us. He consented freely, so Detectives Petrucci, Steppo and I took the somewhat unusual step of chaperoning a murder suspect, essentially into his own neighborhood, to get a fix on a co-conspirator in a major homicide.

At the same time, another car, with Burdick shackled in the back, and Detectives Pisaturo, Steppo and Arcuri escorting, followed closely behind. After the shootings, the Pawtucket man said he witnessed one of the two unknown males getting dropped off at a house in a South Providence neighborhood. He was confident that he could identify the residence, so we called him on it. It was a gamble, but from our chief right on down, it was one we were all willing to take. All the officers were toting shotguns while the suspects were handcuffed in the backseats of the police cars. They were watched closely as we cruised toward the South Providence location at one o'clock that morning.

Looking around, we made our way along Broad Street. I almost checked my watch. It seemed more like 1:00 in the afternoon. There was a cacophony of sound and little activity, as rap and Spanish music blared from cars and open tenement windows. Pungent smells from food trucks parked along the street wafted through the warm night air. There were people everywhere: hookers, drunks, kids playing kick ball in empty parking lots and young children who were unsupervised. One kid, who couldn't have been any more than seven-years-old was riding one of those Big Wheel bikes down the middle of the road.

Many officers, including myself, had children around the same age and they had been fast asleep for hours. Coming from a department in middle-class, affluent suburb of Providence, it was a bit of a culture shock. By comparison, at that same hour in Johnston, the sidewalks were rolled up and it's usually pretty quiet. But this was a hot weekend night in South Providence. Here, we were in an urban war zone. Drugs were everywhere. Violence was a way of life, not an aberration. This was the front line, as far as these harsh realities went. The sight was a real eye-opener for everyone in the cruiser, except Floyd, who didn't seem to notice any of it.

Moving slowly through the crowded streets in our unmarked police car, we stuck out. As our mini convoy of officers and convicts turned onto Prairie Avenue, Burdick became a little confused. The large two- and three-story homes, many predating the first World War, looked very much alike. Stately Colonials and faded Victorians alike were sadly now in various states of dis-repair. The tenanted homes seemed to be surrounded on each side by at least one boarded-up structure. Burdick directed his captors down a side street, away from the lead car. Almost as soon as they broke off, Burdick suddenly shouted out to detectives, whose cars rolled to a stop in front of a tenement-style house with blue and gray paint. This was the location where he said Floyd had dropped off one of the two men the morning after the murders, the place where Floyd himself resided.

A block away, Floyd guided us directly to another tenement and raised a finger toward the second floor, indicating this was Raymond's apartment.

Upon making careful note of the three-story, yellow tenement with the brown front door, we immediately transported Floyd back to headquarters, where we asked him if he would consent to a search of his own place, just around the corner. He agreed. At 1:45 in the morning on June 10, Floyd signed a consent form to search the second and third floors of the apartment where he lived.

With sufficient cause, Detective Tirocchi began to prepare an affidavit for search warrants of both addresses.

There could be no doubt that these apartments were teeming with evidence, sufficient to assist us in capturing the others responsible and securing an ironclad case against each of them. Before anything could be removed or destroyed, we had to get in there.

At that same exact time, Burdick agreed to a videotaped interview. Detectives Arcuri, Pisaturo and I listened as Burdick changed his version of the previous night's events, yet again. This time, he placed himself at the murder scene during the shootings.

The presence of the camera seemed to make him more nervous, but he fought to keep his tears in check. After reading him his rights, I asked, "Do you understand these rights, Harry?"

"Yes, but they made me a promise," he said.

"And what promise is that, Harry?"

"That after I got done doing all this stuff, when I came here, when I told them everything that happened, that I could go home. And another officer came up and told me that, I just asked him, 'Am I going home?' He said the captain said it was alright."

It was one of numerous references that Burdick made expressing a seemingly all-consuming desire to go home. He had voiced this request during the previous night's interview as well. He was clearly trying to enter a plea of innocence even before any formal charges were filed. But what he may have intended to do was not an alibi. What we wanted to know was what he *had* done.

He told us that Floyd approached him as he was waiting downtown for the bus that would take him back to Pawtucket. He said Floyd showed him a gun and told him to hold it while he removed his coat.

"Then," Burdick told us, "I said, you know, I wanted a ride home because I was tired. I just wanted to go home."

Burdick said that Floyd promised to give him a ride, and was led to a nearby car that was being operated by someone Floyd knew by the name of Sammie. He stated that when he got into the back seat with two other males, whose names he did not know, he was taken along on the commission of crimes which he had no prior knowledge and no intention of becoming involved. He insisted that he was an unwitting participant in the carjacking, kidnapping, robbery and the murder of Amy Shute and Jason Burgeson.

According to Burdick, it was only after all this that Burdick got his ride home, by Floyd, and in the victim's truck.

"When I was getting out of the truck," Burdick related, "he goes, 'Hey!' I said, 'What, man?' He goes, 'Don't say nothing, man, because I'm going to shoot you if you do,' and of course, I'm afraid. You know what I mean? And that's what happened. They did it because they were either having fun about it or they just did it to piss people off. I don't know. I was just trying to go home. All I wanted to do was go to the house and go to sleep. That's all I wanted."

In Burdick's account, Floyd and one of the other men got out of the car and took the white truck with Amy and Jason inside. Sammie followed behind with Burdick and the other male as Floyd drove the SUV to the golf course, where they all piled into the truck, rode around spinning the wheels and making donuts in the sand, with no discussion about raping Amy or taking her jewelry. Then, according to Burdick, Floyd fired four or five shots at the victims. He also referred to Sammie as Sonny at one point.

"I mean, personally, okay, I'm trying to remember every word by word, detail by detail, to help you guys with this because I can't afford to have this on my back. I had noth – no idea, nothing – basically, you guys may say I had something to do with it because I was there."

"So," I asked him, "is the version you're telling us now, is it different from the one you told officers before?"

"I'm just, like I said, trying to remember everything word by word, detail by detail, for you guys, and I'm not lying about it."

"Is the version that you're telling us now the absolute truth of what happened?"

"Sir, yes, it is."

It wasn't close to the truth. And everyone in the room knew it.

The interview concluded at 2:26 AM, and a half hour later, Steppo responded to the home of a superior court judge, who signed both search warrants, which were to be executed simultaneously that same morning.

With the signed warrants in hand, Steppo contacted Providence Police Sergeant Francisco Frank Colon, who had responded earlier that evening to the Fricker Street traffic stop of Gregory Floyd. Now, his department was being asked by the Johnston PD to further assist in our ongoing double murder investigation, which was leading us back into the city of Providence.

Colon was one of the city officers who had responded to the South Providence neighborhood shortly before dawn on the morning of June 10. A phalanx of law enforcement agents quickly assembled outside the two street addresses. It was difficult to tell who was who. There were probably thirty or more detectives and patrol officers on scene. Marked and unmarked vehicles drove up and down the streets with the lights off. Others were stopped and blocking access into and out of the area. It looked like a police station parking lot. It was a moonless night, so it was very dark. The air was humid and still. High, spectral clouds hung in the sky like a tapestry, blotting out what little illumination that the stars might have provided.

The men and women in blue organized themselves into two groups. One team hit the blue and white apartment building on Taylor Street at around 3:30 AM. They approached the front of the residence en masse. Detective Nardolillo knocked loudly on the solid wooden door and clearly announced their purpose to the occupants. "Police. We have a search warrant."

Wearing street clothes and armed with flashlights and department-issue firearms, they were ready for anything. This was not our city, so we didn't know exactly what to expect.

When the attempt at contact elicited no initial response, Nardolillo gave the signal and they breached the entrance of the dwelling amidst the warrior cries of officers and the sounds of splintering wood and shattering glass. They responded first to the second floor, whose door was also breached. Three shrieking females were discovered and detained while other officers continued up to the third floor.

The deplorable condition of the house became immediately apparent to the officers who stormed the house. There were holes in the walls, missing pieces of rug and broken windows covered by sheets. The smell of animal urine, beer and cigarettes permeated their nostrils.

At the top of the stairs off to the right, Detective Warren was the first to enter a bedroom where he encountered a surprised male, sitting on the edge of a bed, having just been awakened.

"Get down on the floor," Warren ordered the subject. "We're executing a search warrant."

The subject did as he was told, and he was subdued without a struggle by officers.

"What's your name?"

"Kenneth Day," he spat, grimacing at the inconvenience of being awakened and the discomfort of the manacles digging into his skin as his wrists were handcuffed behind his back. He was short, with close-cropped hair. He told the officers that he had just fallen asleep, returning home about an hour earlier from a temporary job at a bottling plant in Warwick.

Warren read him his rights and asked if he understood.

"Yeah," he responded. "I understand."

He was taken into custody and removed from the premises while the second and third floors were thoroughly searched.

The ground floor, occupied by the landlady, was not listed on the warrant and could not be searched.

At the same time that a search was being conducted on the upper two floors at Taylor Street, the second warrant was being executed on a residence a block away. At the Marlborough Avenue address, Providence Sergeant Colon and Johnston Detective Arcuri were the lead respondents. The moment that Colon was greeted at the door by Raymond's father, the veteran Providence officer realized that the "Raymond" whom Johnston PD was seeking was Raymond Anderson. Colon was familiar with the younger Anderson, from previous run-ins he had with the youth, including a prior arrest. But the suspect was not home, and Colon advised the middle-age man to be sure his son contacted the police as soon as possible.

By now, a commotion had begun to stir outside. The voices of the officers carried, and word quickly spread that a third suspect had been taken into custody on Taylor Street. Sonny DeTora, who was among the officers at Marlborough, was requested to respond to Taylor, where evidence needed to be collected. Everyone else migrated over with him as well.

The second floor, divided into separate one-bedroom apartments, provided us only with potential witnesses. One occupant, Kenneth's mother, was asleep when she heard shouting outside her bedroom. She thought she was dreaming when her door was kicked open and she saw police officers in street clothes enter her room. The beams from their flashlights cut swatches through the darkness and she could see that their guns were drawn. She screamed and was ordered to drop to the floor, face first, and raise her hands above her head.

Kenneth's mother, along with her thirteen-year-old daughter and her sister, were ushered into the second floor bathroom, which was secured by Detective Nardolillo until a thorough search of the residence was completed.

The detective explained to the wide-eyed mother that one tenant, Gregory Floyd, was in custody, and that they were executing a court-ordered search warrant of the premises, all part of an on-going investigation into yesterday's double homicide. Kenneth's mother told Nardolillo that her son, who lived upstairs with Floyd, had moved to Providence from Durham, North Carolina, a few months before, looking for a fresh start, a good job and a better life.

She also recalled for the detective a chilling encounter she had with Floyd a couple of days prior. She said that she had gone up to the third floor apartment to bum a cigarette. When she entered, Floyd was dozing in his chair. He awoke suddenly, startled. Next to him on the floor, lying atop a pile of clothes, she saw a black and silver handgun. When he saw her, he made a quick movement, reaching for the gun. She thought for a moment he was going to pick it up, but instead he covered it with the clothes. Neither of them said anything about the gun. She just took her cigarette and left.

"Do you remember what the gun looked like?" Nardolillo asked.

She pointed to the gun Nardolillo was wearing and said, "It was like yours."

Kenny's mother's statements, as well as those from the other residents on the second floor, were useful to the investigation, but the floor above was where the biggest prizes were found.

Although the top floor had been split into two apartments, only one was habitable. It was this small room, we soon learned, that both Day and Floyd shared. It had only a single closet, one bed, where Day slept, and a recliner, upon which Floyd hung his head. The top floor's only bathroom, sink and tub were all in the room across the hall, which, though larger, was not livable. In fact, it was a sty, cluttered with refuse, strewn clothing, empty food wrappers and suffused with the stench of cat excrement. The smaller room to the right, where Day was apprehended, was also where Detective Faella had discovered what turned out to be the murder weapon, a black, silver-topped .40-caliber semiautomatic Smith & Wesson. The handgun was in plain view, on the bottom shelf of a small entertainment center. Next to the weapon was an ammunition clip, containing two live rounds. On a nearby night table was a single .40-caliber hollow point bullet and an empty black nylon "Uncle Mike" holster. Also recovered from the residence was a phone bill in Floyd's name and reflecting that street address.

As Day was being escorted out of the bedroom, Detective Warren had asked the suspect, "Who does that weapon belong to?"

"It's not mine," Day said. "It's Greg's." As he was led away, Warren made note of the incriminating comment, which only affirmed that Floyd had been continually lying to us about his involvement. I was sure we had the trigger man in custody already, and I was confident that once we apprehended all those involved, every finger would point to Floyd.

When Detective Sonny DeTora arrived to assist Detective Warren, the Johnston BCI team began their crime scene investigation by photographically documenting the Taylor Street apartment, snapping 35mm stills of the bedroom and all the items recovered as evidence. Afterward, the property would be confiscated and returned to Johnston headquarters, where it would be placed in the Evidence Room with the other pieces of the puzzle that we had collected so far.

Sonny couldn't get out of the South Providence tenement fast enough. He felt like there were bugs crawling all over him by the time he finished up in there.

Sergeant Colon, like the others, had left the Marlborough Avenue premises and responded to Taylor Street around the corner. Day had already been taken into custody and the murder weapon recovered. However, there was still a lot of police activity. Most of the officers were milling around outside, keeping the scene secured, so it was more than a little odd what transpired next.

It was around 4 AM when Colon and other officers observed a blue car, with a Rhode Island registration, traveling slowly down Taylor Street. Miles became instantly suspicious of the vehicle, its leisurely rate of speed and the hour of the morning it was being operated. He approached the vehicle, which came to a stop amid a veritable gauntlet of detectives and cruisers, right at the intersection of Marlborough.

Colon instantly recognized the driver, Ray's buddy. Suddenly a lanky male stepped out of the passenger door. His hair was cropped on the sides, topped off by a short afro. An earring on each lobe glinted in the crisscrossing headlight beams. He was wearing a light blue sweater with a loose turtle neck collar. He stood in the street and looked around with a big smile on his face. "What's going on?" he asked.

"That's Ray!" Colon shouted, and within seconds the man was tackled by officers before he get away.

"What's your name?" the sergeant asked him when he was in custody.

"Dion," Anderson replied.

"I'll ask you one more time. What's your name?"

"Dion."

"It's Ray Anderson," Colon confirmed. "He lives over on Marlborough, with his stepfather."

His friend was also handcuffed and taken into custody. They were arrested and driven in separate cars to Johnston headquarters for questioning.

Detectives Steppo and Arcuri drove with Anderson. As they passed the gas station at the intersection of Potters and Elmwood Avenues, Steppo turned toward the murder suspect. "Is that where you guys bought the gas last night?" he asked.

Anderson looked back at him and said, "You fucking guys know everything." Following this remark, he stated that he was going to tell the truth about what happened. The well experienced detective just nodded. He wasn't about to hold his breath.

Detective Faella was one of the last officers on the scene. He stood by the

Taylor Street/Marlborough Avenue intersection as Hooklock's Towing Service removed the car in which Anderson and his friend had been apprehended, then escorted the vehicle to the Johnston Police Station, where Detectives Nardolillo and Petrucci and myself had already begun our interrogation of Anderson. We immediately learned that the murder suspect had an active court warrant out for him, but that was the least of his troubles.

At 5:17 AM, a video camera was set up and Anderson let us record his statement. It was obvious to me that Anderson was high on something. My guess would be that it was pot. He exuded a very cavalier attitude right from the start. Here we were, investigating the murder of two innocent young people, and he was smiling and laughing looking as if he was without a care in the world. He exhibited complete detachment, and refused to acknowledge any responsibility or display a shred of contriteness. That is always a difficult situation for an officer. Sometimes you really have to work to hold your emotions and temper in check. This was one of those times. In view of the horrific crime he'd been part of, Anderson's jaunty manner of speech and demeanor rubbed me the wrong way, but I'm sure I wasn't the only detective at that interview who wanted to reach across the table and shake some sense into him.

I believe the account that Anderson ended up giving us, however, was perhaps the closest to what actually happened that night. In it, he said Burdick and Floyd kidnapped the couple, then drove off with them in the van while he and Day followed behind them in a second car, owned and operated by the elusive Sammie. And, as expected, Anderson impeached Floyd in the shootings of both victims.

"Greg and this kid, Harold, or whatever his name is," Anderson began, "they went and robbed some, went, went and robbed some, two people, and this white truck, I guess, Massachusetts plates, and met up with me, Sammie and Eli waiting on the other block, and they were just joy riding in the car.

"Then they decided, find a place to drop them off, so we went to the golf course to drop them off, and Greg was like, Greg was like, 'Well, we got to do something with them, we got to do something with them.'

"Then Har—then Harold was like, he didn't want nothing to, no part of it, and he was walking away. Then he came back, and he was like, 'Here, sit there and watch,' and then the two people were talking to me, and I told the guy that he had to get out the car and sit down.

"Then I was talking to the girl, and she's asking me to just see if I can do anything as far as getting her out of there, and so then, after that, like, it was like, well, he told the girl to get out the car.

"The girl got out the car, and they're both holding each other, and Greg kept pulling out the burner and pointing it to the girl, I mean, pointing it to the guy, saying, 'Shut up, shut up.'

"And me and Eli, both, started walking away, and Sammie, I think, was in the car. I don't know. We started walking away, and then he just did it. He just shot, he shot the guy one time in the, in the top of the head, and it went in and it came out, and I guess it exploded because of the hollow-tipped bullets and, and hit the girl, and the girl slowly went down. He wasn't sure she was dead, so she, he shot her again, shot her some more times. I think he shot her two more, yeah, he shot her two more times. That was it. And then we left, and I was like— that was it."

I just stared at him. *That was it*, he said, just as heartless as can be.

He downplayed whether there'd been any discussion about raping Amy and confiscating her rings. But he did place all four suspects at the scene of the murder. Burdick, he knew only as Harold, and Floyd only as Greg. Eli, a.k.a., Ken, though he did not know his last name either. However, he was the first one to put a last name to Sammie. And as common as the surname Sanchez might be, especially in South Providence, we finally had a known identity of the fifth and final murder suspect.

Chapter 16

Nowhere
to Hide

A t 5:20 AM, Providence Patrolman Marcus Huffman arrived at the Johnston Police Station. He was introduced to Detective Arcuri, to whom he provided a statement describing his brief encounter with Gregory Floyd a little more than twenty-four hours earlier.

"Yesterday morning," Huffman began, "at approximately 0300 to 0400 hours, I was traveling north on Pine Street, while on duty, I observed a man known to me as Greg Floyd. This male was operating a white SUV with two to three white passengers inside. I did not notice the license plate, but I did observe him following a brownish colored vehicle, also no plate obtained. This was very suspicious to me, knowing that Greg does not have a vehicle like this one."

Arcuri presented Huffman with a photo pack containing six males. Asked if any of the photographs included the individual operating the white van, the patrolman pointed to the second photo, indicating Floyd. He noted that prior to observing the white vehicle go by him, he was alerted by the squealing of tires from the area of Hayward Street and Somerset Street and looked up.

"Did you see where Floyd went in the vehicle after passing you?"

"He turned onto Pine Street and passed by me. He then waved to me, saying, 'Hi, what's up.' He then drove off."

"Is there anything else you would like to add to this statement?"

"No."

At 5:30 AM, Raymond's friend was questioned by Detective Ross and released when it was determined that he played no role and had no knowledge of the double homicide. The friend, however, did reveal that he had a cousin by the name of Sammie Sanchez, who consorted with Anderson and some of the other suspects that were in custody.

At 6:15 AM, Kenneth Day was videotaped by Detectives Tirocchi and Petrucci, providing further confirmation that Floyd was the triggerman as well as corroborating the identity of the fifth suspect, Sammie Sanchez. He described his features, scanty beard and mustache, slight build, markedly smaller than his own 5'7" frame.

With regard to his own involvement, Day's attempt to portray himself as an unwilling bystander failed on every level. Tirocchi listened as Day offered one self-serving and animated statement after another. As a consequence, the detective observed, Day's true nature was revealed, defined by his lack of genuine remorse for the victims. His culpability was further amplified by his self-pity for the consequences of a situation which he was very much responsible.

When I viewed the tape myself later, I was somewhat amazed at what I saw. Day continually fidgeted and bounced around in his chair, pulling his right arm in and out of his shirt sleeve as he spoke to the detectives. Many times he responded to questions without speaking, emitting sound variants of "uh huh" while nodding his head, like a Bobblehead doll. His words and thoughts were as disjointed as his appearance. I've seen people with ADHD, but this didn't seem to be the case. It was almost as if they were interviewing a five-year-old. He wasn't much bigger, either.

When asked if he could tell them what happened on the night of the homicides, Day said, "Okay. I know we was all together. I know it, me, Ray, Sammie, Greg Floyd and I think his name is Harry, or something like that, we was together. We, we in Sam…We in Sammie's car, the…the…car. We in, we in Sammie's car. And we were all talking about getting somebody, getting somebody, getting somebody, getting somebody."

Day would interpret *getting somebody* to mean robbing them, and if the terms, in fact, were synonymous in street parlance, I came to suspect that they had something more unconventional, more deviant, in mind for kicks that night.

"Okay, so, what did you do next?" Detective Tirocchi asked Day. "What happened?"

"All I know is Sammie parked somewhere. Greg and the fat dude hopped out, and the next thing I know, they come out this little alleyway in a white truck and got two people up in the back. All right. Sammie, the driver, so he just followed, you know, he just followed. Next thing I know, we end up at this like, it looked like a desert. That's the way I can explain, like a big old desert. And since they didn't have no money, that was, I guess that was, actually, grand theft auto, kidnapping, and since they didn't have no money, I guess he, he wanted to kill them."

"Who wanted to kill them?"

"Greg."

"Okay. What happened next?"

"All I know is that the girl, the girl sitting down, they were sitting there hugging each other, and he shot the boy. When he shot the boy, I just turned around and just started running, man."

"Did you see the girl get shot?"

"No. I heard three shots though."

"Did Greg tell you why he killed those two people?"

"Nope. I know, I know for one, it had to be, because they didn't have no money. Two, they was going to tell on them, and three, what was he going to do with their truck? So I guess he didn't have no choice but to kill them. I mean, I don't know."

Day was shown a photo pack and asked to point to the person that he saw do the shooting that night in the desert, as he called it. "Number two," Day responded.

"And who is that?" Tirocchi asked.

"That's Gregory Floyd. Come to think of it, yup, that's him because he got my shirt on. Yup, that's him."

At 6:26 AM, the tape went blank. Detective Tirocchi's interrogative, "Is this statement the truth to the best of your knowledge?" was answered by Day's final words, "It's the honest to God truth. Go get a Bible."

It was light again. I wasn't sure what day it was. Once we apprehended Floyd, the concept of time seemed to distort, no longer linear. It was one thing after another for eighteen hours, and we were still going. Spikes of adrenaline and a constant intake of caffeine kept us on our feet, but I was starting to feel the toll on my body by dawn on the morning of June 10. We had nabbed all four suspects involved in the murders of Jason and Amy, and we weren't about to stop until we got the fifth man.

With the statements from the other suspects regarding Sammie Sanchez more concrete at that hour, we were able to establish a last known address, which to no one's surprise was in the same South Providence neighborhood where three other suspects resided. It ran perpendicular to Taylor Street, and was right around the corner from Floyd and Day.

We knew we had enough information to secure probable cause for an arrest warrant, which Detective Steppo prepared. An hour later, Detective Faella went to the home of Justice of the Peace Lauren D. Wilkin, who promptly signed the document.

At 7:30 AM, Jason Burgeson's autopsy began at the Medical Examiner's Office. BCI Detectives Warren and Sonny De Tora were present to document the postmortem exam and to collect the clothing and all personal effects from the subject, including a hair sample and other physical evidence, for use in our investigation.

Portions of the bullets recovered indicated a downward trajectory of their paths into Jason's body through the top of his head. A bullet jacket was lodged in the left temporal cortex of his brain. A fragment of a bullet core was located within the deep tissue of his left mandible. The portion of another bullet core and jacket, deformed but largely in tact, was embedded in the muscle tissue along the lateral left aspect of the victim's neck. Because of the close proximity of the projectiles, and the possibility of a crossing of bullet tracts and deflection, the exact correspondence to the entrance wounds and path of the bullets through the brain could not be determined to any degree of medical certainty. This limitation, however, did not hamper the medical examiner from determining a cause of death, not by a long shot.

The cause of death that the doctor recorded was a simple and violent one. One sentence, factual and to the point: *Skull fractures and brain injuries DUE TO gunshot wounds (2) of head.* But this finding could not begin to tell the story of what happened to Jason Burgeson the night his life ended, or the true damage that those hollow point .40 caliber bullets caused.

The bullet fragments were recovered and presented under Chain of Custody to Detectives Warren and DeTora.

By 9 AM, a dragnet had been organized for the apprehension of Sammie Sanchez. The same South Providence neighborhood was besieged by officers from several jurisdictions. This time, camp was set up outside his residence. Unfortunately, it was full daylight, so the element of surprise had been severely compromised. The strength we had in the number of visible officers would have neutralized the perpetrator's fight-or-flight response, if he had not fled already. We put on quite a public exhibition earlier that morning, and if Sanchez had not known that his co-conspirators and neighbors had been rounded up, then either he wasn't home or he was a really good sleeper.

We approached the front door without delay and a young woman responded to the initial knocking. She was informed that we were police officers, here for Samuel Sanchez, and we had a warrant. She identified herself as Sammie's sister. She said her brother was not home, but confirmed that he was at the home of his girlfriend on Wesleyan Street. While several officers stayed and searched the Glenham residence, the rest of us proceeded a couple of blocks north to Wesleyan, with a Providence officer escorting.

Once there, we observed a gold car with a Rhode Island registration parked on the street in front of the apartment house. The vehicle matched the one described by the co-defendants as belonging to Sammie.

Inside, Sanchez saw us approach. Observing the wave of cops engulf the front of the house, he suddenly felt trapped. With all of us bottlenecked out there, he thought he could slip quietly out the back door and make a clean getaway.

He was wrong.

With no immediate response to our appeal for authorized access, several officers proceeded around to the back of the dwelling.

Just as Sanchez pushed open the screen door trying to get away, he was met by Detective Nardolillo, who immediately observed he fit the description. The detective blocked his escape. "Going somewhere?"

Sanchez said nothing.

"What's your name?" Nardolillo asked the man, who refused to answer. This was not a game that the detective wanted to play at this stage of the investigation, especially not after working through the night. Patience was not a commodity in abundance among any of our detectives, not by a long shot. But Nardolillo maintained his professionalism.

"Sammie?" the detective called to him.

The man looked up and responded, "Yeah?"

It was all Nardolillo needed to hear. Sammie Sanchez was arrested on the spot. And even though he had been trying to protect himself with his strong adherence to silence, before he had even been read his rights, he made an incriminating spontaneous utterance. Upon overhearing a discussion I was having with some of the other detectives about impounding the car and bringing it back with us to headquarters, Sanchez responded, "What are you towing my car for?"

As arrangements were made to confiscate the vehicle, we learned that his car actually belonged to Sammie's mother. In recent months, however, her son had become the primary driver, and his mother believed that he had been using the car for the purpose of job-hunting and the like. She did not know that he had been operating it with a whole other objective in mind, none of which involved gainful employment.

As Sanchez was taken to Johnston headquarters to join his cohorts, Detectives Faella, Ross and Pisaturo stood by until the towing service truck arrived.

At the station, Sanchez denied even knowing the other four defendants, "I don't go outside my mix."

But the others sure knew him. Upon seeing Sanchez enter the cell block, Day said, "What's up, Sammie?" They all identified him as being at the scene of the murders, while he continued to maintain his silence about any knowledge of the crime.

Thirty-six hours had passed since Amy Shute and Jason Burgeson were brutally killed. Now all five suspects were in police custody. The men were processed and held, all charged with two counts of murder, two counts of kidnapping, one count of carjacking and one count of conspiracy to commit carjacking.

In Lakeville, the media began its relentless pursuit of the Burgesons. In the days immediately following Jason's death, they had not been given a moment's peace from the press. Beginning at 7:30 AM, the phone rang and rang. Nadine Burgeson was too grief stricken to talk to anyone, so it became the chore of Kellie and her father to sit next to the phone and take turns answering it. Mr. Burgeson would take one call and then Kellie would take the next. They quickly wore themselves out rehashing everything over and over to the different agencies. They all wanted pictures of Jason alone and with his family and friends. Kellie and her father poured through every album they had and told stories about Jason, crying so hard they couldn't breathe. They tried to accommodate everyone as best they could. Kellie felt that the media was circulating so much misinformation, that she had to step in to set the record straight. The more she talked, however, the more they called. No amount of information she gave them was enough. She needed to believe that she was helping her little brother in some small way by doing this, but she wished she could do more.

All the while, the wake and funeral services weighed heavily in the back of her mind. She was dreading the thought of her brother's final interment, yet at the same time she could not wait for it to be over. But they could not set a definite date until the medical examiner released Jason's body to the funeral home. In the middle of this hellish nightmare, this was one more abhorrent detail that had to be taken care of.

Amy's family found the media was just as aggressive and bold in their pursuit of an exclusive interview. Carol, like Nadine Burgeson, was unresponsive, and relied on her family to keep the wolves from the door. Even sedated, she thought she saw photographers outside the windows, their lenses pressed right up against the glass, and she screamed. It was not her imagination.

At 11:40 that morning, at the same time that Amy Shute's body was being prepared for autopsy, the basement of the Johnston Police Station was transformed into a makeshift courtroom. The five shackled murder suspects were presented before the bail commissioner. Floyd was garbed in a police-issue white jumpsuit, while the others wore the clothes they were arrested in. They remained mostly quiet and impassive throughout the proceeding, staring straight ahead or down at the floor. All of them, except Day, that is. He glared either in defiance or with a strange sense of curiosity at reporters. It was as though he did not know why he was there, or more disturbing, that what he had done did not warrant him being detained. It was as if we had all inconvenienced him somehow, getting him out of bed so early. But whether he knew it or not, he had spent his last night sleeping in a room that did not have bars.

The hearing lasted only minutes, with no family present. The bail commissioner ordered the five men held without bail at the Adult Correctional Institutions (ACI), in Cranston, Rhode Island. A formal arraignment was scheduled for June 12, in District Court. Afterward, three patrol cars transported the perps to prison.

At 12:10 that afternoon, the forensic examination of Amy Shute got underway. He found her cause of death to be similarly simple and violent. *Skull fractures and brain injuries DUE TO gunshot wound of head.* The tract of the single bullet that killed the young woman was traced from the wound at the top rear portion of her head, into her skull and through her brain. A portion of the bullet core and jacket were recovered from the right side of her upper jaw. Both projectile fragments were turned over to Johnston BCI Detectives Warren and DeTora, who were on hand. Like the gunshots that killed Jason, the powerful impact of the bullets fractured the cranial bone in numerous places. In Amy's case, the tremendous force split the sagittal suture along the midline of her skull as well as splitting the frontal suture, which extends from the midline into the right and left portions of the skull. The only thing which eased their family's worries was, due to extensive damage to the brain and internal bleeding, that both their lives ended quickly without prolonged pain or suffering. But the horror of the deaths of these two promising young people brought waves of grief to all that were touched by them.

Chapter 17

The End of
a Long Day

Moving fast and corralling all five murder suspects was the key to attaining corroborating eyewitness accounts from each of them. While some of the assertions they made along the way were obviously false, exculpatory attempts to minimize their own involvement in the crimes, a comparison of their statements revealed clear consistencies that made it easier for us to substantiate certain facts of the case. The worst thing any of them could have done for themselves and each other was talk. If they had kept their mouths shut, it would have made our jobs two thousand times more difficult. Fellowship went right out the window the moment Floyd was pulled over in Providence. As soon as he decided to talk to us, lies or no lies, it became every man for himself. Had they been given more time to think about sitting down and answering our questions, or if they had exercised their rights to speak to an attorney beforehand, they may not have been willing to cooperate. Their impulsive speech, like their choices the previous night, and likely those they made their entire lives, had brought them down. Had any of them given some prior thought to their actions and its consequences, Amy and Jason would be alive today.

Our detective and FBI section certainly caught some early breaks in identifying, locating, and bringing in the killers. Without some good fortune, no case can realistically be solved. Somebody has to see something. Someone has to come forward. Something has to be left behind for us to find. But the men and women in our department worked hard, and our job was not over when these five killers were taken into custody. It was really only the beginning. There was still a lot we did not know. We had other witnesses to locate and follow-up interviews to conduct. There was more evidence to collect, all of which had to be analyzed and preserved for potentially numerous and protracted trials. We had to build our case, and we had to make it stick.

First, we had to catch the killers, then we had to gain convictions, and most challenging, to attain justice with the only appropriate sentence that the five murderers deserved – death.

It was our intention to convene with the Rhode Island Attorney General Sheldon Whitehouse about the possibility of prosecuting the five men under the federal carjacking statute, which provided for the death penalty if this crime results in murder. It wasn't a response to public outcry, or even the inducement of the families that had us initially looking in that direction. Actually, it's not even our decision to make. State prosecutors, as many people know from watching *Law and Order*, are part of the same criminal justice system that work together to punish the guilty to the extent of the law that is both fair to the accused and protects society. Rhode Island statutory law does not provide for capital punishment, and we believed life imprisonment was too easy a sentence for these guys after the heinous crime they committed, so we were all on the same page as far as what we wanted to accomplish from that point forward.

When the faces of Floyd, Day, Burdick, Anderson and Sanchez were in state custody with the good people at the Adult Correctional Institution, it marked the end of one phase of our investigation and the beginning of another. Finally, this long day - day and a half, really - was coming to an end. Though the case was far from over, we could afford to take a short break and get some sleep before going back to work. We were a long distance from securing prosecution against the five killers, but at least we were on our way and headed in the right direction.

By 4 PM, my day was officially over. The high that I had been riding since the previous afternoon suddenly began to abandon me, and I was completely worn-out. There was still a lot on my mind, particularly all the paperwork that had to be done by the other detectives and myself. It was not something we could afford to get behind on. When information comes in that quickly, it's not always easy or possible to get it on paper right away. We had done so much since the previous afternoon, there was a real danger that something could get away from us, a significant fact left out or forgotten which might jeopardize the case. That's why it's so important to have everything documented in writing. And there were many reports that still needed to be filed, including my own. The devil is in the details. That is true.

When I got home, however, these concerns were superseded by my physical exhaustion. I flopped on my bed, clothes and all, fell right asleep. Thankfully, my phone didn't ring and I didn't wake until the following morning.

For the families, the torment continued and sleep was impossible. It was difficult to say which was worse, the insomnia or the nightmares. Night terrors vied with the waking horror of reality. Jason's sister, Kellie, could not sleep for more than a few hours at a time, but there was no respite from the frightful visions she encountered when exhaustion overcame her and she closed her eyes. In her dreams, she was always running toward Jason, trying to get to him before five menacing figures did. But she never made it in time. They always got to him first. Though her brother did not appear to be far away, it took forever for her to reach him. Her legs were moving, but she could not get any closer. By the time she arrived where Jason had been standing, she found his body lying on the ground with blood everywhere. All she could do was reach down and hold him. She just sat there on the ground with her dead brother, cradling him in her lap, crying and crying and crying. All around her were fragments of brain and skull, which she frantically picked up. She tried to put Jason's head back together, but it just fell apart again, time after time. She wound up sitting there rocking him back and forth and screaming, hoping to wake up.

It wasn't much better for any of the Burgesons or the Shutes when the lights went out and they were left alone with their thoughts. Between the constant phone calls from reporters and the steady stream of family and friends, the Shutes and the Burgesons were kept busy all day. But night time was no consolation. It was so quiet, there was nothing to do but think.

For Jason's sister, at least, it was difficult *not* to imagine how Jason and Amy's last moments played out, how scared they must have been, wondering what their thoughts were. Even as they were being driven in the back of the SUV, not knowing what was happening, did they believe that they were going to be robbed and let go, or did they realize that they were going to be harmed? If they knew they would be killed, then why didn't they just run away? Or jump out of the vehicle at a stop light? Why? Why? Why?

The questions never stopped. Even if they didn't want to think about it, they came unbidden in the darkness. One thought was more horrid than the next. When Jason and Amy were out there in the dark holding each other, frightened, did they know it was the end? Or did they have some hope that somehow one of the five men would convince the others to let them live or that someone, maybe a cop or neighbor, would drive down and rescue them? And since one of them had been shot first, the one left would have had to confront the grim reality and sheer terror of knowing the next bullet was going to end their young, promising life with so much left undone and yet to be accomplished.

It did no good for family members to parade these images and thoughts through their minds, but reality was just as bad. As Ernest and Nadine Burgeson and Nick and Kellie Surdis, as a family, made the drive across town to the funeral home to set up services with one of the funeral directors, they understood this. The hardest part for them was walking into a room filled with caskets for the purpose of picking one out for Jason. It seemed such a frivolous matter to Kellie. It was absurd enough that a twenty-year-old was being laid to rest. Did it really matter what the box that Jason was inside beneath the ground looked like?

One was chosen in spite of its futile necessity.

Through blurry, stinging, swollen eyes and with minds that were not functioning properly, they made all the decisions required of them, and then they returned home. As they walked in the front door the phone was ringing. Kellie answered it.

"How are you doing?" someone from the Associated Press wanted to know.

"We just had to pick out Jason's casket," Kellie informed him.

"And what was that like?" a masculine voice on the other end of the line asked.

Kellie, who was trying to be as polite as she could to everyone in the media, despite how frazzled the experiences of the past two days had left her, could no longer maintain her restraint and decorum.

"WHAT WAS THAT LIKE?" she repeated, and then wisely hung up, not wanting to tell the caller what she really felt, that he was an insensitive jerk and she was tired of answering all their stupid questions and she didn't want to do it anymore.

In those first couple of days, not only was rest hard to come by, eating became a problem, as well, though not from lack of it. Besides the constant deliveries of flowers and cards, there were the many baskets of fruit and food that people were kind enough to send. And so many people were cooking and bringing them groceries, nutrition was never a worry. Appetite, however, was another issue entirely.

At this point, both the Shutes and the Burgesons weren't thinking too much about anything besides getting through these trying times. However, with all five killers now in custody, what would happen during the lengthy trial phase ahead would become a major focus of their daily thoughts, and the subject of their nightmares, for some time to come.

Part III

The Long Road to Justice:

June 11, 2000–
August 16, 2004

Photograph courtesy of the Johnston Police Department

Aerial view of Buttonhole Golf Course, where the bodies of Amy Shute and Jason Burgeson were discovered.

CLOCKWISE FROM TOP LEFT: Amy Shute; high school graduation photo of Amy; Amy with her two younger sisters; Amy with her mother, Carol Shute.

CLOCKWISE FROM TOP LEFT: Jason Burgeson; high school graduation picture of Jason; The Burgeson Family: (from left) Kellie, Jason, Nadine and Ernest; Jason DJ'ing at his college radio station.

THE ACCUSED MURDERERS (top): Harry Burdick and Samuel Sanchez **(middle):** Gregory Floyd **(bottom):** Kenneth Day and Raymond Anderson

The spot where Jason's truck was parked. Jason and Amy were leaning against the back brick wall when they were approached by Floyd and Burdick.

The parking lot of the restaurant where Jason parked his vehicle. This is also the location where both victims were carjacked and kidnapped.

The alleyway that Floyd and Burdick drove down with the victims after they were kidnapped.

Buttonhole Golf Course

Detective Raymond Pingitore, at Buttonhole Golf Course, points to the location where the bodies of Amy and Jason were discovered.

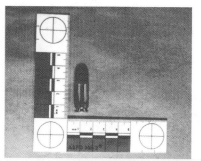

Shell casing found at crime scene.

The .40-caliber Smith & Wesson used to murder Amy and Jason. The gun was later discovered in the home of Floyd and Day.

Floyd and Burdick car-jacked both victims, forced them into the back seat of Jason's vehicle (seen here) and drove them to the Buttonhole Golf course.

Surveillance video taken on the early morning of June 9, 2000 of Harry Burdick and Gregory Floyd moments before they car-jacked and kidnapped Jason and Amy.

Surveillance footage of Gregory Floyd returning to Jason's stolen vehicle on June 9, 2000 after the crime. Floyd was seen by witnesses driving the truck just hours after the murders.

Photograph by John Freidah, courtesy of the Providence Journal

From Left: Gregory Floyd, Harry Burdick, Samuel Sanchez, Raymond Anderson and Kenneth Day in police custody on June 11, 2000 for the murders of Amy Shute and Jason Burgeson.

Chapter 18

The Unusual Suspects

Ira Nasberg was a local cowboy of sorts, though not in the traditional, romantic sense of the word. Though I was not familiar with Nasberg at the time of the murders, in the coming days he would become a person of major interest in the Shute-Burgeson homicide investigation.

Nasberg first made his presence known to us when he called the station the day after the bodies were discovered. We were all very busy at the time. He spoke briefly with an officer, telling her that he believed the weapon used in the double homicide belonged to him. The patrol woman took the man's personal information and passed the call on to Detective Nardolillo.

In cases like this, you don't know how much credence to put on such a call. The bigger the headlines, the more people you get calling in confessing to the crime itself, as well as other crimes, which may or may not even be related. With everything that's going on, you just can't afford to waste time chasing false leads.

The first question the detective asked Nasberg was why he believed the gun used to kill the two victims was his. Nasberg stated that he was acquainted with Gregory Floyd, and that a .40 caliber Smith & Wesson semi-automatic handgun belonging to him had been stolen four months prior.

Furthermore, he said that Greg was with him the day the weapon was taken out of his car.

This last admission immediately raised Nardolillo's suspicion, and he continued to gather as much information as possible from the caller while he had him on the phone. Nasberg claimed that he had filed a police report in Providence the day of the theft. With this information, the detective concluded the call, advising the caller that he would be contacted after the matter was looked into further.

The detective electronically submitted an ATF Firearms Trace form, and just as promptly ran the serial number of the murder weapon, which Nasberg claimed was his, through the National Crime Information Center. The NCIC is a computerized database that provides criminal justice agencies with prompt access to shared information, which can assist agencies in apprehending fugitives, locating missing persons and locating and returning stolen property. Nardolillo's inquiry, however, determined that the gun used to kill Jason and Amy had not been reported stolen.

During this time, Nasberg called back, insisting that it was his gun that had been used by Floyd in the Johnston homicides. When Nardolillo spoke with Nasberg a second time, he informed the persistent caller that the weapon confiscated from Floyd's apartment was not in the NCIC database. The detective promised that he would research it further and get back to him.

From that moment on, we learned a lot about Ira Nasberg very quickly. And what we discovered left more than a few of us scratching our heads.

On June 11, Ira Nasberg appeared at the Providence Police headquarters to clarify the facts relating to the handgun that he had recently reported stolen, and his statement was taken. He was immediately asked about the February 12 larceny.

Nasberg began to spin a quasi-stylized descriptive narrative, as if he were a character in a Mickey Spillane novel. He said he was driving his cab on the night in question, and business was slow. He was also pulling double-duty, freelancing his videography skills, which involved independently filming accident crime and scenes, upon which he would sometimes be the first arrival. He was sort of a middle-aged Peter Parker, who captured images of death and suffering instead of acts of heroism. He would sell his celluloid horror tableaus to the local television station who offered him the most money. He had previously sold photographs of such scenes to *The Providence Journal*. As he shuttled people around the city of Providence in his car, his camera was always at ready for any breaking news. But it was slow on that front, as well, at the moment.

It was around 3:00 AM, and Nasberg was sitting in his tan car, parked on Weybosset Street, when Floyd approached him and they began to chat. Nasberg told Floyd that he was not going to be on-duty much longer, and that he would be heading home soon. He then asked Floyd if he wanted to join him to play *Half Life*, a popular science fiction first-person shooter game played on the Internet. The two, Nasberg affirmed, had hung out together in the past. Though the forty-one year old male and the nineteen year old youth seemed an odd pairing, they had one thing in common, "the wall." This inner city landmark might just as well have been a symbol of the restrictive quality of life that is a reality on the streets of Providence, which for many becomes an oppressive and often violent home that limits human potential and becomes a formidable barrier that is nearly impossible to overcome.

Floyd had been driving an old truck at that time. It was red and had a series of bungee cords holding the hood in place. He followed Nasberg to his Providence residence and they played *Half Life* for about an hour. Afterward, the two drove together to an all-night convenient store and gas station to get some cigarettes. Nasberg had a Smith & Wesson .40 caliber semiautomatic on him. He had a permit to carry a concealed weapon and the gun was registered. But Nasberg did not have a holster and the gun was irritating his skin, so he removed it and left it in the space between the front seat and the passenger seat. Then he got out of his car and entered the convenient store alone, leaving Floyd behind in the vehicle. A couple minutes later he came out of the store with a pack of cigarettes and he and Floyd drove back to Nasberg's residence. Upon returning, Nasberg told the officer that Floyd got into his truck and left while he went into his apartment for the night. However, upon discovering that he was out of dog food for his pet, he got back into his car with the intention of returning to the convenience store to buy some. It was at this time, he claimed, that he realized his gun was missing. It was no longer between the seats. He began to search the vehicle frantically for the weapon, but could not find it anywhere.

Disregarding the trip to the convenient store for dog food, he went directly to the Providence Police Department instead and filed a missing gun report. However, he neglected to mention in his statement that Floyd had been in the car alone with the weapon when he went inside the convenience store to buy his cigarettes. When the officer asked him why he left this information out, Nasberg responded, "I never thought of him as being a bad person."

After the murders, Nasberg recalled that he was at the pizzeria when he overheard people talking about the murders and he learned that Floyd was involved. It was only then, he told the officer, that he knew for sure that his .40 caliber had been used in the double homicide.

Ira Nasberg was very concerned by this admitted oversight, and he had every right to be. He was in a lot of trouble, and he knew it. He wanted to do the right thing. More than that, he wanted to go back and fix what he did wrong. But it was too late. Two people were dead, five others had been arrested and he was right in the middle of it. I'm sure if he had to do it all over again, he would have done whatever he could to keep that gun out of Floyd's hands. But it doesn't work that way.

We were not about to let him out of our sights now, and he dealt with that pressure by staying in constant contact with us, perhaps trying to anticipate our next move. He was overly cooperative, which was unsettling at times because you never know what someone like that is going to do next. However, Nasberg's mounting legal problems were not his only worry. He had various health issues that would compromise more than his ability to assist our investigation.

On Sunday, June 11, April Down began to look closely at the photograph on the cover of the *Providence Sunday Journal*. It showed the five defendants standing together in line at the Johnston Police Department. Kenneth Day was closest to the photographer when the picture was taken, and he was staring intently at the camera, his features most clearly visible. Standing next to him was a taller male, Raymond Anderson, his head down, in profile. These men looked eerily familiar to April, and then suddenly another image surfaced in her memory as she continued to study their faces. In her mind's eye she could still clearly see the silver gun with a white handle that had been pressed against her husband's head. The association sent a fresh spark of terror through her body as she instantly realized where she had last seen the two men. She immediately picked up the phone and called the Johnston police.

Detective Steppo was working that morning, and he spoke to the caller who said she recognized the guys who had robbed her and two people a month before in Providence. She said their pictures were in the Sunday paper.

Steppo responded to the residence of April Down and her husband in nearby Cranston to conduct an interview, bringing a Witness Statement Form and a copy of the Sunday paper. He instructed Mr. and Mrs. Down to identify the robbers by drawing a circle around them. She made a positive ID on Anderson and a tentative one on Day. Mr. Down could make only tentative identifications of both suspects. Then the couple initialed and dated the front page photograph. Steppo put his initial and date on the photograph as well, and then he took a statement. April explained what happened the night of the robbery. She had already filed a report with Providence the day of the incident, but we needed our own statement for our file, as it relates to suspects in our double homicide investigation.

She explained to Steppo that at 7:45 PM on May 18, she, her husband and a friend had just exited the exclusive University Club on the East Side when they were robbed at gun point. Three males approached them, held a gun to Mr. Down's head and demanded his wallet and both ladies' purses, which they turned over to the robbers, who then fled with the items. It was over quickly and the victims were not harmed in the incident. A janitor from the Wheeler School on the East Side phoned her a few days later to tell her that he had found her purse and a billfold in the school playground.

Mel Steppo then advised the Downs that this robbery would be a Providence investigation, and all information would be turned over to that department. Upon returning to Johnston headquarters, Steppo contacted Providence Major Howard Curry and informed him of the interview he conducted with the Downs. Providence Sergeant Jordan Griffith followed up on this information to renew the pursuit of the May 18th robbery investigation, which would, indeed, have an impact on our case.

But April Down and her husband weren't the only robbery victims who looked at the *Journal* photograph that morning and saw a familiar face. Three young people, who had been attacked and robbed recently, instantly recognized Kenneth Day. All three witnesses would step forward in the coming days to update their previous robbery statements made to police.

At 9:00 AM on Monday , June 12, the five murder suspects were formerly arraigned before 6th District Court. Each were charged with two counts of murder, two counts of kidnapping, one count of carjacking and one count of conspiracy to commit carjacking.

Four of them were wearing the same clothes they were arrested in two days earlier. Bound in leg shackles and handcuffs, they were escorted into the courtroom by armed guards. They came in one by one, appearing before the judge, and left quickly. The victims' families were in the courtroom that day, along with a large contingent of the media, who were there to film their reactions as much as the proceeding itself.

Although Carol and her mother were too angry and distraught to attend, Jim went to the hearing with some family members and friends. He was there for his beloved Amy. And he was there for Carol and Erin and Elizabeth, who were all falling apart in front of him. It hurt him terribly to see them in such hopeless pain. Three weeks later, Jim's father died, and he displayed even more fortitude and courage. He was dealing with his own grief, at the same time deflecting the worst of it from the Shutes, and he never missed a court appearance or meeting.

Ernest Burgeson, Jason's father, personified the working class man dressed in a light blue shirt and jeans. He displayed little emotion as he sat with two close friends and his son-in-law in the middle of the crowded courtroom and watched the arraignment proceedings. Other family members and friends were not able to keep their indignation in check, making deliberate facial expressions, shaking their heads and crying. Afterward, Mr. Burgeson told reporters that he took some comfort in knowing that the men responsible for his son's death were in police custody, but there was a reservoir of anger deep inside him. "I had a lot of emotions," he confided, adding, "It took a lot to stay controlled. I wanted to jump up and beat every one of them. I hope I live long enough to see them put to death."

The judge entered no pleas on behalf of the five defendants because District Court does not handle felony cases. They were ordered held without bail pending a hearing scheduled for June 26. At that time, the assistant attorney general requested that four of the men also face hearings on whether or not they violated terms of their probation, on which they had been placed following past convictions. Each would have a public defender assigned to represent them. The defendants were immediately returned to the Adult Corrections Institution. A gauntlet of sheriffs protected the men as they left the courtroom, not an enviable or a very popular job at that moment.

Also in the courtroom that day was Jeffrey Harper, Amy's former boyfriend. The photographers zeroed in on him as he sat quietly clutching a stuffed bunny and sobbing. But not everyone could fit in the limited-seating legal arena. Outside, people called for the death penalty for the five defendants.

"These guys have no regard for human life; they're animals," said one store owner. She told reporters she had plenty of customers ready to sign her petition at the store demanding a death penalty trial. "The only cure for these guys is a bullet between the eyes."

Her sentiments were shared by many people, who responded to an initiative started by the Burgesons, asking state residents to write letters to the government, including the U.S. Attorney General and U.S. Attorney Margaret Curran, to petition for a federal death penalty trial against the killers of Jason and Amy. This vigorous letter-writing campaign would turn into an all-out battle that the victims' families would embark upon in a concerted effort to ensure that justice was served.

Immediately, more than 1,000 letters flooded the office of the Rhode Island Attorney General, Sheldon Whitehouse. Still others called the office directly to voice their opinion that the only way to completely protect the public from known predators was to put them to death. The Burgesons and the Shutes were not the only ones determined to have the case reviewed by, and hopefully prosecuted by, United States Attorneys. Long before the arraignment of the five suspects, our state Attorney General was already conferring with federal prosecutors to determine how to best pursue the case.

Kellie Surdis told reporters that day that Mr. Whitehouse had spoken with her family about the potential for federal prosecution and the death penalty. Because of the extensive criminal records of the defendants, she went on to say, "This is not trying to be vindictive. But imprisonment isn't enough of a deterrent."

A District Court clerk handed out thick packets to the media which listed, in legal shorthand, the entire criminal histories of four of the double murder suspects. For such young men, they were voluminous. The information, contained in forty-one pages, documented all the individual complaints and charges filed against the men, whether or not they ended up in convictions.

Gregory Floyd was only nineteen, but had a known history of vehicle theft, and was currently on probation for separate offenses at the time of the murders. *The Providence Journal* has indicated that Floyd pleaded no contest to both charges using an alias, Michael Banks. The newspaper also reported that in 1998, while still a minor, Floyd, a.k.a Michael Banks, fought with another youth on Weybosset Street and wound up pleading no contest to disorderly conduct for the altercation.

On November 20, 1998, he mugged a tourist near the city's landmark Biltmore Hotel. Actually, it was a family from Staten Island, whose daughter was interviewing for residency at area hospitals. They made the mistake of stopping to ask Floyd and a friend for directions. As soon as the woman rolled down her window, someone grabbed her hand while the other reached into the vehicle and stole her purse. They got away with two hundred dollars in cash, credit cards and a spare car key. Floyd used the panic button on the electronic key fob to locate the car parked in the city and then stole the car. Floyd immediately drove to the pizzeria, where he worked part-time, and bragged to the owner and others about how he had stolen the car.

I don't know if the woman ever received her specific medical training in Rhode Island, but the family who left New York only to get their car stolen in Providence did get their car back. Floyd was arrested later that day by Woonsocket police, who also recovered an unloaded airgun from the glove box and a small amount of marijuana. They reported that Floyd gave them an alias and told them that a friend gave him the car. He was charged on February 28, 1999 in Woonsocket with possession of a stolen vehicle.

Then, on June 20, 1999, he stole a new car and wound up being apprehended after crashing it on Log Road in Smithfield. The following month he pleaded no contest in Superior Court to both car theft charges. Judge Mark Pfeiffer gave him a five year suspended sentence and five years probation.

On Sept. 24, 1999, Providence police charged Floyd with possession of stolen property, less than 500 dollars. Also in 1999, State Police arrested Floyd in Warwick for driving a car with plates stolen from the Urban League of Rhode Island. Providing authorities with false identification, he pleaded no contest.

Floyd showed a propensity for belligerence, missing five court appearances in two years. Each time, a warrant issued and he was arrested. He was no stranger to Superior Court either, though he was somehow able to avoid jail time on his felony arrests. Floyd was outwardly quiet and soft-spoken, and his criminal activity did not involve the use of violence. This may have played a role in his lenient sentences. However, his repeated failure to show up at District Court compelled the Chief Judge Albert DeRobbio to impose a thirty day jail term against him for a minor obstruction charge in May 2000. He had been released only a few days before the murders.

Floyd was somewhat of an aberration, however, with a duplicitous nature which ranged from occasional outbursts of violence against a girlfriend and general street hooliganism to a more thoughtful young man who was categorically respectful of authorities and at times considerate toward strangers. He was known to go out of his way to help stranded motorists, and give money to hungry runaways to buy pizza. After stealing the new car in 1999, it was alleged that he was caught after driving off the road and smashing the vehicle while attempting to avoid hitting a cat.

Harry Burdick, at the age of twenty-one, had a long record of armed robberies, his first at the age of seventeen, and was known to beat his girlfriends. There are indications that Burdick used heroin, a habit he supported with robbery. Though he spent time on the streets and homeless, he was from a large family, with six siblings and living parents, who reported having no contact with him. He was on probation at the time for a 1996 larceny conviction. He had also pled guilty to a disorderly conduct charge as well as a domestic violence offense.

One of two former girlfriends who accused Burdick of abuse was so afraid of him that she wrote to a judge, advising the court that Burdick needed serious help dealing with his anger. He pleaded no contest for disorderly conduct and to violating a no contact order. A psychiatrist found that Burdick had "poor impulse control," and "traits of antisocial personality disorder." The doctor imposed domestic abuse counseling, but he stopped going in winter 1999-2000. Burdick's probation recommended that he get fifteen days for violation of his parole for non-compliance, and on February 23, 2000, a District Court judge issued a warrant, but Burdick failed to show up to court three times. The warrant was in force the night of the double homicide.

He had a tendency to get on people's nerves, and even his friends described him as a punk, a bully and a hot head. He would act tough all the time, but it was much worse when he was drunk or high. He would circle the block around Weybosset Street and harass people, frequently just picking on them, but sometimes robbing those who were the least threatening and most defenseless as he brandished a foot-long knife. Mostly, he targeted college students, who often had money and were the easiest to intimidate. He walked up to people all the time and demanded money. "Give me your money," Burdick told them, "or you know what's going to happen."

Once, at Waterplace Park, he confronted a man who confided that he had no money. Burdick responded by throwing the man into the Providence River and laughing about it with his friends.

Burdick hung out at the Welcome Arnold Homeless House in Cranston as well as the Amos House in Providence, where he took advantage of the free breakfasts. He sometimes asked for spare change and hustled for money, selling bootleg silver chains at a nearby cafe. The bartender would frequently be forced to ask him to leave the bar if he wasn't going to buy anything.

Raymond Anderson was not a fighter. He was known as a pretty boy by his street associates and had a reputation as a ladies man. But his clean-cut good looks were not what attracted the attention of the local police. Recent arrests included charges of drug possession and obstruction. He was regarded as a rather polite, quiet kid in this tough, impoverished neighborhood. He was raised primarily by his grandmother, who urged him and his brothers to stay in school and participate in sports, driving them to both to ensure that they made it safely and without being sidetracked. Anderson moved from his grandmother's house in 1998 when his father, who had his own trouble with local law enforcement, took up residence around the corner. No longer in school and not working, he made a few dollars cutting men's hair out of the house.

Samuel Sanchez, at twenty, was a one-man crime wave. He had been linked to numerous serial armed robberies of convenient stores and neighborhood markets, at least six over an eight day period in early 2000, in Pawtucket, Providence and Cranston. It was generally agreed that he was probably the worst offender of the group, the one who was most inclined to do serious harm to someone. He was a person who seemed born to commit crime, who would just take whatever he wanted and would do so with a sense of entitlement, without remorse. And he would not stop until he was put away. He had convictions for robbery, conspiracy and felony assault. But it was a lesser charge, disorderly conduct, which landed him on probation, a term that he was presently serving. Earlier that spring, he had missed two meetings with his probation officers.

Kenneth Day, who was twenty-one, had no adult rap sheet in Rhode Island, and his out-of-state troubles with the law were not included on the list of local complaints and convictions filed against the double murder suspects, which the court provided to the media. However, Day had only recently returned to Rhode Island from North Carolina, where criminal charges for drug offenses were pending against him. Also, back in 1995, as a minor, he had been convicted of assaulting a woman, sentenced to house arrest and required to wear an electronic monitoring device for thirty days. He was given twelve months probation, during which time he repeatedly did not comply to the terms, including absconding from supervision and failing to report.

The fresh start he was hoping to make when he returned to his native Rhode Island lasted less than two months.

If the court of public opinion held sway on the morning of June 12, all five men accused of murdering Amy Shute and Jason Burgeson would have been convicted and condemned for their criminal actions that very day.

Many people voiced opinions on one of the most shocking and brutal murders that the state had seen in recent history. Death penalty opponents were called to task. There was little middle ground to be had. It may have appeared as though Amy's grandmother was the one exception. She did not attend the arraignment and could not even bring herself to discuss the case publicly. "It's too upsetting to talk about," was all she could say. But she definitely had a strong opinion on the men who killed Amy, and it was anything but grandmotherly.

Still, there were a few who tried to remain impartial until all the evidence was presented. Reporters were able to approach Raymond's father, and they spoke to the thirty-seven-year-old grandfather outside his South Providence home. "The only thing I can say is," he began, "Raymond is innocent until proven guilty. How's a man supposed to feel? My son's nineteen years old, has a newborn baby, four-weeks-old. It comes down to me, the grandfather."

Asked to describe his son, he said, "All he does is, he plays sports. He's always been a good boy. He tries to help out kids. He's the type of kid, if a cat was limping down the street with a bad leg, he'd try to help the animal."

The owner of the pizzeria that Floyd and Burdick frequented told reporters that he was surprised that Floyd and Burdick would be involved in the carjacking-murders. "That kid, Greg, he would give you the shirt off his back. I mean, as far as I know, every time somebody has no money he'd give them some, buy people food."

As he spoke these words to the media that afternoon, both Floyd and Burdick were being escorted into Superior Court to face possible sanctions for violating terms of their probation for previous crimes.

Because of the implications that this statute had on the case and the direction of the criminal trials, it is worth discussing formally and in some detail. In order for a defendant to be sentenced for a capital crime in Rhode Island, which is one of only twelve other states that did not have the death penalty, the suspect has to be charged with a federal offense and prosecuted by United States Attorneys. The federal government, however, does not litigate homicide cases, at least not those involving civilians who are not employed by the government. The United States does allow capital punishment for other, non-homicide crimes, some sixty overall. One of those crimes was applicable to the five accused murderers of Amy Shute and Jason Burgeson. So the only way that the five men responsible for these deaths could be sentenced to death was if they were indicted, tried and sentenced on federal charges of carjacking, death resulting.

Carjacking is defined by the crime of stealing a car by force, intimidation or violence "with the intent to cause death or serious bodily injury." To punish and deter such a brutal crime as that seen in the case of Amy and Jason, the current federal carjacking statute that is currently on the books (Title 18 United States Code Section 2119) provides the death penalty if, during the commission of this crime, murder results. Life imprisonment is the other possible sentence that could be imposed upon someone convicted of this offense. And, of course, in the federal system, a sentence of life imprisonment always entails no possibility of parole.

How this law works precisely when it is pursued is much more complicated than this definition implies, however, and it is very rarely applied. It is initially the obligation of a United States Attorney, who decides whether or not to try a case federally and whether to seek the death penalty or life imprisonment.

With regard to the five we charged in the murders of Amy and Jason, there were several avenues of prosecution to pursue, but none were more attractive than those which would bring about the harshest punishment. Convictions for carjacking, death resulting, as well as use of a firearm during a crime of violence, are both punishable by either life imprisonment or death. Conspiracy carries a statutory maximum penalty of five years in prison and possession of a firearm by a felon is punishable by up to ten years. Each offense in the indictment also carries a potential fine of up to $250,000.

Next, after the U.S. Attorney makes a sentencing determination, these death-eligible offenses automatically trigger an administrative review process prescribed by the Department of Justice. Under that process, prosecutors submit appropriate information to the review committee, made up of Justice

Department lawyers appointed by the Attorney General of the United States. Defense counsel at this time may make arguments before the committee. Families of the victims may also submit information. After hearing arguments and reviewing all pertinent information, the panel has fifteen days to submit its findings and make a recommendation to the U.S. Attorney General, who conducts his or her own review and then decides whether to seek the death penalty. A decision usually follows recommendations of local prosecution by the U.S. Attorney.

In the Shute–Burgeson case, the heinous nature of the murders, in which both victims were reasonably tortured as they pleaded for their lives, made a strong case for the death penalty. The age of murderers, however, did not favor such a conviction. In this instance, perhaps the most discouraging factor of this law's application was a political one. Since Rhode Island did not have the death penalty, if the government were to step in and kill Jason's and Amy's killers, it would set a dangerous precedent, namely, that for any state that did not have a death penalty of its own, the government would do it for them. And the Department of Justice did not want to become a federal watchdog agency for state capital punishment cases. There are still many people today who oppose the death penalty for any reason. To all of them, the Burgesons and Shutes would ask how they might feel if it had been their son or daughter who had been killed. Would they feel the same way about their own child's murderers?

The federal death penalty was reinstated in 1988, after a sixteen year moratorium which began in 1972, when the United States Supreme Court ruled that all state death penalty statues were unconstitutional because they allowed for arbitrary and capricious application. The federal death penalty statutes suffered from the same infirmities as the state statutes, however, and as a result no federal death sentence case employing the older federal statutes has since been upheld. Furthermore, between 1927 and 1963, only thirty-four individuals have been executed by the federal government.

A federal carjacking statute soon followed the 1988 return of government-sanctioned death, when four years later, a Maryland mother, while taking her daughter to preschool, was forced from her car and dragged a mile and a half. She was killed as thieves drove away in the vehicle, and the statute was quickly enacted and enforced. Since 1992, 135 of 418 carjacking-murder cases were approved by Justice Department Committees, resulting in twenty-nine people in death row as of June 2000. However, not one of those convicted carjack-murderers had been put to death up to that time. In fact, overall, no federal inmate had been executed between 1963-2000, and only three federal prisoners have been put to death since then, including Oklahoma City bomber, Timothy McVeigh, in 2001.

One columnist provided perhaps the most illuminating statistic of all. Don Feder, in his article titled, "Advertisements for Death Penalty Walking" in *Insight, Jewish World Review*, reported that between 1973 and 1997, half a million Americans were murdered, and only 432 state executions carried out. He said that, "A murderer is more likely to get struck by lightning than pay the ultimate penalty (for his crime)."

The Shute-Burgeson case, being prosecuted by a team of federal and state prosecutors, led by Assistant United States Attorneys Gerard Sullivan and Mary Rogers, Assistant Rhode Island Attorney, Stephen Dambruch, and Special Assistant Rhode Island Attorney General, Peter Neronha, were looking to buck that trend. And so were the victims' families, as well as many individuals in the state and around the country. They were all hoping that justice would prevail in federal court.

Chapter 19

Joining forces

Late in the day on June 12, the Burgesons received word from the funeral home that the Medical Examiner's Office in Rhode Island had completed its autopsy and Jason could be brought there. There were no mixed emotions about it, his father, mother and sister wanted to see him, but the anxiety ran high. Since his death had been so violent, they didn't know what he would look like. Kellie's nightmarish visions kept coming back to her. They were also concerned that they might not be able to have an open casket.

Immediately, Kellie and Jason's father drove to the funeral home to confer with the director and make the final decision. His mother, Nadine, remained at home awaiting the determination. They were all relieved when they found out that Jason's body could be viewed, but it was a dreadful determination just the same. Finally, they completed the arrangements. There would be a public wake Wednesday evening at the funeral home and the following morning Jason would be buried at Precinct Cemetery.

The task of picking the clothes in which Jason would be buried was the next chore asked of the Burgesons. While it would be impossible to rank from least to most the level of distress and anguish among all the painful duties that the family needed to perform during this extremely traumatic event, this was among the most tormenting. There was a sad finality to deciding what your son, your baby brother, was going to wear in his casket, and it was overwhelming. Nadine and Kellie cried as they walked into Jason's room for the first time since he was murdered, feeling a little like intruders. When the latest spate of their tears subsided, the two women decided against anything formal, such as a suit. That was just not, Jay. Thankfully, they did not have to rummage for long, finding his favorite pair of blue pants, which he wore all the time for dancing and the pants were made of lightweight nylon and had numerous pockets up and down the legs. Kellie knew how much he liked them.

When it came to choosing a shirt, more thought was required. Jason had a ton of crazy loud shirts in a variety of prints that he loved to wear. They would like to have picked out one for him, but these were all short-sleeved and they thought that something with long sleeves would be more appropriate. Instead, they chose a lightweight cotton Patriots shirt. Instinctively, Nadine took the two items to have them washed and ironed, just as she had always done for Jason.

Detective Nardolillo, following up on the Nasberg-murder weapon connection, pulled the Providence Police theft report that Nasberg filed in February. It was determined at this time that the gun recovered from his residence, and believed to have been used in the double homicide, was, indeed, the same gun that Nasberg had owned and reported stolen four months prior. The serial numbers matched, and the fact that it did not appear in the NCIC database was an oversight that we fortunately caught. Nardolillo then informed Nasberg of what we had learned. It was no surprise to Nasberg, but we still didn't know how Floyd got his hands on the gun. Floyd said he bought the weapon from Nasberg, but he didn't have that kind of money to throw around, and we suspected Nasberg just gave it to his friend and falsely reported it stolen to cover himself. But what we thought didn't matter. It was only what we could prove that counted.

That same afternoon, a conference between local, state and federal authorities took place at the U.S. Attorney's Office in Providence. It was the first collective step we all took together in moving this case forward to determine the most effective way to conduct the investigation and prosecute the suspects. I sat down at a large conference table and across from me were Captain aRusso and Detective Nardolillo, representing the Johnston Police Department, members of the United States Attorney's Office, the Rhode Island Attorney General's Office, FBI and ATF. The primary topic underlying everything else we discussed was the question of whether or not the five defendants would be prosecuted federally. Steven Dambruch and Peter Neronha represented the State Attorney General's Office, Gerard Sullivan, the U.S. Attorneys Office, Special Agent Ann Goodwin the FBI and Special Agent Wing Chau the Department of U.S. Treasury ATF Division.

One hard fact was laid on the table right away: though this was a remorseless, savage crime, we all felt strongly it merited the most serious sentence. Even if federal charges were filed, a death sentence could not be guaranteed, conviction or not. All of us were well aware that the path to death row was long and rutted, and this fact-finding meeting was just the beginning.

Because many people have strong feelings about capital punishment, jury selection alone in death penalty-eligible cases usually take a longer period of time to conduct than most entire trials. And even if the trial should end in a conviction, and it is upheld, the appeals process can defer a death row inmate's fate indefinitely. Of course, there is always the possibility that the conviction might simply be overturned, with prosecutorial misconduct or incompetent defense lawyering the main reasons cited for such reversals. These are factors that often make prosecutors very leery about even seeking the death penalty.

Public outrage had already sparked loud calls throughout Rhode Island for the death penalty in this case. However, this was not seen as an influential factor, at least as far as Justice Department guidelines were concerned. While some legal experts were of the belief that the heinous manner of the execution-style killing could possibly trigger a federal death penalty push, by a matter of law, federal prosecutors could not decide to try the Providence carjacking federally solely because the state did not have its own death penalty sanction, and were not likely to do so.

Additionally, a decision made by the First Circuit Court of Appeals in Boston earlier that same year set precedent for any federal carjacking case litigated in the United States. The case involved two drug dealers who carjacked and killed a woman leaving a doctor's office with her baby. The court reversed the convictions of the two drug dealers because they found insufficient proof that the drug dealers intended to do serious harm at the time they began the carjacking. The requirement, that the carjackers show a readiness to do harm in the Shute-Burgeson case might arguably hamper efforts to apply the federal statute. It is certainly more complicated than someone's car being stolen and somebody dying.

Particularly foreboding was the United States Attorney Margaret Curran's silence on the matter. Her only public comments had been that her office would not comment on the prospect of the death penalty in this case.

As we talked further in the Rhode Island Attorney General's office that afternoon, Agent Chau of the Bureau of Alcohol, Tobacco and Firearms enlightened us about Ira Nasberg, who we learned had alleged that an unbelievable total of five different guns were stolen from him between 1992 and 2000. They questioned whether an almost conspiratorial relationship between Nasberg and Floyd existed. At the very least, they felt, it evinces Nasberg's careless approach to lethal weaponry and make him partially culpable in the shooting deaths of Amy and Jason.

On July 8, 1992, Nasberg had filed his very first larceny report with the Providence Police Department, claiming that a .22 Magnum Derringer belonging to him had been stolen from his residence in Providence.

On September 4, 1997, Nasberg reported to Providence Police that a stainless steel .357 caliber revolver belonging to him was missing. He stated that he had last seen it several days before under his mattress, where he usually kept it beside a .380 caliber automatic, which inconceivably hadn't been taken. Nasberg, who was working at a pawn shop on North Main Street during this period, reported that no else had been in the apartment during that time frame, but confided that he had misplaced other weapons in the past. Police found no signs of forced entry. A short time later, Nasberg did phone police to report that he had located the missing .357.

On August 24, 1999, police responded to Nasberg's residence once more to take a report for a stolen gun. This time, Nasberg told them that his Makarun .380 caliber pistol was missing, though he was unsure if it had been misplaced or lost. As usual, there were no signs of forced entry, but he did produce a bill of sale from DB Guns for the weapon in question. Nasberg described the gun as black and loaded at the time that it was lost or stolen.

Then, on February 12, 2000 police responded to Nasberg at another address to take a report of a stolen .40 caliber Smith & Wesson handgun. Nasberg told a Providence patrol officer that while he was shopping inside the store at this address, an unknown person or persons opened the door to his vehicle and removed the weapon from between the front seats, where it had been left unattended. Nasberg supplied police with the serial number of the weapon, but there were no witnesses to the theft.

Finally, two months later, on April 14, 2000, police responded to Nasberg's second floor apartment for the final time to take a report of a stolen weapon. At that time he explained to the reporting officers that he had been unable to locate his 10 MM handgun that morning and immediately called the police. When asked if he had any company the previous night, he told them that Sammie Sanchez, of an unknown street address on Union Avenue in Providence, had been at his apartment, both in Nasberg's presence and later alone, when Nasberg was not home. He presented them with a gun permit at that time, and soon afterward reported that he had once again located his misplaced weapon.

Agent Chau furnished individual copies of these reports to all the agencies present, with particular emphasis on the .40 caliber semiautomatic handgun that Nasberg reported stolen from his car in February 2000.

We were also informed that afternoon that Agent Ann Goodwin would be lending her full-time assistance to the investigation. She had been an FBI agent for sixteen years, and was currently designated to the Providence Resident Agency, Boston Division. We were all grateful to have her professionalism and expertise, and took her assignment as a positive sign that a federal trial was imminent.

At the same exact time that the multi-agency conference was taking place in Providence, Ira Nasberg was sitting down at the Johnston Police Department being interviewed by Detective Mel Steppo. Assisted by Detective Sonny DeTora, they got right to the point. Sonny brought in the gun that was used by Gregory Floyd to kill Amy Shute and Jason Burgeson. Upon viewing the weapon that once belonged to him, and pointing out a distinctive tear on the handle grip of the weapon, Nasberg began to cry. But Mel didn't want Nasberg to be distracted in any way that might slow the interview or cloud the facts.

Mel needed to hear everything about that winter morning when the .40 caliber handgun that was now on the table between them had allegedly been stolen. Slowly, Nasberg reiterated the account he had given the Providence Police the previous day.

"Floyd gave you up," Mel began when he was through. "He said he got the gun from you. If that's true, you can be implicated in the deaths of those two kids. It was your gun that was used to kill them."

Nasberg began to cry anew, this time it was more obvious they were self-pitying tears.

"Mr. Nasberg, do you have a permit to carry a firearm?"

"Yes," he responded, and produced a valid pistol permit, which was due to expire on January 27, 2001. He also produced a valid DEM Blue Card for the detective to examine.

In the course of Nasberg's tear-laden dialogue, Mel tried to determine what specific need this man might have for carrying a concealed weapon, if he not had supplied them to street criminals and falsely reported them stolen. He learned that Nasberg, who was presently employed by a cab company in Johnston, had previously worked at a store, the same one where he later reported that the .40 caliber semiautomatic had been stolen from his car with Floyd sitting in the passenger seat the night in question. Nasberg had also been an employee of the pawn shop where he and Sanchez first became acquainted. Now, besides earning a living from driving his cab, he made extra money as independent videographer, chasing crime scenes and videotaping them. Real film noir stuff, Mel thought, as the moonlighting hack hocked his grisly productions to television stations and police departments. At one time, he purportedly had posted some of the more macabre stills onto his website, including a series he had taken at the scene of a previous carjacking incident in which a man was fatally shot in the head.

Of the murder weapon, which Nasberg had reported stolen four months previous, he stated that he purchased the .40 caliber weapon brand new from a gun shop in Woonsocket, Rhode Island in 1999 for 200 dollars.

Mel then displayed photographs of the five suspects implicated in the murders. Nasberg immediately picked out Floyd. He said he knew him as Greg, but did not know his last name. According to Nasberg, he first became acquainted with him five years ago when Floyd had been working at the pizzeria.

"You've known him for five years, but you don't know his last name?"

Nasberg shook his head.

When shown a picture of Burdick, Nasberg said he recognized the heavy set youth from the downtown area, as well, indicating that Burdick was friendly with the tow trucker drivers who haunted Weybosset Street. He also described Burdick as "a pain in the ass," often loud and abrasive. Nasberg admitted that he would more readily accommodate other kids downtown who wanted to ride along with him when he went out looking for news-worthy stories to document on film. However, he said that he would often refuse Burdick's requests just because he was so annoying.

Sanchez knew Nasberg from the pawn shop, and although he was unable to identify Anderson or Day, he was sure that Floyd, Sanchez and Burdick were all well-acquainted.

"How many guns have you bought in the past five years, Mr. Nasberg?"

He thought about it a moment. "Four," he answered.

"How many guns have been stolen in the past five years?"

"Three," he responded right away. "This .40 caliber, a 10 caliber, which I suspect Sammie Sanchez stole from my house, and a 380 Makarov." For the Makarov, he was ready with a bill of sale from D-B Guns. Bob observed the sales date: March 20, 1997.

All three guns had been reported stolen to the Providence Police.

"Mr. Nasberg, did you ever sell or give any of your guns to Gregory Floyd?"

"No. Never."

"Would you be willing to submit to a polygraph test if needed?"

"Yes, I would take a poly."

Nasberg was released and asked to return to the division to sign the state-ment he had just given regarding being the owner of .40 caliber weapon that was used in the double homicide. Nasberg stated that he would return.

As a result of the multi-agency conference in Providence that afternoon, Sheldon Whitehouse, the Rhode Island Attorney General, provided a press release for the public. It stated simply that his office was continuing to evaluate information, statements and evidence gathered by Johnston and Providence Police in the carjacking-double murder case, and that they had been in contact with the US Attorney's Office and the FBI to discuss the case. "This terrible crime only reinforces my determination to continue to address armed violent criminals through every legislative, law enforcement and community means available," Whitehouse said.

It was not unusual for the Rhode Island Attorney General and the U.S. Attorney to coordinate their efforts on matters of overlapping jurisdiction. They did so frequently. In fact, they had already established a protocol to review all cases involving firearm, a policy that Whitehouse instituted shortly after he took office.

Whitehouse said, "It is a mutual objective of the U.S. Attorney's Office and this office to pursue the best avenue of law to prosecute these crimes. The most appropriate course of prosecution will be determined after careful and thoughtful review of the facts at hand." He added, "I commend the police and prosecutors, Assistant Attorney General Stephen Dambruch and Special Assistant Attorney Peter Neronha for their efforts thus far investigating this case which continued unabated through the weekend. The prosecutors have been present and on duty along side officers from the Johnston Police Department from the onset of the investigation and I appreciate the praise (Johnston) Chief Richard Tamburini has had for their efforts."

He also mentioned that an FBI agent and a federal prosecutor had been assigned as liaisons with the Department of Attorney General on this matter. There was a lot of potential in his words, but there was still no definitive answer to the question that everyone wanted to know, though none more so than the Shutes and the Burgesons.

When Erin Shute received her high school diploma, her whole family attended the ceremony at the Providence Performing Arts Center. It occurred just three days after Amy had been killed, and at a site not far from where she and Jason had been abducted. Erin's high school graduation will forever be stained by her sister's murder, but Carol refused to let the killers take everything away from her family.

Before the start of the commencement exercises, a moment of silence for Amy was called for by the principal of Coventry High School. As everyone bowed their heads, the only sound Carol heard were her own sobs and the sobs of her family. Half the town may have been inside the auditorium that night, and this setting only seemed to represent just how isolated and alone she felt in her grief. Then, when Erin's name was called, everyone stood and began clapping, a resounding standing ovation that the family did not expect. The show of emotion and support was overwhelming, and it touched them all deeply. It is something they will never forget, least of all Erin.

Chapter 20

Jason's Homecoming

Tuesday, June 13, began with further deliberations between our investigators and attorneys from the state and federal government. It was a rather solemn day, knowing what was going on in Lakeville, but there was still a lot of investigation left. No matter where these five alleged killers would be tried, we had evidence to collect and witnesses to get ready for testimony.

Nothing was determined on the best avenue of prosecution, and the Rhode Island Attorney General, Sheldon Whitehouse, was equally circumspect, informing the media that discussion between himself and the United States Attorney, Margaret Curran, would continue on a regular basis, in a deliberate and thoughtful manner, until all relevant issues have been resolved.

That afternoon, Captain aRusso and I spoke with U.S. Attorneys about the authorization of a federal search warrant to remove evidence from the car that had been used in the carjacking/murders. The gold car, driven by Sammie Sanchez, was registered to his mother, and the warrant was prepared without delay by the Assistant United States Attorney, Stephanie Brown, with Special Agent Ann Goodwin of the FBI the affiant. The warrant was signed by U.S. Magistrate Robert Lovegreen, and it was determined that all evidence obtained from this vehicle, as well as from Jason's SUV and the crime scene, would be processed by the FBI Crime Laboratory in Washington, D.C.

Later still, Detectives Steppo and Arcuri met with the Chief of Investigations of the Rhode Island Department of the Attorney General, to inquire about the video surveillance camera outside their building and any tapes that may exist with images recorded during the early morning hours of June 9. Based on the confessions of the suspects, their movements that night were traced to that area of South Main Street. He advised the detectives that he would gather the tapes himself and get back to them when they were secured.

The criminal timeline took the detectives next to the Providence/Washington Building across the street from the Attorney General's Office. There, they intended to question the security personnel who may have witnessed a near-robbery by the five suspects of an ATM customer. The machine was outside that building, which three people were using just before 1:30 AM on June 9. The receptionist provided them with the name of the individual who had been on-duty at that hour. The detectives learned that the man working the midnight to 8 AM shift handled those services for them.

The detectives then turned their attention to the towing agency which had been contracted to work the Arcade area of the city of Providence on June 9th. A representative advised them that the towing company had been called to service a vehicle in that section of the city the morning in question. With this information, Steppo and Arcuri responded to the towing company and met with the manager, who disclosed the name of the tow operator who had responded to the call. They were able to question him at that time, and he told them that a call came in at 1:40 AM to tow a vehicle from the intersection of Weybosset and Orange Street to a residence in Warwick. When asked if he had observed a white van in the area on that morning, the operator responded that he could not recall seeing a vehicle fitting that description. He was able to provide the detectives with the corresponding paperwork for the 1:40 AM tow request. The individual whose car had been towed and the address of the Warwick residence were included, and this information could be followed up on at a later date if necessary.

Finally, the two detectives responded to the gas station on Elmwood Avenue in Providence to ascertain the identity of the clerk who had taken money from the murder suspects to buy gas for both the SUV and the car at around 3 AM that same morning. The manager was able to provide them with the clerk's name and his phone number.

Upon returning to headquarters, all the information that Steppo and Arcuri collected was given to Detective Mancini, who would see to it that the clerk and the other potential witnesses were contacted and requested to respond for follow-up interviews.

That evening, Jason's wake was held at the Lakeville funeral home. To the surprise of the Burgesons, hundreds of people showed up to offer their prayers and condolences to the grateful family. They knew Jason had many friends, but the family had no idea just how many until they all came together in the same place at the same time. The support of strangers was just as heart-warming to the Burgesons. The display of love and compassion all around helped them make it through the services that night. Even men came in and sobbed. One man had written a letter, which he gave to Nadine Burgeson without saying a word. He could not speak. All he could do was cry. After the man left, the family read what he wrote and learned that he had been a co-worker with Jason. He expressed how deeply Jason's death affected him, and then went on to relate several touching stories about Jason that the family never knew. One year, during the middle of the Christmas season, when the shipping industry always had more packages to deliver than time would allow, Jason stopped to help a little old lady bring her groceries into her house. Nobody could get even get mad at him for that. Jason was just that kind of young man, a caring, thoughtful person who brightened people's lives wherever he went.

The president of a local staffing service which had employed Jason most recently, wrote the Burgesons to express her sorrow and to let them know what a nice and well-mannered son they had raised. "He seems like the type of child that a mother would be proud of," she wrote. She admitted that, though she had planned to attend Jason's wake, she simply could not do so. "I am overwhelmed with hurt and sadness as if Jason was my own family member. I will miss Jason very much and I will always remember him as the happy and wonderful human being that he was."

Another friend told the family how every time Jason drove to Boston to visit some of their buddies at Newbury College he would stop at this one particular gas station where an elderly man worked the night shift. He would pull in even if he didn't need gas just to say hello or spend some time talking with the lonely old man. Those kinds of stories were told about Jason all night, and it helped the family get through their toughest day yet.

But there was at least one bad element that was doing everything it could to dilute the remedial benefits that so many people were providing in their words and letters. While some press coverage was expected, none of the Burgeson's thought that it would denigrate into a complete media circus to the point of being intrusive and disrespectful. It seemed as though every newspaper and television news show wanted to capture images of the grieving family. One journalist even managed to finagle his way into the funeral home. Kellie, who was standing in the receiving line as mourners streamed in, hugging and crying and accepting their condolences, suddenly noticed the man out of the corner of her eye. She saw him raise a camera and could not believe her eyes. When she saw the flash go off her heart dropped and she immediately excused herself. She was livid. She made a bee line for the photographer and confronted him.

"What do you think you're doing?" Kellie said in a voice as soft and restrained as she could manage. "Get out of here!"

"Oh, I was told that I could be here," the man said. "Don't worry I won't take any pictures of your brother in the casket."

"I don't care who told you could be in here," Kellie screamed, not caring who heard. "Get out."

The man gave her a disapproving look and left reluctantly. It wasn't enough to have to go through the emotions of such an event, but also to be subjected to such an invasion of privacy was inexcusable.

The outpouring of affection began again the morning of Jason's funeral. Many people who did not (or could not) attend the wake the previous evening arrived at Dahlborg-MacNevin Funeral Home early the next day. Leo Hancock was one of those people. And his experience, perhaps more than any other, describes the scene for many. There were plenty of people there that he knew, and many more he did not. There were some classmates from grade school who hadn't seen Jason in many years, other people from around Lakeville who hadn't seen him since he left for college in Minnesota. It was a homecoming of sorts for Jason Burgeson, and everyone wanted to see him one more time.

Hancock attended Apponequet Regional High School, and because of the alphabet, Jason Burgeson sat in front of him for those four years, as well as the four previous years of middle school. Hancock knew Jason as a fun loving kid who relished hanging out with friends, playing hockey, writing, acting and a slew of other activities. He and Jason had acted together in several high school plays.

Leo was battling a feeling of nausea as he made his way across the funeral home parking lot when he spotted a number of people who had been some of his closest friends in high school. Still, there was not much to say now as Hancock looked at them and they looked back at him in silence.

Then his friend Gary said to him, "We always thought you'd be the first to go."

It was an odd thing to say to anyone at any time, but this was just such an obvious attempt to lighten the mood, they all just laughed at first. It was supposed to take the focus off Jason, but it just made them think of him more. Jason was so full of life, he was the last one any of them would have thought would be here. After that, they all just started crying, and it was the first time that Hancock recalled crying in many years. He hugged his old friends and dried his eyes before heading toward the entrance of the funeral home. He dreaded what was next. He didn't know how he would react to the pain of seeing Jason in a casket, and he didn't know what to say to the family.

He knew one thing – he would not be going to the cemetery. That would be too much for him to take.

An employee of the funeral home opened the door and held it for him, offering him such a well-practiced somber look it was almost permanently etched onto his face. Now there was nowhere to go. So many people were packed inside that he couldn't see anything but the shoulders and heads of the mourners in front of him. As the crowd slowly shuffled forward, he could make out two homemade collages, large poster boards filled with pictures of Jason. They were displayed just outside the funeral chapel, where he could now see an open casket facing into the large room.

As he looked around, he saw many faces that he hadn't seen in years, their eyes either red or running with fresh tears. It was a surreal sight. It felt like a nightmare. Only everyone there was experiencing the same nightmare. Hancock knew he should go up and pay his final respects to his friend, but he was worried he might not make walking up to the casket without fainting or vomiting. He was perspiring and needed to rest a moment. Every chair was filled. There was nowhere to sit so he stood back and tried to steady himself as he looked around, shaking his head. He could not believe that Jason was dead. All he could think of was how his friend had died. Of course, it was all over the news. As he turned toward the collages to look at the images of Jason captured when he was alive, he recognized Natasha Spears, Cathy Antonio and Jennifer Laurence standing nearby.

Leo tried to smile as he nodded a half-hearted hello to the girls. Then he turned hurriedly back to the collages. There were hundreds of photographs of Jason, from baby pictures on up to more recent ones taken of him with Amy. He was seen clowning around, wearing oversized glasses, eating ice cream, riding his first bicycle, holding up a string of fish he'd caught with his dad, riding his four-wheeler, posing in a cap and gown, dressed as a nun for Halloween. Jason's own prophetic words were emblazoned through the juxtaposed images on one of the poster boards: "IF I HAD TO GIVE YOU ONE PIECE OF ADVICE, IT WOULD BE TO LOOK INTO THE FUTURE, FOR THE PAST HURTS TOO MUCH." This personal epithet came from a birthday card Jason had written to Cathy a few years before. The three young women who Hancock had just acknowledged created this pictorial tribute together. The other one had been put together by the Burgesons.

The reverend and pastor for South Christian Church of All Nations in East Freetown, Massachusetts, encouraged people to express their sorrow or share their thoughts with the rest of the congregation.

Cathy, Jennifer and Natasha were good friends and they knew Jason perhaps better than anyone. A couple of days before, they had gotten together with some of Jason's other friends, including Arnold Banker and Stephen

Cone, and decided that each of them would say something at the service. This came about after Cathy related a conversation she had with Jason, not very long ago, in which he had asked her to speak at his funeral someday. Never knowing that someday would come so soon, Cathy said she would. Now, using both Jason's words and their own, they paid a personal tribute to their friend.

"I know things are weird, and somewhat crazy, but hang in there" Cathy read from an old Valentine's Day card Jason had given to her. "Do not ever think that I don't need or want you...You are my life partner, even if it doesn't mean we are destined to be together. During the next four or five years, I don't want to lose you in the shuffle, the shuffle which is going to happen. I love you, don't forget that. You always meant the world to me, so when you think I'm not there, not listening, not with you, I am.

Natasha recited a poem she composed after Jason's death. "...We cannot see you/We cannot touch you/But we know you are there."

Jennifer also read a Valentine that Jason had given her and she had saved. He always had a way with words, and he frequently expressed his feelings in cards, letters and poems that he'd written to all of his friends, male or female.

Their depiction of Jason as good-natured, trustworthy and generous rang true to everyone in attendance who knew him. And although he could be a clown at times, he was also sentimental and affectionate.

Natasha, who was a year behind Jason and her friends in high school, recalled the prom in which she and Jason had attended together, when he showed up in a baby blue sports car that he borrowed from his father. He provided her a single rose. "Red," he told her, "because I love you."

Jason's thoughtfulness was exemplified in a story she related about the time he unexpectedly stopped by to see her at work. After talking with him earlier on the phone, she revealed that she was bored. When Jason showed up later, he handed her a bottle of chocolate milk, something which he knew always put her in a good mood. Cathy contributed a story of her own, recalling how one Christmas, when she and Jason were shopping at the mall, she suggested getting a picture taken together with Santa Claus. Jason rebuffed the idea, refusing to wait in line. When Christmas arrived, however, inside her present from Jason he had placed a photograph of himself with Santa Claus.

She was touched, but could not feign surprise.

They spoke of his love for prose and verse, which he had occasion to write himself. In contradiction to this romantic bent, he had a dry, offbeat sense of humor that was reflected in the *Monty Python* lines he often quoted. The principal of Apponequet High School once referred to Jason as the guy who would take Jay Leno's place. He said of Jason, "You recognized that if he applied himself, he would have been an astounding kid."

Arnold Banker and Stephen Cone were stuck in line and could not get into the building to speak. They arrived at the funeral home late that morning and there was no getting through that crowd. Earlier, reporters were kindly asked to leave to make room for friends and family, but that yielded only five seats.

"I came from Praise-The-Lord Church," said the reverend, who had baptized Jason as a born-again Christian. "When I baptized Jason in water, he said to me, 'Brother John, do you think you can hold onto me?' And I said, 'I can't, but the Lord can.'"

He encouraged Jason's only sister, Kellie, to stand up and say a few words.

"A few days ago," she began, "I was sitting in Jason's room and crying. When I looked up, this was taped to the wall. It's called, *Happiness*."

She read the adage out loud: "We convince ourselves that life will get better after we get married, after we have children, after our children become teenagers. The truth is, there is no better time to be happy than right now. Happiness is a journey, not a destination."

The reverend read scripture and told stories revealing Jason as a typical, fun loving young man.

"I remember that day," he began, "when Brother Jason took me four-wheeling in the back yard. I hung on for dear life. I told him, 'Be careful. I'm not an angel.' The next thing I knew I was airborne."

After the service, the immediate family prepared to say their final good-byes to Jason before he was placed in a hearse and transported to the cemetery for burial. At that time, everyone else was asked to leave the room. They had made it through much of the service, but the worst was yet to come.

One by one, family members walked up to the casket and touched Jason, kissed him and said they loved him. Kellie did not want to leave him, and was taking extra time to be alone with her only sibling. She was looking at him and crying, but even through blurry eyes she saw something that drew her attention and chilled her blood. When she saw it moving she straightened up immediately. Blinking rapidly, she looked more closely at Jason and that's when she realized what it was. She didn't want to see it, but it was too late. She actually hoped that she was hallucinating, but she was not. There were maggots crawling out of his ears.

Her brother had been lying on that golf course for so long, Kellie thought, that flies had been crawling all over his bloody body, laying their disgusting eggs inside him. It was too much for her, and the next thing she heard was the sound of her own voice screaming loudly. Everyone looked up and rushed over to comfort her, but to no avail. Even after the funeral director was called over by her aunt, who had realized what her niece was screaming about, she could not be consoled. It is an image that she will never forget, and it replays in her mind when she puts her head down to sleep even today, and there is nothing she can do about it.

Jason's funeral procession moved slowly toward Precinct Cemetery, just down the road. As his casket was placed at the gravesite, a bouquet with a cross of red and yellow roses and azaleas was draped across the lid.

"The Old Rugged Cross," a country-sounding church song, played on the reverend's tape deck while each family member placed a single yellow rose on Jason's casket. That officially concluded the funeral services. Five days after Jason and Amy were found shot to death, he was first to be buried. The majority of the mourners departed slowly, while the Burgesons and numerous friends from Jason's high school remained to see the coffin as it was lowered into ground. They cried and bade Jason tearful good-byes. Cathy passed out copies she made of the picture of Jason with Santa.

After the funeral, the Burgesons continued to lobby for people to beseech prosecutors to try all five murder suspects under the federal carjacking statute. The family provided two stacks of separate, but nearly identical form letters, one addressed to Rhode Island Attorney General Whitehouse, and the other to United States Attorney General, Janet Reno. People were encouraged to sign them both in petition of the death penalty as specified in Title 18 United

States Code Section 2119. To the detriment of our investigation, the letters also included many details of the incident which had not been released or confirmed.

The cover letters to Whitehouse and Reno concluded by stating:

I am writing to you to urge you to accept this case under federal jurisdiction that states carjacking that leads to harm or murder and kidnapping are punishable under federal jurisdiction. I believe that the death penalty should be pursued as a punishment. Please accept all five suspects' cases to be tried under federal jurisdiction. Nothing will bring the two young adults back, they were taken from us before their lives truly began; however, something productive must come from this tragedy. We need to deter the criminals of this world. Obviously, imprisonment is not enough punishment for these kind of people because four of the five men alleged in the incident were out on parole. I am outraged at this horrible tragedy. Please help this case become one that brings about changes in our legal system.

To the public, whose signatures would endorse this sentiment, they were called to action with this letter:

IF YOU WOULD LIKE TO HELP, PLEASE TAKE ONE
Jason had the biggest heart in the world. He was always happy, never in a bad mood, never had a grudge. He was the comedian of our family. The void in our lives will never be filled. We do not want Jason to die in vain. The law states that carjacking that leads to murder and kidnapping are crimes punishable under federal law. We did not even have this law until several years ago when two tourists who were vacationing in Florida were carjacked and murdered for no reason; because of this tragedy, the law was changed and kidnapping and carjacking that leads to harm or death became a federal crime. This crime could be punishable with the death penalty. Now hopefully something productive can come from this tragedy. We do not wish to be vindictive. The threat of prison obviously is not enough to deter these people from creating such horrific crimes. Four of the five men involved in my brother's murder were out on parole. Something has to be done to stop all these senseless shootings.

An image of Jason's smiling face in the center of the page divided the text.

Within the next few weeks a decision will be made in reference to whether or not this case will be tried under federal law. So many people have asked what they can do to help. Unfortunately, nothing will bring my brother back. He died a brutal, violent death. There are so many things that are out of control. We have many obstacles to overcome. But there is something that we can all do. Our first obstacle is to make sure this case is prosecuted under federal jurisdiction. We can let the Attorney General's Office know that we support this. We ask you to please take this information and send it to the Rhode Island Attorney General, Sheldon Whitehouse, and the U.S. Attorney General, Janet Reno to ask that my brother's case be tried under federal law. You can write your own letter or just sign your name to the one provided and send it. Please help, it will take thirty seconds to sign this and a few cents to mail it. Some people think that, "Well, one person signing a letter really will not make a difference." BUT IT DOES. One plus one is two, and two plus two is four. They add up quickly.

Thank you for all your tremendous support. The Burgeson family.

PLEASE SIGN YOUR NAME AND ADDRESS BEFORE MAILING

The sister of the murdered young man estimated that 4,000 letters were signed by individuals and submitted to the addressees.

Family and friends of Amy Shute also produced a similar letter to rally public support for federal prosecution:

IF YOU WOULD LIKE TO HELP PLEASE SIGN THE ATTACHED

On June 9, 2000 our beautiful daughter, Amy Shute, and her friend Jason Burgeson, went out dancing with a group of friends at a nightclub in Providence. The two were getting into Jason's car when five thugs carjacked them at gunpoint, kidnapped, robbed and brutally murdered them. If you would like to see this case prosecuted on the federal level please sign your name and address to the attached sheets. This petition will be sent to Janet Reno, the U.S. Attorney General and Sheldon Whitehouse, the Attorney General for the state of Rhode Island.

In the upcoming weeks/months, a decision will be made as to whether this case should be prosecuted on a federal or a state level. Federal law states that a carjacking that results in murder is a federal crime that can carry the death penalty.

We have had such a generous outpouring of love and support, and people asking what they can do to help. By signing this petition you will be helping us have our voices heard.

Thank you all for your tremendous love and support.

The Family and Friends of Amy Shute.

A beautiful picture of Amy's smiling face, taken for her high school year-book, took up the bottom half of the page, which only served to underscore the innocent and youthful life that was taken.

The Rhode Island Attorney General's Office confirmed that they had received innumerable calls and letters from people angered by the double murders and urging aggressive prosecution against those responsible. They responded to all the letter-writers, reassuring them that they were doing everything they could on their end to see that the guilty in this case were punished to the full extent of the law. Whitehouse included an expression of his personal concerns as a father, that he was greatly appalled by the double homicide.

"We will give them (the families) a full explanation of the options, and their views will carry substantial weight with me."

The phone calls were the most arduous to respond to, as the office dealt with each one individually, taking the time to explain the judicial process or just listening to people vent. A spokesperson for Whitehouse told the press that they had received more correspondence on this case than any other.

Chapter 21

Saying Good-Bye to Amy

As Jason was being interred in Lakeville, investigators in Johnston and in Providence were hard at work taking statements. Eyewitnesses are important, however, witness testimony is often flawed, with faulty recollections and biases that often prove to be no more credible than circumstantial evidence. And since memories only get worse with time, it was important to follow up on every lead, get everything in writing and get it signed.

Florence Sander came in and spoke with Detective Ross about her boyfriend, Raymond Anderson, the father of her four-week old child.

Detectives Arcuri and Tirocchi went to the home of the gas station attendant. When it was confirmed that he had been on duty at the gas station the morning of June 9, he was asked to respond to Johnston headquarters to give a formal statement, and he consented. The detectives drove him to the department, where he described Burdick for them, and then picked him out of photo lineup. Tirocchi was quite surprised that the witness was able to identify Burdick so confidently, especially in consideration of the volume of customers he regularly sees and the passage of nearly a week. He recalled in detail how Burdick paid for the gas with a single bill and a fistful of coins.

This angered the attendant, who had to add up each quarter, dime and nickel at a time when the station had suddenly gotten busy.

They had the attendant's statement typed and he signed it. Then he was driven back to his residence. Afterward, detectives stopped by the gas station directly across the street from the station at which he worked. The manager related that the station closes at 10:00 PM every night and that they had no surveillance cameras outside the building. The only ones in operation were for interior use.

Meanwhile, Detective Nardolillo and Agent Goodwin responded to the pizzeria in Providence where Floyd worked and spoke with the owner. He answered questions concerning Floyd's employment status at the pizzeria. He stated that neither Floyd nor Burdick actually worked there presently. However, when supplies were delivered, the owner told them that the young man would help unload the truck in exchange for meals.

A news conference was held at a learning center that afternoon in the Mount Hope section of Providence. A new community policing program was unveiled by Attorney General Whitehouse. He announced that he supported the death penalty in the Burgeson/Shute carjacking-murder case. He stated that he "would be happy to see the person who shot Amy and Jason face the death penalty." In the same breath, however, he warned that it could be many months before he and federal prosecutors determined whether they can charge Floyd, or the other conspirators, under the federal statute, which would invoke the death penalty.

"I am not going to recommend the case to federal authorities until both I and they are sure that they will take the case," Whitehouse said. "Until the time comes to pass the baton to the federal agency, we will go ahead full speed on this case as if it were our own."

Whitehouse took the opportunity to reiterate an earlier call he made for an overhaul of the state's systems of probation and parole by improving on the 314-to-one probationer to counselor ratio. Because four of the five defendants were on probation for other crimes at the time of the murders, it was the right thing to say at the time, regardless of whether or not it was possible to effectuate. He also reminded Rhode Island voters that the FBI and the Bureau of Alcohol, Tobacco and Firearms had all assigned agents to the case. The Providence police chief, who attended the news conference, offered his department's full cooperation in bringing the case to its proper conclusion.

In a similar discourse, the U.S. Attorney Margaret Curran said that her office was working with Whitehouse to determine the "appropriate avenue of prosecution." She added, "On the law-enforcement side, we have to be careful of the due-process rights of any defendant, whatever charges are brought."

The victims' families felt angry at what they perceived as political pussy-footing. They felt the murderers of their loved ones were being treated with far more humanity and dignity than they deserved, and certainly more so than they showed Amy and Jason the night they abducted and shot them to death.

Later, I responded to the United States Attorney's office with Captain aRusso and Detective Nardolillo to meet with Ira Nasberg and his attorney. We were joined by Special Agent Goodwin and Assistant Attorneys General Dambruch and Neronha of the State of Rhode Island as well as two General Assistant Attorneys of the United States office. Wing Chau of the Drug Enforcement Agecy was also present.

Nasberg was initially asked to describe the nature of his relationships with Gregory Floyd and Sammie Sanchez. He told us that he became familiar with them down city, and over time permitted them to ride around with him when he was working for News Channel 10, filming crimes scenes around Providence. Nasberg stated that he carried a firearm, because he had a permit to do so and that both Floyd and Sanchez knew he owned guns. Nasberg also informed us that on two of the occasions when his guns were stolen he had been in the company of either Floyd or Sanchez.

After the interview, Captain aRusso, Detective Nardolillo and I, along with Agent Chau, went to Nasberg's residence. He had consented to a search of his home and accompanied us with his lawyer.

Among the items seized were several firearms and numerous rounds of ammunition. These included a .357 Magnum with two inch Interarms, an IAI Automag III thirty carbine, one clip loaded with eight rounds (.380 ball ammunition), an Uncle Mike's sidekick holster, a clip loaded with ten rounds

(.40 caliber hollow point ammunition), one clip loaded with eight rounds (thirty carbine ball ammunition), one box, half full (twenty-one rounds, .40 caliber hollow point ammunition), one box, half full (twenty-two rounds, .357 Magnum hollow point ammunition), one box, full (forty rounds, .30 carbine ball ammunition). The small arsenal was photographed, tagged and placed in our evidence room by BCI detectives Warren and DeTora.

Then, Warren and DeTora responded to the Adult Correctional Institution in Cranston to process Samuel Sanchez and to photograph and confiscate the suspect's clothing. When they returned to headquarters with this evidence, they were met by two agents from the Boston FBI field office. All evidence collected and secured by the BCI detectives was turned over to Special Agents at that time. Crime scene and autopsy photos were provided by Captain aRusso. Also taken into possession by the federal officers were Sanchez's car and Jason's van. The vehicles were loaded onto separate flat bed trucks and transported to an FBI facility located in Wilmington, Massachusetts.

By the end of the day on Wednesday, June 14, the FBI had officially taken over the case. As part of the ongoing effort to prosecute the suspects on federal charges, this was the necessary and expected step. Johnston Police would be assisting, and I was still representing the department in that capacity. In the next few days, all further evidence secured by the Johnston BCI detectives, including prints and clothing taken from the other suspects, were collected and turned over to the FBI as well.

Subsequent searches of the SUV and the car were completed by federal agents. From the car alone, forty-three pieces of physical evidence and thirteen latent fingerprints were seized. The recovered items and prints were taken into custody by a Special Agent who passed everything in his possession to another Special Agent, Brian Womble. A total of eleven boxes, four bags and an envelope were transported by Womble to North Central Airport in North Smithfield, Rhode Island, where it was all loaded onto an FBI aircraft. The plane and its contents would then be flown to Manassas, Virginia, where the evidence would be transferred to receiving agents on the ground.

In all, over 200 items of physical evidence would be examined at the FBI Laboratory in Washington, D.C. Significant findings from the examination and analysis of tool mark, fingerprinting, DNA, trace and tire evidence would be recorded.

Tool mark examiners found that bullet fragments recovered from the victims during autopsy matched not only the murder weapon, but the spent casings found at the scene as well as the live rounds found both at the scene and in the ammunition clip recovered from Taylor Street.

DNA analysis of various items was conducted and provided solid evidence against the suspects, as well. Comparison of organic matter recovered from the muzzle of the murder weapon to the DNA provided in a post-mortem blood sample obtained from Amy Shute revealed that she was a major contributor of the DNA on the murder weapon, to a reasonable degree of scientific certainty. Also, blood found on Floyd's right shoe matched the DNA profile of a post-mortem sample obtained from Jason Burgeson. Comparison of DNA on the latex glove found at the homicide scene to the DNA provided later, in a post-arrest saliva swabbing obtained from Burdick, revealed that the white suspect was a major contributor of DNA on the glove, to a reasonable degree of scientific certainty.

Fingerprinting analysis conducted at the FBI Laboratory yielded further proof that the accused had been participants in the crimes for which they were charged. Burdick's prints were recovered from the right front door of the SUV, as well as the right rear door window and also the broken ceramic "Tasmanian Devil" coffee mug found in the vehicle. Anderson's prints were lifted from the passenger-side roof of Sanchez's car. And both Sanchez's and Day's fingerprints were recovered from numerous items found in the car.

Trace evidence that had been collected was also examined by the FBI Lab. This included vacuum sweepings of Sanchez's car, which yielded, among other things, head hairs that exhibited the same microscopic characteristics as hair samples obtained later from Burdick and consistent with those originating from him. Sweepings from the van yielded head hairs that exhibited similarities and slight differences to the samples of head hair subsequently obtained from Anderson. A pubic hair that was found in the SUV also exhibited similarities and slight differences to Anderson's pubic hair. Fibers recovered from Floyd's clothing were found to be microscopically similar to fabric found in the SUV.

Furthermore, the impression taken of the tire track left at the homicide scene was analyzed and found to correspond with the tread-design of the tires on the van. Due to limited detail in both the track and the impression, a more positive association could not be made. Taken together, however, the forensic evidence linking the suspects to the crimes was ponderous. Physical traces of all five suspects were found all over both vehicles.

That evening from 4 – 8 PM, wake services were held for Amy Shute at the Potvin Funeral Home in West Warwick. The service was rather quiet and subdued compared to the one held the previous day. Though it was an equally crowded and sad affair, people hardly spoke at all, and the only audible sounds were sniffles and sobs of mourners. Three collages were on display in the front hall by the entrance, a retrospective of Amy's life in still photography. Erin, Elizabeth, Jeff and Carol's sister put together a picture tribute, while Amy's friends made two of their own.

Carol and her family moved around in slow motion as if in a dream. It didn't seem real. It was just face after face floating by, some of them Carol knew, most she did not. She was surprised, however, when she saw a woman who had gone to grade school with her. It had been almost twenty-five years since she had seen her old classmate from St. James School, but Carol recognized her instantly. Much later, when looking over the book, she would become shocked by all the people who had signed it, having absolutely no recollection of many of them ever being there.

There were lots of young people, wearing black, but carrying bright flowers, cards and stuffed animals. They hugged, shed tears and waited in long periods to get in.

Amy's best friend growing up, Sienna Iannelli, arrived thirty minutes early, expecting to be one of the first visitors. However, there was already a massive line wrapped around the building and later was continuously two blocks long. Also in that line was Rhode Island Attorney General Whitehouse and Johnston Police Chief Richard Tamburini. They were thinking along the same lines as Sienna, but it would be an hour and half before any of them would get inside.

While my heart was with the family, I did not think it was appropriate to attend myself. In fact, besides Chief Tamburini, no other Johnston police officers attended, at least not as mourners. There was some undercover surveillance that was being conducted in case someone who "did not belong" or who seemed out of place showed up; someone who may have been involved in the crime in some way, whether they played a primary or secondary role. Of the hundreds of people who came in and out of the front door of the funeral home, one officer noted, there was not a dry eye among them.

As Sienna waited, she looked around, seeing some of the very streets where she and Amy used to ride their bicycles, and memories filled her mind.

Sienna had gone to school with Amy from kindergarten through eighth grade. They went on to separate high schools, and as a matter of consequence they saw less and less of each other, but they always kept in touch and remained close. They also lived around the corner from one another, and Carol Shute practically was her surrogate mother. Sienna even called Amy's grandmother, Nana.

Though Amy's sister, Erin, had related to her that the casket would be open, Sienna was surprised and apprehensive. She was not looking forward to seeing Amy that way. Tears fell from her eyes as she approached her friend. She looked so beautiful, Sienna thought. Amy was wearing a sleeveless sun dress with buttons up the front. The earth tones highlighted her dark brown hair and hazel eyes. Erin, Elizabeth and Jeff chose the outfit for that very reason.

Sienna practically collapsed onto the cushioned kneeler in front of Amy's casket, but all she could do was cry. On top of all this, it was her birthday. She turned twenty-one that same day. Some of Sienna's friends wanted to take her out afterward, but she was not in the mood to celebrate. She was thinking about her friend, Amy, who she will always remember as someone everyone enjoyed being around. She was just so much fun, charismatic and full of life.

Kate Langlais, another grade school friend of Amy, talked with Sienna later that night about the special memories she had of Amy and the many times Amy made her laugh. They both smiled recalling the Halloween that Amy dressed up as Roseanne Barr. Smiling and singing and making other people laugh and feel happy, that's how Kate would remember Amy.

After 9:00 PM, Carol was asked by members of the staff if she would like to have the doors to the funeral home closed and locked. There was still a long line of people waiting to get inside. The family briefly discussed the issue. They were all physically exhausted and emotionally drained, but agreed that everyone deserved to pay their respects. Some people had been waiting two to three hours, so the funeral home kept their doors open until the last mourner filed through. It was close to midnight by the time the family returned home.

Amy Shute's funeral took place the following morning, Thursday, June 15, at St. James Church in West Warwick. It was another night without sleep for the Shutes. The dream-like quality of the previous day returned when they arrived at the funeral home prior to the church service.

Dozens of red roses, which Jeff had bought, sat in five gallon buckets just outside the door to Amy's room. All of Amy's friends took one. The rose was beautiful and fleeting, and it symbolized Amy's life.

While the night before, mourners paid their respects and left over the course of several hours, that day everyone was gathered together at the same time, making movement all but impossible inside the building. Afterward, whether they were in the funeral procession or not, it seemed everyone went on to the church, where even more people were waiting, along with a large media contingency. Television cameramen and newspaper photographers began jockeying for position earlier that morning.

By the time the service was ready to begin at 10 AM, there were close to 600 mourners crowded inside the Catholic church, which Amy had attended since she was a small child. A group of neighbors and other spectators watched the spectacle with sadness and empathy from across the street.

The family stood in the foyer at the entrance of the church as the priest blessed Amy's closed coffin. Crying and shaking uncontrollably, Carol embraced Erin and Elizabeth. As they proceeded to the front of the church at the beginning of the mass, Carol noticed only two people among all those who were packed into the pews on both sides of the aisle. They were two men she worked with, and as soon as her eyes fixed on them she did not see anyone else. They were both standing there watching this grim procession of a mother walking behind her daughter's casket. Tears streamed down their faces. The image is still fresh in her memory, clear as day, and just thinking about it gives her chills.

Often, funerals are a celebration of life, a tribute to the departed who has endured a full and fruitful existence in reaching a ripe old age. But that was not the case with these two young people. Jason and Amy did not "pass." They were taken and ripped cruelly and horrifically from the world, in the springtime of their lives.

Amy was not eulogized in the traditional fashion. "No one could endure one," said the reverend, who baptized Amy and officiated her first communion. He said Amy's was one of the largest and saddest funerals he had ever conducted. The reverend was the only speaker. He could only offer a message of hope and salvation to the grief-stricken family.

One of the most emotional reactions occurred toward the end of the church service, when the popular Christian song, composed by Michael Joncas, *On Eagle's Wings*, played.

Hearing the sad, beautiful words Carol lost control of her own close to the surface emotions. The next thing she heard was the sound of her own heart-wrenching sobs and screams. Erin and Elizabeth joined their mother, and then, like a wave, the grief swept through the entire church.

The Shute family supported one another as they left the church with Amy's casket and walked out together into the midday sun. The pallbearers were all men from Carol's workplace. News photographers captured these images as soon as the family emerged from the church. Soon, a long funeral procession snaked its way down Main Street, headed toward St. Mary's Cemetery, also in West Warwick. Even as the hearse arrived at its final destination, people still were leaving the church.

At the gravesite, the reverend addressed the congregation. He said that Amy had attended the parish's elementary school as a girl, and related that on Monday, the school's president, made an announcement over the loud speaker that morning and asked the faculty and student body to pray for Amy and her family.

"Amy sat where you sit and dreamt the dreams that you dream," he told the students. "How does one ever understand what happened to Amy and Jason? All of us are diminished by such an act of random and senseless violence. Let us pray for Amy's parents, her family and friends and for all those who feel her loss and with intensity beyond our understanding."

He also said, "The Lord has taken a peaceful and merciful Amy."

Referencing her major in psychology at the University of Rhode Island and her five years of employment at Kent County Hospital, he added. "She studied hard. She had goals in life. She was willing to help others."

When the brief graveside service was concluded, Carol instinctively kissed the lid of Amy's coffin. While what seemed like an endless stream of tears cascaded down her cheeks, she removed a flower from the casket spray. Everyone who passed the casket likewise took a flower from the spray. Those who were carrying roses from the funeral home dropped them into the empty grave as they approached.

Afterward, Carol, grief struck, rushed from the cemetery and sat in the family limousine with her family, waiting for a lane to clear so the vehicle could pull out. Then, out of the corner of her eye she noticed a newspaper reporter stopping people as they were dispersing from Amy's gravesite and asking them questions. He was carrying a notepad and a pen.

"Let me out!" Carol said at once. But her family would not permit her to leave.

"Let me out," she repeated, more calmly. "I just need to get some air. And stretch my legs."

Finally, they opened the door and Carol jumped from the car. All at once, she started running back in the direction of Amy's grave. "Get out. GET OUT!" she said. "YOU DON'T BELONG HERE!"

Her family could only watch as she ran off yelling and screaming. None of them could see the reporter. Nearby, Jim's brother realized what was going on and intervened. He grabbed Carol by the waist and tried to restrain her. She struggled in his arms and continued to shout at the stunned reporter. Once he got Carol under control, Jim appeared and escorted her back to the family car. Then, Jim's brother confronted the reporter, and asked him to leave.

In those first few days after Amy's death, Carol was hardly aware of how decisions were being made and how details such as funeral arrangements and expenses were being taken care of. She was in no condition, emotionally, mentally or physically to take on these burdens. Her sister and Jim handled many of these particulars while she felt like she was being pushed out to sea along a dark current, which became blacker the further out it took her.

Everyone had been so helpful and kind, even if Carol was not fully aware of what was happening at that time. She was told when she had to be somewhere and what time she had to be ready. Friends and family members continued their support long afterward, helping with those little necessities in life that suddenly lost all importance, such as shopping, laundry and cleaning. The house was always filled with flowers and people. It was just one thoughtful and considerate gesture after another. Her company offered to pay for Amy's services, and even the state stepped forward to assist with the burial expenses. Everyone was writing checks. Carol did not have life insurance on her children. She never expected to need that kind of coverage. She learned much later that a $5,000 payment from Rhode Island Victims' Advocacy & Support Center (RIVASC) had been granted to both families to help offset the cost of the funeral. Besides money, RIVASC provides other forms of aid and services to all crime victims and their survivors without discrimination. She was instructed where to sign or initial and she made her mark on the documents, not knowing exactly what she was authorizing, but trusting those close to her. The state general treasurer's office said that the Burgesons were eligible even though they lived in another state because the murder occurred in Rhode Island.

Though her grief was ongoing, picking out Amy's headstone was something that Carol felt she had to do. She went with Erin, Elizabeth, Jim, Jeff and Amy's father. It was a difficult decision on more than one level, and it was made worse because there were so many choices and options. They decided on a pink-tinted marble fairly quickly, but what required a surprising amount of consideration had to do with the name that was going to be carved into the stone.

Amy Lyn Shute was her given birth name, but Amy never liked the fact that both her first and middle names had only three letters, so whenever she wrote or signed her full name, she would spell her middle name, Lynn. After some debate, Amy got her name spelled the way she wanted it, and her marker reads, AMY LYNN SHUTE - Beloved daughter and sister. "Step forth and dance like nobody's watching."

While everyone did what they could to support the victims' families, no amount of money or sympathy was going to make up for the loss they suffered. Seeing justice served to the five men who murdered Amy and Jason was the only thing they really wanted. The only thing any of us wanted.

fear
factor

In the days immediately following the burials of Jason and Amy, the media hype slowed down considerably, though it never went away. When some news pertaining to the defendants arose, it would start building up all over again. The families tried not to let the hype affect them. But for the Shutes or the Burgesons, things could never go back the way they were. The horrible reality that Amy and Jason were really gone was inescapable. And there were reminders everywhere.

In Lakeville, there was a golf course that the Burgesons had to pass to get in and out of town. Jason used to work there during the summer. When Mr. Burgeson went back to work, he had to drive by it twice a day on his commute. Kellie saw the golf course when she would visit her parents, but this was often because but she was not ready to return to her job, and she would not be for some time. The slightest elevation of stress would produce an emotional breakdown or a fit of anger, so she stayed with her mother. The days after the funeral were largely spent in the silence, writing hundreds of thank you cards to all of the caring people who showed their love for Jason and support of his family's plight. For Nadine Burgeson, her sorrow was always just below the surface, barely contained. Sometimes it would come out at the most inopportune times. When she would attempt to do her grocery shopping, for example, she couldn't help being overcome as she pushed her cart down an aisle and saw some of Jason's favorite foods that she had always bought for him. Sometimes she started to cry and had to leave the store.

The public was consumed with their own sense of dread during this time. The more information that the press revealed about the suspects and the street life that had spawned them, the more gnawing, anxious fear began to grip many Providence citizens and visitors.

City officials pronounced that all was well, hoping to keep panic from gaining a foothold and to discourage reactionary violence and other prejudicial acts against innocent people who might be homeless or regulars of Weybosset Street and "the wall."

"There is nothing going on in the city of Providence," Police Chief Urbano Prignano said, regarding the concern over increased violence in the aftermath of the Shute-Burgeson carjacking and murders. "The problem is random crimes done by people who believe in violence."

But even the top cop's reassurance did not allay everyone's trepidation. Business owners and civic leaders began to question the effect that the double-killing, random or otherwise, would have on the downtown economy. With the summer tourism dollars at risk, city vendors wanted more than reassurances.

The Providence Public Safety Commissioner did not help the city's cause with his repeated incendiary comments, such as, "There are parts of downtown that you don't want people walking through, especially after the clubs shut down at night." He was critical of what he saw as a public safety vacuum, created when a majority of the city's police force gather en masse in a several block area where the clubs let out between 1 and 2 AM on the weekends. He said that when cops are pulled off their regular beats, a practice called "short-posting," for night club duty and to help direct the bumper to bumper traffic onto the highways, outlining sections of the city which become more vulnerable to crime.

In subsequent articles on the state of the city after the June 9th carjacking/murders, The *Providence Journal* reported that one out-of-state businessman, in light of the recent crime, was considering abandoning his family's plans for a Providence vacation. In researching the city's crime rate in recent years, the newspaper found that it had remained fairly stable, with violent crime, including murder, rape, robbery and assault, occurring once every three days. The *Journal*, however, still found plenty of people to interview who had been recent victims or witnesses of violent crimes in Providence and who gave deprecating remarks about the city's safety. The articles only served to escalate the fear that what happened to Jason and Amy was *not* an isolated incident.

One Providence councilman proposed hiring thirty more officers as a remedy to the perceived problem. It was not that simple, however, and even though Police Chief Prignano himself would like to have seen this happen also, he said that, budgetary issues aside, if he were given thirty new officers and put them downtown, then he would effectively be neglecting the other neighborhoods that also need police service. Mayor Cianci understood that some people would perceive the city as dangerous in the wake of the carjacking, but insisted that Providence should not get a bad rap over a single crime. Not to downplay its tragic consequences to families of the victims, he called the crime an isolated incident, and urged the public to rebuke the suspects and not police, saying, "The city is safe. In fact, it's safer today than it was ten years ago, and safer today than it was two years ago."

Warning of further concerns, the Commissioner said, "You can feel it out there. The kids come through and they're whooping it up and you get a bad mix. You get the booze and you get the older people and the college kids and the people from the gay clubs and the blues clubs. They don't mix."

He also went on record as saying that he was not a fan of bars being granted licenses to hold "under age" nights, where young people who are under the legal drinking age are admitted into clubs to dance. Accordingly, after such a facility checks the ID's of the individuals entering, those under twenty-one are given special wrist bands which identifies them as such and prohibits them from purchasing and consuming alcoholic beverages. The Commissioner however, expressed his belief that this was a problem waiting to happen, especially when there are young people traveling from all around Massachusetts and Connecticut, making the "mix" even more volatile. And because Providence is the only game in town, its clubs and bars closing at 2

AM, whereas the rest of the state shuts down at 1:00, the problem becomes that much more elevated.

Though in one breath the commissioner said that "Providence is basically a safe city," he cryptically predicted, in regard to the recent carjacking, "We're going to have a rash of these." He even urged late-night visitors to take an unusual precaution. "Bring a whistle," he said, "and blow the damn whistle if needed."

He tempered the remark somewhat by saying, "I don't want to make it sound like the O.K. Corral, but at certain hours, downtown Providence is out of control."

Certainly, from a statistical standpoint, a small calculated risk might be inherent anytime someone steps out of their car in any American city after midnight. Having said that, it is the obligation of the police to protect its citizens, and department and city administrators come up with policy as a means to that end. As a practical matter, when citizens talk, politicians listen. That was the case in Providence following the carjacking, kidnapping and murders of Amy Shute and Jason Burgeson. Some of the recommendations put forth by the public and endorsed by local legislators during that time, however, were more feasible and practical than others.

Some city residents called for bulldozing "the wall." The proposal to rip out the two-foot high wall was seen by some as a way of increasing public safety in Providence. But tearing down the now iconic symbol of Providence's center of violence would not do a thing to solve the deeper, underlying problems that "the wall" represented - namely poverty, addiction and homelessness. It would have been little more than a cosmetic fix to a complex problem.

Not surprisingly, Rhode Island Attorney General Whitehouse announced his backing of the proposal, just as he had supported the hiring of thirty extra police officers. He urged the city to raze "the wall" as a public safety measure, and suggested replacing it with some sort of memorial to Jason and Amy. The raised concrete planter was likely to be removed, anyway, as part of a proposed development project that was slated to bring a Sundance Cinema to that area of Weybosset Street.

"I am sure you were as disturbed as I was," Whitehouse told members of the media, "as many other Rhode Islanders were, to read about "the wall" on

Weybosset Street. I'm sure the talents of Providence's arts community can produce an appropriate replacement, which I could suggest might be appropriately dedicated to the memories of Amy Shute and Jason Burgeson." He added that providing more police officers throughout the city would, "go a long way in preventing crime on our streets." The Renaissance City, as Providence has been called, has grown more popular, Whitehouse said, and as a result the demands on the Police and Fire Departments have increased along with it.

"The popularity of the activities and events in Providence's downtown area," he remarked further, "on many occasions result in officers being drawn from the neighborhoods."

The mayor admitted that the extra officers would be "wonderful" for public perception, but questioned whether the hiring would solve the problem. "I'd rather spend the money trying to get rid of guns in the city," he said, but promised that he would discuss the plan with the city's Financial Department. "We might be able to find the money to implement the plan," he added.

The mayor also hinted that the 2 AM closing time that bars in the city enjoyed might soon become a thing of the past. He called for a study to investigate the issue and make a determination. The mayor would not go so far as to say that crime rate would be reduced in any significant way if the closing hour was changed to 1:00 AM, "But my instinct tells me that if the closing hour everywhere else is 1:00, and we close at 2:00, then people are going to come downtown during the last hour and we end up getting the worst of the worst. But let's not jump to conclusions. I want a hard study. We need to look at the numbers of arrests. Compared to other times, is the number of arrests around 2 AM inordinate."

One councilman responded, "I don't think we need to worry about any more studies. I'd like to see a rollback now." He added that many of his colleagues were willing to vote for an immediate rollback, and he was convinced that the $1,500 in extra fees the city collected from establishments that applied for a special license to stay open an hour later on the weekends was not worth the potential risk to civilians or to the police trying to disperse the unruly crowds. He said he was planning to put a rollback proposal on the following month's council agenda, giving the city solicitor just enough time to check on the legality of such a move.

The protests of the club owners fell on deaf ears, and the mayor did not agree with them that a rollback would adversely affect their businesses. "We're talking about two hours a week," he said. "That shouldn't break them."

The mayor also said that he was going to be asking the chief of police to study the effect on overall public safety as a direct result of so-called "over and under" nights. He wanted to know if incidences of violence, complaints and arrests were higher in and around clubs that admitted patrons who were eighteen or older.

"You know how that works," Cianci said. "These young people are supposed to be drinking fruit drinks or Coca-Cola, but they end up drinking something else."

By far, the issue that the public seemed most concerned about was the issue of police officers being called away from their beats around the city to assist with crowd control downtown when the clubs closed. Every Thursday, Friday and Saturday nights, a cadre of officers were visible in cruisers, on foot, some with dogs, and in the summertime on bikes and even horseback along a several block area that runs between Pine and Friendship Streets. This is the location where numerous nightclubs dump out a sometimes raucous and drunken jamboree of young people from all over the state and nearby Massachusetts onto the streets of Providence at 2 AM. Police presence alone is usually enough to keep the peace. The visibility of uniformed officers toting guns and night sticks at their sides will have that effect. But there were always fights to break up, arrests to make and reports to write.

The epicenter of many city disturbances at that time, however, was slightly northwest of this location, along Weybosset Street, in a small area known as "the wall." While there were no popular nightclubs in this immediate area, between the donut shop, cafe and pizzeria, the converging street life made for a volatile mix where violence was always ready to erupt. Things had gotten so dangerous along this virulent hot spot that the city had recently installed a surveillance camera in the Johnson & Wales University tower clock, which was situated directly across the street from the pizzeria. The public safety spy cam had actually been placed there in the aftermath of a shooting that claimed the life of a

University of Massachusetts student, who was killed the previous winter following an early morning robbery on Union Street.

What made this area along Weybosset Street so problematic was not just the bad element that dwelt there, but the innocent young people who congregated among them. It was a late night haven that featured a pizza joint, always a favorite among teens and twenty-something's, and because the pizzeria was one of only a few Providence restaurants allowed to remain open for business until 4 AM, it was *the* place to go after the clubs closed on the weekend. The spot has seen more than its share of assaults, robberies, shootings, stabbings and even murders through the years, yet despite all this, the establishment had managed to maintain its after hours privilege. The Providence Board of Licenses has repeatedly looked into revoking its license, though nothing has ever been done. The week after Amy and Jason were murdered by a former pizzeria employee, the chairman of the license board, told the *Providence Journal* that he was not sure closing the pizza shop early would solve anything. He also said he did not believe that the need for police outside the pizzeria made other parts of the city more vulnerable to crime.

"If police weren't at the pizzeria, would they have been at the Arcade?" he asked. "Probably not. They probably would have been at other busy parts of the city."

The owner of the pizza place told reporters that when he first opened his doors in 1982, "No one would even come down here." But since the rejuvenation of Providence, he does not think it's fair that his restaurant gets blamed for all the trouble. "It's not my fault," the owner said. "How can it be my fault? I don't sell booze here. I sell pizza. Do I own the sidewalks? No, that's the cops' job. You know what I'm saying? If someone drives by and starts shooting guns, is that my fault?"

To make matters worse, the already undermanned city police department had to routinely centralize a small group of officers every weekend to maintain order in this overcrowded crime zone.

What all this leads many people to ask is: did this dynamic make Jason and Amy more vulnerable the night of June 9, 2000, or factor into their abduction as they talked outside the restaurant near the Arcade just a few blocks away?

As a police officer who understands just how difficult it is to be everywhere, all the time, I would say no. As a father, however, that question becomes much more difficult to answer so promptly. To lay blame on anyone other than Greg Floyd, Kenneth Day, Harry Burdick, Sammie Sanchez and Ray Anderson might be unfair, but to say that the two kids were just in the wrong place at the wrong time, as a parent, I would not be satisfied with that logic, either.

Chapter 23

Building
a Case

Almost exactly seven days to the minute after the bodies of Amy and Jason were first spotted by a golf course construction worker, Providence Patrolman Lough arrived at the Johnston Police Station to give a statement. He told Detective Nardolillo what he had witnessed the night of the carjacking and double murder. Lough was driving alone, on routine patrol, and was approaching the Arcade when he said he noticed a young couple sitting and talking on the wall outside Scott's restaurant. Next to them was a white SUV. It was around 2 AM. About ten minutes later, when Lough drove back through the same area, he said the two people, a male and female, were in the exact same location. They were still alone. However, the next time he saw them, only five minutes after that, they were both in the back seat of the vehicle, which was being operated by a young man. A fourth individual was in the passenger seat. The SUV, he observed, had Massachusetts plates, and was being followed by a small sedan with three male passengers.

With the intense investigation and media blasting the story of Amy and Jason's murders, Lough now was well aware of the significance of what he had seen. Despite the tremendous empathy and pain he felt for the families, he knew that given the circumstances on the original night he'd seen them, he had no cause at that time to stop either vehicle. Certainly there had been no apparent signs of distress. They did not even have a tail light out. Still, the sense of guilt that had been projected on him by so many people over the past week was difficult. What made it worse was that part of him could understand everyone's contempt for him and outrage at his inaction. He knew that the Shutes and the Burgesons would never understand why he let the SUV drive past him, and he did not expect them to, but he felt obligated to tell investigators everything he had seen to help their case. If he had known that the couple had been abducted by the others, he would not have let them get away. He made that statement over and over, as if to convince himself, but even if everyone still believed that he could have done something more at that time, he knew this was all he could do now.

A little later that morning, Providence Patrolman Huffman came to Johnston headquarters to provided investigators with a follow-up interview to the statement he made six days earlier. Detective Nardolillo questioned Marcus Huffman about the exact time that he had seen Floyd driving the van on the morning of June 9. Jackson had stated earlier that he figured it to be close to 4 AM. This, however, did not fit in with the timeline we had established from all the other evidence and testimony that had been compiled up to that point. Huffman expressed confidence that sometime between the hours of 3:00 and 4:00 AM, Floyd drove past him in a white SUV bearing what he believed were Massachusetts tags. He recognized Floyd. When the two saw one another, Floyd offered a greeting to the officer. Huffman said he could not identify the male passenger in the SUV, but he "thought there were two white passengers in the back seat," their sex unknown. Huffman also said he thought the SUV had been following a small tan colored car, but could make no determination about the occupants of this vehicle. It was too far up the street by the time he realized that the two vehicles may have been together. Shown several photographs of Jason's SUV, Huffman confirmed that it was the same one he had seen Floyd operating.

Next, Nardolillo displayed photographs of Sanchez's car. "I am now showing you photos of another vehicle," the detective said. "Do you recognize this one?"

"It looks like the vehicle I saw in front of the SUV," Huffman replied.

Much of Huffman's statement seemed accurate enough, but some of the details were troubling, and we weren't sure if his testimony would be helpful at that point. Although we did not doubt that Huffman saw Floyd that morning, we believed the time to be an hour earlier than he remembered, between 2:00 and 3:00 AM. That being the case, his placing of Sanchez's car in front of the van at that time also had to be inaccurate. What seems likely to investigators is that Jackson, not Smith, was the last person to see Floyd and Burdick leaving the city of Providence with Amy and Jason.

As Detective Nardolillo was finishing up with Huffman, Detective Warren responded to North Central Airport in North Smithfield, where he boarded an FBI aircraft. About twenty feet from where the bodies had been discovered, an officially marked Johnston police vehicle had been left for use as a reference point for Warren to focus his camera from high above. Accompanied by a special agent, Warren was flown over Buttonhole Golf Course where he snapped numerous aerial photographs of the crime scene from an altitude of 2,000 feet. Had he been using a telephoto lens, he would have seen Detectives Nardolillo and DeTora, as well as Special Agent Goodwin, on the ground below. They had returned to the golf course to collect soil samples in the area where the tire impressions had been taken.

An abundance of investigative activity continued into the afternoon of June 16, as judicial consent was given for a search of the apartment in Providence where Sanchez had been apprehended.

Led by Agent Goodwin, the FBI was busy as well, conducting their own follow-up investigation in order to more conclusively substantiate the exact movements of the killers prior to the abduction of Amy and Jason. With full cooperation from Providence and assisted by our investigators, the feds began by canvassing the downtown area. Goodwin wanted to talk with anyone and everyone who had seen one or more of the five suspects during the evening of June 8 and into the morning of June 9. The FBI spoke first with known witnesses, hoping to broaden the scope of the investigation and generate new leads. They interviewed the security guard from the Providence/Washington Building who had witnessed the gang as they approached two women at an ATM located outside. Further record checks and interviews provided agents with information used to locate the two females and their male companion, all of whom corroborated the security guard's statement. A bank receipt determined that a transaction had been completed at 1:19 AM.

In the course of her investigation, Agent Goodwin reviewed all video-tapes made by security cameras mounted outside city buildings. A security tape with a time stamp of 1:23 AM and capturing an image of the five men as they moved along Westminster Street, away from South Main Street, was immediately confiscated. Although the quality of this tape was rather poor, one of the individuals clearly resembled Burdick, based upon his physical size and the clothing he was wearing that night.

Ann Goodwin also conducted her own interview with Providence Patrolman Lough, who once more told what he had witnessed that night. His observations were supported by footage from surveillance cameras in opera-tion around the area of the Arcade. They provided some quality prints of Floyd and Burdick as they walked along the alleyway from Westminster toward Weybosset. The time print on the final frame featuring the carjackers was 2:09:59, seconds before Patrolman Lough drove past Amy and Jason a second time, and only minutes before they were abducted.

Videotape confiscated from security cameras outside the Travelers Aid Society in downtown Providence clearly showed a light-color sport utility vehicle pull to a stop outside the building and a male resembling Floyd emerge from the driver side door. As he entered the facility, videotape from interior sur-veillance cameras captured better quality images of Floyd's movements. He appeared to be looking around for someone briefly and unsuccessfully before exiting soon afterward, getting back into the vehicle and driving off.

All five men were clearly in the vicinity of the abduction/carjacking. The federal case was strong for carjacking, and the evidence placing them at the scene of the murder was just as compelling. It was only a week into the inves-tigation, and we were still building our case against the suspects. We felt the evidence was strong and were confident that it would hold up in court, but we intended to let no detail go unchecked. We didn't want any surprises.

The following morning, on June 17, Detective Petrucci took formal typed statements from Arnold Banker and Stephen Cone, who had driven to

Providence on June 8 to meet their friend, Jason, and his girlfriend, Amy, and hit a couple of clubs together. The two boys were with the doomed couple most of the night, right up until the end. Banker and Cone were transported to Weybosset Street and asked to identify the exact location in Scott's parking lot where their cars had been parked. They pointed out two spaces, marked as #7 and #8, specifying that the front of both their vehicles that night were facing the wall. Photographs were taken of the lot and the entrance from the street. The digital prints and photo disc were immediately turned over to BCI Detective Sonny DeTora. Though these were destined for the FBI as evidence, this was the chain of command. Banker and Cone were also asked to voluntarily provide fingerprints, to which they gave their consent. These, too, were turned over to Sonny the following day, to be used for elimination purposes only. Their fingerprints were likely all over the SUV as well, and having their prints on record would make it easier to distinguish them from the killers.

On June 19, the Chief District Court Judge Albert DeRobbio appointed defense attorneys for each of the suspects in the carjacking-double murder case. After moving the proceedings from the open courtroom to his chambers, the lawyers were named. Members of the media were permitted to attend the hearing, and they reported that the Chief Judge was direct and stern with the litigators that morning.

"I think you understand how I handle bail hearings," he told the assemblage. "I expect the highlights. I assume you are going to be zeroing in."

The lawyers would have to zero-in, because they only had a week to sort through the volumes of witness statements, suspect confessions and other evidence in preparation for the June 26 hearing. The judge advised the attorneys that the bail hearing would not run for more than two days. He told them that if he found that the state had proven to a reasonable degree of satisfaction that a defendant participated in the crimes, then he would likely order the defendant held without bail. Then, the judge instructed prosecutors to turn over all evidence to the defense counselors at once. What he excluded from each of the defense lawyers was privilege to the statements that had been made about their client by the other four defendants in the case.

State prosecutor, Dambruch, made no objections. He said that the state had more than ten witnesses, including investigators, who would be called to testify.

Each of the defense counselors were carefully considered before they were chosen. Because the interests of one defendant might conflict with the interests of the others, the public defender's office could represent only one of them. Private lawyers had to be appointed for the other four, the names drawn from a short list of qualified defense attorneys. This was standard practice, and every court in the state keeps such a list, or "panel." The lawyers must petition the court to be included on a court's panel, and demonstrate that they are qualified to handle the types of cases that would be assigned to them in that particular court. For example, the county Superior Courts, which try all felony cases, keep two panels, one for lawyers qualified to defend Class 1 felonies, including murder, and another for attorneys qualified to defend Class 2 felonies, in which the sentences imposed cannot exceed ten years. Court-appointed attorneys in murder trials must prove that they have tried at least two previous homicide cases to a verdict, either as lead counsel or second counsel. Other stipulations apply, such as carrying their own malpractice insurance and enrolling in ten hours of continuing education in law every year. If they fulfilled all these requirements, they were placed on the panel and paid a state rate of fifty dollars per hour for the work they did on any case they were assigned.

Gregory Floyd was to be represented by state public defenders, Anthony Caparo and Robert Marro, both lifelong Rhode Islanders and Providence College graduates. They were also the most experienced lawyers in the state's Public Defender's Office.

Harry Burdick would be defended by Mary June Ciresi. She was also a local product who was a PC graduate. She had represented Burdick on a prior violation of probation charge, and was familiar with him, so she was assigned to be his counsel.

Kenneth Day's attorney, Joseph DeCaporale, was fresh from a highly publicized corruption trial. Now in private practice, he was the former head of special prosecutions.

Making arguments on behalf of Raymond Anderson would be Robert Mann, perhaps Rhode Island's most recognizable and talented defense attorney at that time. He had logged a long and renowned career by 2000, representing several high profile clients during his twenty-seven years of litigating. A Yale graduate, he served as an Army Intelligence officer in Vietnam.

Finally, delegated to the defense table of Samuel Sanchez was Mark Smith, known as much for the trademark bow ties he always wore in court as he was for his considerable trial experience, defending more than fifteen murder suspects in his twenty-seven years of practice.

The murder suspects were well-represented by defenders who were more than capable, but the prosecution team was certainly of their equal. Assistant Attorney General, Stephen Dambruch, who would prosecute the case for the state, and Special Attorney General, Peter Neronha, were both sworn in as Special U.S. Attorneys. Dambruch, a local boy, graduated from Providence College and Boston College Law School, and had been with the Attorney General's Office for the thirteen years. Neronha, out of Boston College, had been practicing in Rhode Island and the Attorney General's Office for the past five years

The two U.S. Attorneys prosecuting the case for the federal government, Gerard Sullivan and Mary Rogers, were likewise sworn in as Special Attorneys General for the state of Rhode Island. These cross-designations would give both state and federal prosecutors the latitude to prosecute the offenders in the dual court system and ensure they receive the maximum punishment allowable.

And, of course, Rhode Island Attorney General, Sheldon Whitehouse had promised to work closely with United States Attorney, Margaret Curran, in collectively guiding the case into the most appropriate jurisdictional venue. So far, both were only in agreement that it was likely to be a very long time before any decision was made on the matter.

Now, with the sides chosen, the legal battle was officially underway. It was shaping up to be a major prizefight, if it went the distance.

The rest of the morning and that afternoon was spent getting ready for the following Friday's bail and probation violation hearing. This involved taking formal statements from prosecution witnesses, including a bus driver and the mother of Sammie Sanchez. It also required getting subpoenas prepared and into the hands of these individuals. We were requesting them to appear in courtroom four at Sixth District Court, 1 Dorrance Plaza in Providence, on June 26th to testify against one or more of the five murder suspects.

Once more, Ira Nasberg flew onto the radar screen of law enforcement investigators working on the Shute-Burgeson case. This time, it was ATF Agent Chau who had some follow up questions he wanted Nasberg to answer. The two met at the Detective Division of the Providence Police Department. Chau conducted an exhaustive two-hour interview with Nasberg. One by one, Chau went over every stolen gun report that Nasberg had filed in the past. When asked if he knew where any of the weapons were during the times they were missing, Nasberg's memory was off, and on two occasions he had completely forgotten about filing a report on a particular gun.

In speaking about the .40 caliber Smith & Wesson semiautomatic that wound up in Floyd's possession, Nasberg admitted that when he first realized the gun was missing, he suspected all along that Floyd may have taken it. However, he was not 100 percent sure, and because of this he did not want to accuse his friend. So any surprise he expressed previously after learning that Floyd had been involved in the shootings had to be a lie.

In reference to Sanchez, Nasberg said that the youth had been to his apartment only one time, and described for them that night in April when Sanchez called him and asked him if he could hang out. Nasberg agreed and the two had a few drinks in his apartment. He said Sanchez left around midnight. The following day, April 14, when Nasberg noticed that one of his guns was missing, he went to the police to file a stolen gun report. In it, he had been asked if he had any visitors to his apartment recently, to which Nasberg identified Sanchez. He now admitted to Chau that he felt bad for incriminating the youth because he later found the gun under his bed.

His statement had obvious discrepancies, and the federal agent was not about to let him off the hook so easily, not in light of the two fresh graves that had been turned over, one in Lakeville, Massachusetts, the other in West Warwick, Rhode Island. Despite the relentless interrogation, however, Nasberg stuck to his story, holes and all, that he had never given permission to Floyd, Sanchez, or anyone else, to use any of his guns. Suddenly, with more certainty he further stated that he had not been aware of anyone being in possession of his weapons during the time that they were reported missing.

It was duly noted that Nasberg was very nervous during this interview, and upset that he was even remotely being viewed by police as a criminal. He stated that he wanted to do everything he could to cooperate, but was leery about submitting to a polygraph test. He did, however, agree to go to the Alcohol, Tobacco and Firearms office the following Monday afternoon to speak with the polygraph examiner to find out what the procedure entailed.

218

Chapter 24

To Catch a Thief

On June 20, Kenneth Day was arraigned on two counts of robbery, unrelated to the Shute-Burgeson case. His wrists were bound in front of him and he was wearing a blue prison jumpsuit with a number on the breast pocket as he was escorted into court to answer these charges. As Judge Patricia Moore read each charge against him in succession, the suspect looked more and more surprised. He entered no plea, as is expected with felony charges presented in District Court. He was ordered held without bail pending a bail hearing, which had already been scheduled for him and the four other carjacking-murder suspects on June 26.

The separate complaints were filed against Day based on testimony provided by three teenagers.

The first robbery occurred at Waterplace Park in Providence on April 1. Two teenagers, a male and a female, were walking from the State House after participating in a mock legislative session involving students from various high schools. They were making their way to a mobile food truck that was perennially parked next to City Hall and is practically a downtown landmark itself. It was just before sunset, and as they were passing under the cobblestone-paved pedestrian walkway that linked the park and downtown, they were ambushed. Three men jumped out of the shadows under the bridge, one carrying a gun and another clutching a baseball bat.

"Give me your stuff," the man with the gun said. The victims would later identify the gun-toting thief as Kenneth Day from a photograph of the five double murder suspects that appeared in the *Providence Sunday Journal*.

"I don't have any money," the young man told him.

It was the wrong reply, as the second assailant responded by swinging the aluminum bat. He struck the male twice in the spine and in the head, which opened up a gash in his scalp that required eight stitches to close. As the victim dropped to the ground, the third perpetrator, a small, buxom female stepped in front of the young lady and said, "Give me your money and everything you have on you."

Terrified, she surrendered her watch, cell phone and pocketbook, which contained her keys, credit cards and four dollars cash. The bandits ran off with her belongings, disappearing down the far end of the tunnel toward the city. There were no other witnesses to the robbery. However, after seeing Day's picture on the front page of the Sunday paper on June 11, the male victim contacted Providence Police. Upon arrival at the station later that day, the teenager was shown a series of mugshots, from which he was able to positively identify Kenneth Day as the attacker. Now, both had filed robbery complaints and were willing to testify against Day.

Another victim, a male teenager, went to the Providence Police on June 16, five days after the picture of the suspects appeared in the *Journal*. He told a detective that Day was one of a gang of five men who beat and robbed him of twenty dollars at the bus depot in Kennedy Plaza just before 10 PM on June 7, mere hours before he would take part in the abduction-murders of Amy Shute and Jason Burgeson. It was reported that he was waiting for Bus #57 to take him back to North Providence when he was confronted by two males.

"What's in the backpack?" Day wanted to know.

"Nothing," he responded, and then Day punched him in the back of the neck.

As he recoiled from the blow, three other men appeared and all five began beating him. They took his backpack, his wallet and twenty dollars before fleeing. Several witnesses observed the gang of robbers getting onto a bus headed for Broad Street, information which was promptly reported to the police. A nearby Providence unit responded, and ten minutes later they stopped the bus, but Day and his posse were no longer aboard. The victim suffered an assortment of cuts and bruises, and his right eye was swollen shut, but he was not seriously hurt. His mother picked him up at the police station and took him to a nearby hospital for X-rays, just to be safe. No breaks or internal injuries were found.

The information he provided was used to charge Day with a second robbery, and he would swear under oath in an open courtroom to the statement he gave police. Together, the accounts of the three teenagers were credible enough to make the charges stick. To some, it may have seemed superfluous to even bring these charges against him, considering what Day had hanging over his head in the pending double murder case. Later on, however, securing guilty verdicts on the two robberies would prove very important, indeed.

On June 21, a set of full major case fingerprints were requested to be taken of the five double murder suspects. The affiant, Detective Nardolillo, prepared the search warrant for District Court Judge DeRobbio, who signed the document. At 2 PM, Detective DeTora and FBI Special Agent David Little executed the warrant to obtain the prints, proceeding to the Intake Services Center at the Adult Correctional Institutions in Cranston, Rhode Island. Upon arrival, they found that Floyd, Day, Burdick, Anderson and Sanchez had already been gathered into the same cell, which was somewhat triangular in shape and had a single door at the base with benches along the two angled walls. The Special Agent set up a printing station using a desk that he brought into the cell and placed in front of the door. Sonny handed an individual Search Warrant to each of the subjects. Little identified himself as part of the Federal Bureau of Investigation and explained the process by which major case prints are taken, these merely being a more comprehensive fingerprinting, involving the full palm and the entire finger and thumb pads, all the way around both sides of the fingernail.

The subjects were further advised that they would not be questioned regarding the incident for which they were incarcerated, or any other crime in which they may have been involved. Little cautioned them not to speak about the case, and he assured them that any and all overheard statements or comments they made regarding the homicides, or unrelated crimes, would be documented and presented to the prosecution for possible inclusion as witness testimony during trial. When asked if they understood, each subject in turn replied in the affirmative. None of the young men, however, heeded the federal agent's advice.

Prison authorities requested that Sanchez be printed first, a procedure that would take about ten minutes. As the four others waited their turn, they sat on the bench along one wall, though unevenly spaced and not immediately next to one another. It was Floyd, Day, Burdick and Anderson, left to right, with distances between them ranging from eight to ten feet. They sat in silence for a moment, but very soon the four of them began to speak openly and in friendly tones to one another. At one point, Sanchez, who was being fully cooperative with the agent as Sonny printed him, turned abruptly to the others and said, "Shut your fucking mouths. Don't say a damn thing." However, when the conversation turned to cell assignments, Sanchez joined in. Soon, the exchange became light-hearted and relaxed once more, and they all participated, discussing everything from women to when they could get haircuts.

Following a brief silence, Floyd suddenly blurted out, "Hey, this is the first time all of us have been together since that night."

Sonny and Little, both hearing this statement clearly, immediately looked up at one another in acknowledgment. None of the suspects seemed to give the remark a second thought. Anderson, Day, Burdick and Floyd, respectively, were printed and then each removed from the cell by prison officials. The investigators left the facility two hours after they arrived and with more than what they came for. The prints were sent to the FBI lab in Washington and where reports were filed, detailing the conversation they overheard between the subjects.

On June 22, a friend of mine contacted me out of the blue on behalf of Ira Nasberg. My first reaction was to roll my eyes, much the way that many others might do after hearing this man's name again and again. Like the proverbial bad penny, Ira Nasberg kept turning up.

My friend related that Nasberg wanted to meet and speak to me directly. No lawyers, no prosecutors, just the two of us. I didn't even question why Nasberg went through a mutual friend, rather than contact me himself. It was just the way things were done in Rhode Island. It was not even surprising to me that someone I knew would be acquainted with Nasberg. In fact, it's the rule, not the exception in this state, where everyone knows everyone, and if not they have a cousin who knows them. The rest of the world may be connected to each other by six degrees of separation, but here, it seems more like two or three degrees.

I agreed to meet Nasberg, and the next thing I knew he showed up at the Johnston police station around 11:00 one night, shortly before my shift ended. He came in alone. I sat down with him in my office and looked closely at him. He was disheveled, had a stubbly beard, reeking of coffee and cigarettes. The clothes he was wearing looked liked he had been sleeping in them for a week. His face was pale, bloodless. He was extremely nervous and smoking like a fiend. I thought he might drop dead right there in front of me.

"What is it, Ira?" I asked.

"Can I make a deal with you?"

I shook my head. "You know I can't do that."

"What if I told you everything about the gun, and Greg? How much time will I get?"

"It's not up to me. You should already have told us everything."

"Ray, I can't do time," he said, exasperated.

"Does your lawyer know you're here, talking to me?"

"I don't care about that. I just can't do time. I can't!"

"There's nothing I can do, Ira. The best thing you can do for yourself is tell someone involved in this investigation, including myself, everything that you know. Do you remember something now that you want to add to your previous statements?"

Nasberg obviously wanted to speak off the record, and I was trying to discourage him from saying something he would regret. This was not some misdemeanor weapons charge he was tangled up in. His gun had been used to kill two people.

"I can't do time," he repeated, practically mumbling now. He knew he was in a world of trouble before he came in to see me. He was out of options. The system had him dead to rights.

Just then the remote radio he was carrying crackled and he announced that he had to leave. He had driven over in his cab and he had to go on a call.

"We'll be in touch, Ira," I told him. In spite of his desperation, I wasn't overly concerned about his movements, because we knew where he was and I felt he wasn't going anywhere.

Boy was I wrong.

He walked out of the building still muttering that he couldn't do time. That was the last time I saw Ira Nasberg.

By coincidence, that same day, Brett Mills, of the Firearms/Toolmarks Unit of the FBI Laboratory in Washington, D.C., filed his examination report regarding the .40 caliber Smith & Wesson semiautomatic weapon used in the double homicide. The live round found on Jason's sneaker at the murder scene was determined to be have been loaded and extracted from the cartridge case that was recovered with the murder weapon. Both the jacketed hollow-point bullet found at the scene and the cartridge case bore the head stamp of IMI (Israel Military Industries). The fragments of bullets that were recovered from the victims were also identified as having been fired from the seized handgun in question.

On June 23, the Burgesons and the Shutes met with state and federal prosecutors for about an hour to discuss the status of the investigation. The two families were all together for the first time. They had not formerly met previously, even during the short time that Amy and Jason had dated. It was an emotional moment as they hugged and expressed their sympathies.

"We've come together and we're going to go forward together," Jason's sister, Kellie, told reporters afterward. "We're all in the same boat."

State Attorney General Whitehouse was the first to the podium. He began by extending his deepest condolences to the families and assured them that he and U.S. Attorney, Curran, as well as the team of prosecutors from both offices, were resolute in going the distance and doing everything possible to meet their wishes in seeing that those responsible for this senseless and reprehensible crime were punished to the fullest extent of the law. He explained how the case would proceed if it was prosecuted as a federal crime. He also told them what to expect if it went forward in state court. In conclusion, however, he once again tempered both options with his noncommittal disclaimer, impressing upon them that they were still in the early stages of the investigation and that no decision had been reached yet with regard to the death penalty. He informed them that it could be a "substantial amount of time" before prosecutors knew whether one or more of five men charged would be prosecuted under any federal statute that carries the death penalty.

Still, Kellie said, "They were very informative. We came away with a good sense that everything that could be done was being done."

With the bail and probation violation hearing only a day away, the state was lining up all its ducks in a row, issuing the last of the subpoenas to the witnesses who had provided credible and compelling statements. In case these individuals were needed to give testimony during the proceeding, they had to be present. So the detectives in our department spent much of June 24th and 25th delivering the writs, commanding the witnesses to appear in court under penalty of law for failing to do so. There was only one glitch in performance of this task.

Patrolman Robert Lemieux served a subpoena on witness, Johnny Harrison. As a juvenile, however, the boy was unable to sign the document himself. Lemieux requested Harrison's grandmother, who was present, to sign it for him. The woman, however, refused, stating that the boy's mother, perhaps fearing repercussions from the suspects or their associates, insisted that her son not to sign the document. The officer's attempt to contact his mother was met with negative results, and a copy of the document was left with Sellers, who was advised of the instructions and penalty contained therein.

As it turned out, his presence was not required. In fact, none of the witnesses were called to give testimony. On June 26, in Room Four of 6th District Court, the five murder suspects, knowing there was too much evidence against them, all waived their right to a bail hearing. In doing so, neither side had to present evidence or call witnesses on their behalf.

Now the prosecution had six months to fully develop its case before going to trial and presenting their evidence to a jury, although which court would be hearing testimony was still in question.

Chapter 25

Pre Trial Days

On June 29, state Senator William P. Tocco, Jr. (D–District 28) recognized the members of the Johnston Police Department introducing a Senate Resolution in their honor. The Tocco resolution specifically addressed the carjacking-murders of Amy Shute and Jason Burgeson. Addressing the media at a news conference, the Senator, a former State Police officer and one-time Chief of Police in Johnston, called the June 9 crimes a horrific tragedy, and said, "Members of the Johnston Police Department worked extremely hard under difficult circumstances to apprehend the individuals responsible for this heinous crime. In less than one day, they worked feverishly to solve the crime and they deserve to be thanked and recognized for their diligence."

In addition to Senator Tocco, several Johnston legislators praised the members of our department, many of whom were in attendance with their families.

It became a typical PR event in many ways, but we all felt pretty good about what we'd been able to accomplish so far. We were fortunate to have apprehended the suspects who were now awaiting trial for Amy and Jason's murders, but we needed to concentrate. There was still plenty of unfinished business to attend to, to gain justice for the young couple who had been killed in such a heinous way.

On July 3, Jim's father died. Carol wanted to be as strong for Jim as he had been for her. She went to the services, paid her respects, but when she looked in the flag-draped coffin, she did not see an elderly war veteran, she saw Amy lying there. She stayed as long as she could, and it seemed like much longer than five minutes before she had to run out of the funeral home.

To this day, Carol only goes to funeral services of people who are close to her for that very same reason. She knows she would invariably envision her twenty-one year old daughter in the casket, and she would lose it.

Ira Nasberg, the overexposed freelance crime photographer/cab driver whose "stolen" gun was allegedly used in the killings, died unexpectedly on July 5. The week after he came to see me at the police station, he was found unresponsive in his apartment. No foul play was suspected, but suicide could not be ruled out after it had been speculated that he had stopped taking his prescription medications for various ailments from which he was suffering.

Nasberg's death had little impact on the case as a whole or in the rutted path for justice. Family, friends and supporters, who had begun to wage a private war to see to it that the crimes committed by the five suspects were tried as capital offenses, dug in for a long battle as the U.S. Attorney General's Office considered whether or not the case would be tried in federal court. They continued the letter campaign in earnest, hoping that such efforts would sway opinion and policy in their favor.

Over the course of the next couple of months, through the summer of 2000, the case seemed to move forward slowly, bogged down by bureaucracy and a strained federal judicial system. No word was coming from Washington about which direction the prosecution might go, and I wasn't sure if that was good or bad.

Sonny and I returned to the crime scene on Friday morning, July 14, to look for further evidence, in particular, the final unaccounted for shell casing. It had been nagging me that we had not collected it previously.

Sonny began breaking up the hay bales, while I raked through the contents searching for the elusive evidence. We went meticulously through eight of them, hardly saying a word. The heat and humidity was stifling that day. Then, all of a sudden I noticed something glinting in the sun.

"Hold it," I said. Looking closely, I saw that it was a live round. The bullet was a .40 caliber, like the others, approximately five feet from the spot where the victims were found. As Sonny was photographing the object, I caught sight of the final spent casing, lying about eight feet from the location of the bodies. I took it as a positive sign when we came away with more than what we set out to find that day, and if that was also luck, I just hoped that it would continue for the next couple of months and we could make our federal case.

On Sunday, July 16, a benefit dinner was held in memory of Amy. Two seatings were scheduled at the VFW Post No. 449 in West Warwick. The Shute family friend wanted to give the community an opportunity to show its support for the Shutes. She also hoped that, in some small way at least, the benefit would ease some of the family's burden.

It was a compassionate and loving gesture that Carol Shute, even in her persistent state of mourning, appreciated very much.

On July 19, I appeared in United States District Court, Room 314 of the John O. Pastore Federal Building, Two Exchange Street in Providence, to give testimony before the Grand Jury. I was questioned about the investigation and the role I played.

In late July, Sonny and I responded to the residence of Harry Burdick's girlfriend, Elizabeth Zatkoff, in South Attleboro, Massachusetts. In the basement apartment, where Burdick sometimes stayed, and from inside the trunk of Zatkoff's vehicle, we seized numerous items of clothing belonging to Burdick.

Sonny and I also accompanied two Special Agents in serving a search warrant for the third floor of the dwelling, where Day and Floyd lived. Speaking with Day's mother, we were advised that she had cleaned up the third floor apartment herself recently, and had removed two black leather jackets, which she then turned over to Special Agents, who provided a receipt for the items. The following day, another search warrant was executed for the second floor of the residence. A variety of clothing belonging to both Floyd and Day were confiscated.

That month, Special Agent Bowers appeared at the Photography Laboratory of the Boston field office of the FBI. Strong provided an FBI photographer with three videotapes, including one that was taken by a security camera in the alley next to the Arcade. Bowers requested that still photographic copies be made of the images on the tapes, particularly those of the Arcade alley recorded on 06/09/00. This was an important piece of evidence, because it showed Floyd and Burdick walking in the direction of Scott's restaurant parking lot moments before Amy and Jason were abducted. Jurors could clearly see the two defendants as well as the time stamp, 02:59:59, on the bottom left of the photo.

The photographs were made using a PELCO Genex Duplex Color Multiplexer. If that sounds like something out of a *Men in Black* movie, I think it is. Still images were also requested and taken from the cassette tape recorded by a surveillance camera outside the Traveler's Aid Society, posted at 177 Union Street, on the same date. The third tape was made outside the Rhode Island Department of the Attorney General on South Main Street, showing the building across the street and the robbery attempt at the ATM.

As the investigation moved forward, those whose lives the murders of the two young people had touched continued to grieve in their own ways. Cathy Antonio had created a memorial web page as her personal response to the murders of her friend, Jason Burgeson, and Amy Shute. She wanted to do something to help, and the Internet tribute page was conceived as a call to action to bolster support for the letter campaign.

When she began to receive a flood of e-mail from people who wanted to tell her just how special Jason and Amy were to them, this gave her even more incentive to keep their memories alive. Of course, she had been close to Jason and knew most of his friends, while she had only met Amy once, on that fateful night in Providence. Cathy, however, was not surprised by the outpouring of love she received about Amy from the many people who had known her.

Alex Green was one of those people. He met Amy in 1993 when she arrived at LaSalle Academy as a freshman and he was a junior. Despite the difference in class status, the two became close friends. What struck Alex immediately about Amy was how confident and secure she was. Typically, high school students find a clique that they fit in with and do not stray too far these groups. Amy, however, appeared comfortable around anyone.

The two spent many hours on the telephone talking late into the night. They would spend time together before he had to be at basketball practice, and Amy would often go to his games and cheer wildly for the team. Alex thought of Amy as open-minded, free-spirited, a loyal friend and a very caring person. Someone who was very honest, sometimes brutally so, with a sarcastic wit that was never mean-spirited. Despite being so outspoken, Amy was also very sensitive. She did not have a negative bone in her body and her intentions were pure.

Alex recalled fondly the time Amy's mother took them and two other friends to a Janet Jackson concert at the Providence Civic Center. He had such good time with Carol and Amy that he considered it the best concert he had ever attended. Alex always felt welcome around Amy and her family.

Not long after moving on to college, Alex lost touch with Amy, and they began to drift apart. Hearing the news of her passing, he was naturally shocked and saddened.

"Overall," he would say of Amy, "she was a genuine person who saw the truth in a person beyond the exterior. She had a wonderful heart and is by far the best personality and person I have ever met. Her life was way too short."

The more Cathy found out about Amy, the more she saw just how much alike she and Jason really were, and she understood why they had been drawn together. Like Amy, Jason could fit into any social group.

Maureen Petroskie was in seventh grade when one of her friends planned a party at an ice skating rink. Despite the fact that she had often been picked on by bullies and had never skated before, she was a very confident young girl and thought it would be a fun time. They shared the public facility in Taunton, Massachusetts with a lot of people, all of whom could skate. Even her friends skated quickly past her as she kept falling down. It was mortifying. She noticed a group of "cool" eighth-graders, some of whom played hockey, and were getting a lot of attention. It was like no one noticed her at all.

Finally, Maureen had fallen so many times she became thoroughly discouraged. Then, to her surprise, one of the hockey players, beside whom she had just collapsed, reached down to help her to her feet.

It was Jason.

"I'm going to teach you how to skate," he pronounced, and proceeded to take her by the hand and skate around the rink with her. Soon, she was keeping up with him on her own, and still he held her hand. At the end of the day, expecting an awkward good-bye, Maureen was surprised again when Jason asked her out with him. She could not say "yes" fast enough. For the next two weeks, he would meet her at her locker at school, walk her to the bus and pass notes back to her. People even stopped picking on her. In seventh grade, two weeks is like an eternity, and eventually, like seventh graders do, Jason had a friend of his break up with Maureen for him. She was saddened, but happy she had gotten to know Jason, who had restored her faith in herself and made her feel special.

When Maureen ran into Jason again it was in high school, and she was certain that he would not remember her or want to talk to her.

She should have known better.

On her desk one day in study hall, someone had left her a note. It was from Jason - her first ever boyfriend. He asked her to please not hate him and he said he hoped they could become friends, which they did. Jason helped her through some trying days during her sophomore year, and she will never forget all the days he had picked her up for school or the breakfasts at a small restaurant in the morning.

As August rolled around, we began to field reports from inmates who claimed to have spoken or overheard one or more of the double-homicide suspects admit to various aspects of the crime. In a murder case such as this one, they are all taken seriously and investigated in order to determine their legitimacy and to evaluate the possibility of presenting the individuals or their statements in trial. Credibility, however, is always a concern when inmates inform on other inmates. Lies told to advance personal grudges and vengeance, or as an attempt to curry favor with prosecutors, hoping to reduce their sentences, are all influences that are common among squealing inmates.

On August 11, I, along with Agent Bowers and an investigator of the Rhode Island Department of Corrections' Special Investigation Unit, responded to the Adult Correctional Institutions in Cranston, Rhode Island to interview one such inmate.

Felix Landry, a forty-eight-year-old man, provided us with information about Sammie Sanchez that he thought would be helpful to us as well as to him. The first day that Landry entered the ACI in July, he told us that he had been placed in a cell next to the one occupied by Sanchez, who has since been transferred to a cell elsewhere in the facility. During that brief time, however, Landry said he heard Sanchez make several incriminating, if vague, statements about his involvement in the carjacking/double murder case. He also informed us that Sanchez admitted selling cocaine and heroine with an uncle. Landry further claimed that Sanchez implicated himself and his uncle in a couple of murders in New York, and that Sanchez and his father were working a scheme to "retag" cars and arrange for them to be sold overseas. Sanchez indicated that he was primarily involved in stealing the vehicles while his father altered the vehicle identification numbers.

As it turned out, Landry's information, though interesting, didn't prove to be building our case.

Several days later, I was back at the ACI. Investigators with the Special Investigation Unit of the Rhode Island Department of Corrections assisted in transporting four inmates to the Hospital Section of the Intake Service Center at the ACI. In the presence of Agent Strong and I, a registered nurse from Maxim Healthcare Services, combed and tweezed head hair samples, tweezed pubic hair samples and took saliva samples from Floyd, Anderson, Day and Burdick, successively. Tony Capraro, Floyd's attorney, was present when the samples from his client were taken. A law student working for Anderson's Attorney, Robert Mann, was also present. The hair samples were placed in individual envelopes provided by Bowers and taped shut by both Bowers and myself. The swabs were placed on individual index cards provided by Bowers, who taped the respective applicator sticks to the card identifying each inmate, then placed them into separate evidence bags.

About an hour and a half after we arrived, Bowers left the facility with the DNA samples and returned to the Providence office of the FBI, where he placed them in the Evidence Room for temporary storage. Strong made sure that he removed the index cards, with the applicator swaps tapped to them, from the evidence bags to allow them to air dry overnight. The following day, he retrieved all the samples from the Evidence Room and submitted them to the FBI Crime Laboratory in Washington.

On August 23, I appeared once more in United States District Court, Room 314 of the John O. Pastore Federal Building, to give further testimony before the Grand Jury. Once again, I was questioned by an Assistant U.S. Attorney Gerard Sullivan. The focus of my testimony that day was on key evidence that had been collected against the defendants, including the recorded confessions, the positive identifications the suspects made of each other, incriminating statements, the casino coins, condom and "rave" fliers.

On September 5, Natalie Escrow of Burrilville, Rhode Island was interviewed by Special Agent Goodwin at the Providence office of the FBI. I was present along with a social worker with the Department of Children, Youth and Families (DCYF). After being advised of the identities of the interviewing agents and the nature of the interview, Escrow provided information that we felt might have a strong bearing on the double homicide investigation.

Escrow reported that she had known Gregory Floyd since October, 1999. She said she hung out at "the wall" on Weybosset Street and originally met him there. She stated that she was a runaway and living on the streets when Floyd asked her to stay with him sometime around Thanksgiving that year. The two became boyfriend and girlfriend, occupying the second floor of an apartment together, along with several stray cats that she took in with her. This was prior to Kenneth Day relocating from North Carolina. She was gone by the time Day moved into the residence, returning only to retrieve her cats, at which time she believes she may have briefly encountered Day.

She told us that Floyd worked for a small flooring company during the day and hung out downtown most nights, but did not take her with him. When he was home, she said that he was often on a telephone chat line, a free service which operated pretty much like today's computer chat rooms. Once he found someone he liked, he would press "36" for a private conversation. He went by the name "G," and often spoke with someone named "Marjorie." Escrow said Floyd met Marjorie in person and started to hang out with her in Providence. That's when he found out her real name and that she was from Pawtucket. Escrow claimed that she got on the chat line once herself, using the name "Tika," and informed Marjorie that she was Floyd's girlfriend. When Floyd found out, he got upset and Escrow never called again.

When asked to direct her dialogue toward the knowledge she had of any crimes her former boyfriend may have committed, Escrow stated that just before Thanksgiving, Floyd and several others had stolen a car. The incident, she recalled, occurred after a drunk male was walking by "the wall" and said something to Floyd that caused them all to chase the man, who dropped his keys while he was running away. She did not know their names, but she said that after they picked up the keys and stole the man's car, they drove over to the apartment, where someone named "Champ" lived. Floyd allegedly admitted to her that he had once stolen a car and got caught. He said he had found the keys that time, then located the car and took it.

Of the four other suspects, Escrow recalled only Burdick, whom she had met at "the wall." She was also familiar with someone called, "Super Todd," a twenty-nine-year-old guy, who Floyd knew from Weybosset Street. She was acquainted with Pamela Crawford, as well. She said Crawford was known as "Pain," and described her as a good friend of Floyd, who had dated him for a long time and had been engaged to him for a short period of time. They broke up, Escrow said, when Floyd caught her cheating on him. However, they remained good friends, and Escrow believes that Floyd was trying to get back together with her at the time of the murders.

Though she broadly characterized Floyd as nice, Escrow said that he often lied to her and was quick-tempered, yelling a lot. She told us about the argument they got into on their last night together, when Floyd told her to leave. She said that he picked her up by the back of the neck and threw her onto the bed. Then he grabbed her by the arms and dragged her downstairs. A friend of hers was visiting that night and witnessed the assault, which she did not pursue with a criminal complaint. She said that Anna Brown, as she called the landlady, had a dog named "Henry" who attacked Floyd a couple other times when he tried to choke her. She had also heard that Floyd had slapped Crawford on at least one occasion.

In February, 2000, Escrow said she went back to DCYF because she was pregnant and did not want to have the baby taken away from her. She said Floyd was not the father. She added that Floyd told her he could not have children. But even after she left, she continued a relationship with Floyd by telephone, and he would occasionally come to visit her at DCYF. When she called him long distance, he would not accept the charges, but he always called her right back.

Around Valentine's Day, she said Floyd told her that he had gotten a gun for protection because some kids jumped him recently. He said he kept the gun in the red pickup truck, belonging to his boss, which he was driving at the time. Escrow said it was not registered. The gun, not the car. She believed it was a Smith & Wesson, and that he had gotten it from the "guy in the newspaper, the reporter who took the photographs." She was referring, of course, to Ira Nasberg. She said Floyd hung out with Nasberg a lot, and he trusted Floyd. Escrow said she met Nasberg a couple of times and had sat in his car once.

Escrow was asked to specifically address Floyd's behavior on June 9. She told us that on the Friday morning after the killings she had spoken to Floyd. She could not determine who had initiated the call, but she said that he did not seem any different. Escrow had been fifteen and in a foster home at the time and asked him to come over on the bus. He told her he wanted to, and that he had an SUV which he borrowed from his cousin, which she figured was Nick, though he did not name anyone. The last thing Floyd said to her was that he would come by to visit her before her foster mother got home around noon time. However, he never showed up that afternoon or called, and when she tried to call him around 2:30 PM, Day answered and told her he did not know where Floyd was.

She further advised us that she had written to Floyd once since his arrest, and that he had written her a letter back. She said she read the letter and then her foster mother took it, and she did not know where it was now. Esrow told us that, in the letter, Floyd said he did not kill the couple and that he could not prevent them from being killed. However, he wrote, he did stop the girl from being raped.

It was at about this time that Carol Shute returned to work. She had taken an extended leave of absence in June, and all the while her employers remained supportive and accommodating, allowing her to take as much the time she needed. Since then, she simply could not have done her job effectively or function in any way on a managerial level. In fact, for weeks at a time after the murders, Carol did not go anywhere or see anyone. Other than her visits to Amy's grave, which she made twice a day, she did not leave the house, remaining curled up in bed, crying, distraught and unable to move. Now, after Labor Day, she thought she was ready and tried to go back to work, putting in short days at first. As Halloween approached, however, she experienced an emotional setback and slipped back into deep depression. Unable to function, she had to take another leave of absence.

Sleeping pills became her escape, but they soon became a trap, holding her prisoner, and impeding the facilitation of the healing process. She stayed in bed for days at a time. When she began to look at the pills as more than just a way to dull the pain, but as a permanent way out, she knew she was headed down a path of self-destruction. And her family knew it, too. She didn't know where to turn, but with their help, she began taking the first steps toward counseling, which she had resisted up until then. The appeals of Jim and the rest of her family made Carol realize that she still had two teenage daughters, girls who needed a mother to be there for them, a mother who was awake and coherent.

In the fall, a deputy with the Providence County Sheriff's Department (PCSD), was interviewed at the J. Joseph Garrahy Judicial Complex, at One Dorrance Plaza, by Agent Goodwin. He had been assigned to the courthouse cell block on Monday June 12, the day the five double murder suspects were arraigned. He advised Goodwin that he knew all five of these individuals from previous appearances. Each had been placed in separate cells. However, because the cells were all in close proximity to one another, the suspects were able to carry on personal conversations. The deputy recalled it being very noisy, with 200-plus prisoners in the cell block that day. He vividly remembered Floyd, Day, Burdick, Anderson and Sanchez all screaming at one another. At one point, he had been standing by Floyd's cell when he heard Day shout to Floyd, "You better tell the truth about what happened." Floyd responded that he was not going down by himself. "You guys hyped me up to do this."

It was Halloween when the owner of the condom company was contacted by Agent Goodwin. After being advised of the identify of the interviewing agent and the nature of the interview, the owner provided information pertaining to a particular condom, which had been found both in Sanchez's car and at the scene of the double homicide. The owner informed the agent that her company supplied condoms as well as antibacterial products to nonprofit AIDS and hepatitis C outreach programs nationwide. It was learned that some of the condoms purchased were initially shipped to a warehouse in where they were then distributed to various customers. The company, the owner said, which had recently moved, bought the condoms intermittently in boxes of 1,000, so she was unable to trace them by lot number. She was, however, able to track the condoms by brand and style.

The lot consisted of assorted color condoms, Goodwin asked if it could be determined where this type was shipped by the company between March 6 and June 8, 2000. The owner provided a printout containing all the customers receiving the assorted color condoms during this time frame. She advised the FBI agent that the records are maintained by order dates, and it is possible that the condoms were ordered two weeks before they were shipped because the company ran out of condoms on occasion. She, therefore, provided a second printout which covered the period from February 15 – June 8. The owner stated further that while she did have customers in the Providence are, none of them had ordered or received any of the assorted color condoms between February and June.

However, the owner provided specific information on the Alliance Community Initiatives' Journey Outreach Program, which was close to where Jason Burgeson attended college and where there was a casino with unique tokens like the ones that were found in both Sanchez's vehicle and in Jason's SUV.

It was a rather unexpected, though useful bit of information. We figured the condoms had belonged to one of the suspects, but this worked out even better, because we did not have to burden ourselves trying to prove ownership. The condoms, like coins, belonged to Jason, and because they were found in the car with the killers, it placed them indisputably at the scene.

Chapter 26

Making a Federal Case

On November 20, after more than five months of waiting and silence, federal charges, detailed in an affidavit supporting the complaint, were filed against the five defendants in U.S. District Court in Providence. Because the charges were felonies, the complaint was merely an initial charging document, not an indictment, but it was the first formal step towards federal prosecution of the case. For the case to move forward in federal court, an indictment had to be returned by the Grand Jury within thirty days.

Special Agent Ann Goodwin submitted the carefully-drafted affidavit in support of an arrest warrant for Gregory Floyd and a criminal complaint charging him with conspiracy to commit carjacking, carjacking resulting in death, use of a firearm during a federal crime of violence and being a felon in possession of a firearm. The affidavit was further submitted in support of arrest warrants for Harry Burdick, Samuel Sanchez, Raymond Anderson and Kenneth Day and criminal complaints charging them with conspiracy to commit carjacking and carjacking resulting in death.

The affidavit listed all the facts and information she gleaned during the course of the investigation she conducted, crediting information that was shared with her from myself, the Johnston Police Department, the Providence Police Department, Special Agent Justin Bowers, Brett Mills, Forensic Examiner in the FBI Laboratory and Special Agent Wing Chau with the ATF.

In her forceful conclusion, she wrote that "there is a probable cause to believe that Floyd, Burdick, Sanchez, Anderson and Day all conspired to commit carjacking, and aided and abetted each other in that crime, which resulted in the deaths of Amy Shute and Jason Burgeson." She further concluded that there is probable cause to believe that Floyd used a firearm during this federal crime of violence and that, at the time he possessed that firearm, he was a convicted felon.

This affidavit was subscribed and sworn before U.S. Magistrate Judge Robert Lovergreen.

When the decision was announced, collective sighs of relief around Rhode Island were drowned out only by the cheers coming from the Shute and Burgeson households. They could not bring their children back, but they could gain justice for them and ensure no other families would suffer as they had because of the five men who had snuffed out Jason and Amy's lives.

Exactly four weeks later, on December 18, a federal grand jury returned a four-count indictment charging the defendants with a variety of crimes related to the carjacking and murders of Amy Shute and Jason Burgeson.

Gregory J. Floyd, the admitted triggerman, was charged with conspiracy to carjack, carjacking; death resulting of a firearm in a federal crime of violence; causing death, being a felon in possession of a firearm and using a firearm during a crime of violence.

Day, Burdick, Sanchez and Anderson were each charged with conspiracy to carjack, carjacking; death resulting and as aiding and abetting to each of these offenses.

The indictments carried forward federal charges initially brought in a complaint filed the month before in U.S. District Court and allege offenses that carry potential death sentences, namely carjacking; death resulting and using a firearm during a crime of violence. Life imprisonment, however, was the other possible sanction for the crimes.

The five defendants were scheduled for an initial appearance before U.S. Magistrate Judge Lovergreen at 2 PM.

The four-count indictment was jointly announced by Johnston Police Chief Richard Tamburini, U.S. Attorney Margaret Curran and Special Agent Charles Prouty of the FBI.

We all thought this was it. We were on our way. Half a year had gone by, and a lot had changed. The political landscape had been altered on all levels of government. A Republican was back in the White House after Texas Governor George W. Bush edged out Democratic Vice President, Al Gore, by the slimmest of margins when he took Florida by a mere 537 votes and wound up winning a majority of the all-important electoral votes, despite losing in the overall popular vote to Gore. Janet Reno was out as U.S. Attorney General and John Ashcroft was in. In our own police department, some had retired and the rest of us were working on other cases. Nevertheless, we had fought hard to bring this case against five heinous criminals to court. We believed in and worked hard to achieve the same goal. Now, it was this indictment that became the crowning achievement for everything we did. And it brought everyone together again. It was a truly joyous occasion.

The delight, however, was short-lived.

Three days before Christmas, 2000, Santa dropped two big lumps of coal in everyone's stocking when two of the accused, Burdick and Anderson, made deals with the government to spare their lives by agreeing to plead guilty. Their non-binding plea agreements required both of them to fully cooperate with the prosecution and testify against the three other defendants, who had all entered pleas of innocence. Burdick and Anderson, however, would not have to face the death penalty as part of their convictions, and the newspapers reported that both families approved of the deal. To clarify, it was not as if they were consulted. The decision was made solely by the U.S. Attorney's Office. Furthermore, the Shutes and the Burgesons did not exactly render a ringing endorsement of the agreements. They were well aware that there were no guarantees that the remaining three defendants would be condemned to die, but they believed that the testimony of Burdick and Anderson would help lead to death penalty convictions against Floyd, Day and Sanchez. They would have preferred that all five be given death sentences, but falling short of that, three out of five would suffice.

If the news of the plea deals themselves weren't bad enough, it couldn't have come at a worse time. The families had gotten through Thanksgiving a month earlier, but Christmas took every ounce of strength they could muster. For both the Shutes and the Burgesons, the Christmas after the death of Amy and Jason was the hardest to celebrate. A holiday that once had so much meaning and was so much fun was now dreaded and unwelcome. It was just too painful.

In the case of the Burgesons, they would have preferred to be anywhere but home for Christmas, which had always been Jason's favorite holiday. Even at nineteen, he would still get up early and make sure everyone else in the house was awake to open presents. In the weeks preceding December 25, he would make up silly songs and rhymes about the presents he was giving and hoping to receive. They were always good for laughs. This year, there was no laughing.

As a way to anesthetize some of the torment, they allowed their minds to trick themselves into believing that Jason was away at school, and that he would be home as soon as finals were over. On that first Christmas morning without Jason, this unreality was shattered as soon as they woke up and Jason was not there to rouse them from sleep. They did not even want to get out of bed. When they did, they got dressed in silence and went to the cold, empty cemetery to visit him.

For the Shutes, the heartache was just as acute. Typically, Carol decorated her house for every holiday, and the family would begin getting ready for Christmas right after Thanksgiving. But this Christmas, there would be no tree, no decorations and no presents. It was unanimously agreed upon. No one felt joyful.

Then, one afternoon, a few weeks before the holiday, Carol went out and returned with a gift bag in her hand.

"I bought Amy a Christmas present," she announced.

Everyone was speechless, exchanging glances with one another as if she had lost my mind.

"I didn't buy her pajamas or slippers or anything like that," Carol said. Still, no one said anything, so she just opened the bag and removed a small pin that she had purchased. It was an angel. After everyone cried, Jim located Amy's Christmas stocking and hung it. Carol ceremoniously pinned the angel to the stocking and everyone cried some more. After that, Christmas began to infiltrate their home little by little. A few days later a tree was in the house, then a couple of presents appeared, another day some decorations went up. It wasn't much, but they were all together, even Amy, if only in spirit. And a tradition was born. Now, each year, one family member buys a pin for Amy and fastens it to her stocking on Christmas Eve. They take turns, Carol, Erin, Elizabeth, Jim, Amy's grandmother and Sienna, Amy's best friend growing up. They can get any pin they choose. It is usually personal and always very emotional.

After the holidays for those awaiting trial of Amy's and Jason's killers, the New Year would pick up right where the old one left off. On January 9, 2001, Raymond Anderson admitted his guilt in federal court, officially fulfilling his part of the deal reached with the federal government. In exchange for this plea and his testimony, the Office of U.S. Attorney would not seek the death penalty against him. The U.S. Attorney Curran, however, made no guarantee as to what the final sentence recommendation would be.

Burdick, who reached the same plea agreement with the government the previous month, did not appear in federal court as scheduled. His hearing was postponed until Friday at 2:00.

On January 12, 2001, the Burgesons were in court when Burdick pleaded guilty to his part in the murders of Jason and Amy, effectively avoiding the death penalty. Now the harshest sentence he could receive was life in prison. The judge did advise the defendant that testifying against the other three men could allow for a lesser sentence, but the final sentence is up to the presiding judge, who does not have to reduce the sentence if he does not think it fit.

February 15, 2001 would have been Jason's twenty-first birthday, something that he had been looking forward to for a long time. Kellie said that her brother had been planning the celebration for at least a year. She was looking forward to sharing their first legal drink together. Not wanting to disappoint him on that special day, she went out and bought a six-pack of beer and then drove to the cemetery. She also bought a "Happy Birthday" balloon, which she tied to a beer bottle and placed on Jason's headstone.

"Happy Birthday, Jason," Kellie said, and stood alone in the cold as she drank a toast to her brother and cried. It was certainly not what Jason had in mind when he was planning his twenty-first birthday, but she wanted to make sure that they had their drink together.

On Friday, March 30, 2001, members of the Burgeson and Shute families spoke at a state senate panel to encourage its members to let voters have a say on whether the death penalty should be reinstated in Rhode Island. It seemed that last June's double-murder had greatly renewed public interest in adapting such a bill, and now the Burgesons and the Shutes wanted to take it to the next level. Despite the historical fact that the last execution in Rhode Island took place in 1845, when the brother of the first Rhode Island Governor, and the father of the second Governor (later U.S. Representative and U.S. Senator), was murdered and his killer hanged, they stood before the local legislators and presented their arguments.

Armed with the signatures of 5,000 citizens who supported federal prosecution with the possibility of the death penalty for her daughter's killers, Carol Shute addressed the panel. Choking back tears, she spoke quickly to keep from crying. "Don't vote *your* beliefs," she said. "Give your constituents the opportunity to be heard." Amy's mother carried the signed petitions with her inside a large white binder with a photograph of her murdered daughter on the cover. "These are the voices of the people of Rhode Island," the Coventry woman told Judiciary Committee members, requiring two hands to hold up the thick binder for everyone to see.

When Kellie Surdis stood at the podium, she spoke of the pain she and her family experienced since her brother's murder. "Jason and Amy were minding their own business," she said. "They killed them for no apparent reason than to watch them die. How many of us need to die before stiffer penalties are enacted?" she asked. "You can make a difference in the next case. I see no other reason for my brother's murder than maybe my presence here."

Democratic Senator Leonidas Raptakis, from Coventry, was sufficiently motivated by the tragic deaths of Amy Shute and Jason Burgenson to sponsor a capital punishment referendum bill which would give voters a real voice in the death penalty debate. The bill, which first had to be submitted for review before the General Assembly, would go to a referendum vote only if it passed there. Then, a consensus of Rhode Island citizens would decide whether or not the state should invoke capital punishment. In case of just such an event, however, state lawmakers would have numerous collateral legislative issues to consider, just one of which would be passing a measure specifying how executions would be carried out. It was a multi-edge sword, and policy makers were afraid to get too close to either side of it. That alone did not favor the passing of the Senator's bill.

With more and more states introducing legislation to repeal their death penalty provisions, and considering that Rhode Island has not carried out an execution in more than 150 years, the families and the senator had their work cut out for them, to say the least. Despite the quality of arguments in support of the death penalty through the years, opponents have successfully fought every attempt to reinstate capital punishment in Rhode Island.

"This case is all about emotion," Raptakis said. "You can't tell people they shouldn't get angry about violent crimes in their community. We have the right to seek justice."

But opponents at the meeting came prepared for a debate. First, they raised questions of morality as the reason for the continued abolition of the death penalty.

"The death penalty is an affront to God and dehumanizing to society as a whole," said a prison minister and advocate for the Rhode Island State Council of Churches.

Capital punishment adversaries also cited fairness issues raised by other states in the application of the death penalty to minorities and the poor. One example involved an Illinois Governor who had issued a moratorium on executions the previous year. He had appointed a commission to study the process after thirteen death sentences were overturned there. Nationally, the numbers of inmates who are removed from death row due to their sentences being reversed or concerns about evidence are staggering.

Of course, the death penalty's arguable ineffectiveness as a deterrent and the monetary burden of capital case proceedings were also mentioned. These contentions, however, generally carry little validity among death penalty supporters. The last thing a victim of violent crime ever wants to hear is that they are being denied justice because of the fiscal burdens of prosecution.

In a bid that showed an immensely more likely potential for success, the Coventry Senator Raptakis also pushed a state bill that would raise from twenty to thirty-five years the minimum sentence for murderers who get life with the possibility of parole.

"Life sentences up to twenty years make a mockery of the courts," the Senator said.

The victims' families testified in support of both bills, neither of which was acted upon by the committee.

"It is very hard for me to be here," Mrs. Shute said after the hearing. "The people speaking against the death penalty are not victims of the heinous crimes. It's not about vengeance; it's about justice."

On April 17, 2001, Constance Fisher, an examiner in the DNA Analysis Unit of the FBI Laboratory in Washington, D.C. forwarded her findings to Agent Goodwin in Providence.

The specimen samples derived from clothing items confiscated from the five suspects in June 2000, as well as DNA markers obtained from hair and saliva samples taken from them in August 2000, all established a clear physical link of their presence at the crime scene and inside the vehicles used in carjacking-murders.

All processed DNA from the specimens examined were delivered to Goodwin, along with the submitted evidence items themselves, for use as prosecutorial exhibits in the federal court proceedings. In case further testing became necessary, Fisher recommended that the processed DNA samples be refrigerated, or frozen, and isolated from evidence that had not been examined.

On April 26, 2001, the Rhode Island General Treasurer Paul Tavares, held a Crime Victim Compensation Conference in commemoration of National Crime Victims' Rights Week. More than 100 victim advocates, policy-makers, law enforcement officials and members of the court gathered at the Holiday Inn in downtown Providence to discuss the critical improvements recently made to the once-ailing program that the treasurer inherited in 1999. In particular, the group focused on efforts to outreach Rhode Island victims to ensure they are fully aware of the benefits of this program, which provides financial assistance to Rhode Island victims in the aftermath of violent crime.

Carol Shute, who had received the New Survivor Benefit, was in attendance to discuss how improvements to the program helped her and her family in a time of need. In fact, the Shutes were one of the first recipients of the new Burial Benefit, added as a result of the revamping of the program, which help survivors with funeral and burial costs.

Also on hand was the Hospital Association of Rhode Island (HARI) President, who received an award for the organization. The award recognized HARI's efforts on behalf of victims by agreeing to reduce the amount of money that HARI's eleven hospitals were owed by the program. The negotiated agreement reduced the debt to the hospitals by almost half and allowed the program to pay eighty victims who had waited five to ten years for payment.

On June 4, 2001, Assistant United States Attorney, Gerard Sullivan, received a letter in the mail from Wade Carlson, a thirty-nine year old inmate at the Donald W. Wyatt Detention Center in Central Falls, Rhode Island. Carlson had enclosed a copy of a handwritten note, which he had written on May 28, sending the original to the *Providence Journal*. It included detailed statements allegedly made by a fellow inmate, Raymond Anderson, relating to the murders of Jason Burgeson and Amy Shute. Most interesting to federal prosecutors was the allegation that Anderson admitted to lying to federal authorities in order to receive a lighter sentence.

Carlson, incarcerated and awaiting sentencing on federal bank robbery charges had been housed in the same unit with both Burdick and Anderson, the two defendants who had agreed to testify against the other three co-defendants in the double homicide trial. They have both since been transferred to another holding facility. Carlson wrote in his letter that while Burdick had exhibited some remorse for the killings, Anderson had not, but had been boasting that he was going to receive the least amount of time of them all. Carlson purportedly heard Anderson laughing as he said, 'I've been lying my ass off' to federal authorities and, 'them other suckers can go and get the death penalty.'

The jailhouse snitch also informed that Anderson vividly described how, after discussing among them whether or not to rape Amy, he made the couple get out of the vehicle and kneel down before they were shot to death while begging for their lives. 'If it wasn't for Harry (Burdick), we would have raped that bitch like I wanted,' was the quote Carlson used.

"How Assistant United States Attorney Sullivan," Carlson wrote, "can use the testimony of, let alone ask for a lesser sentence for, someone as unremorseful as Anderson is beyond me. Sullivan should withdraw the deal he's made and let Anderson stand trial with the rest. To do otherwise would be to make a mockery out of our system of justice."

It was doubtful that the thirty-nine-year-old bank robber, who had a history of heroin, cocaine and marijuana abuse, was exercising good citizenship rather than grinding a personal ax he had with Anderson when he made these supposed observations known to authorities. Also, Carlson's claims could have been greatly exaggerated or completely fabricated so that he might put himself into a position to barter with prosecutors for a reduction of his own sentence, or for some kind of prison perk altogether. However, even though he would not be considered a very credible witness and would likely never be called to testify, once the allegations were made public, Carlson knew that prosecutors would have to at least look into them. That's why he sent the same letter to the newspaper.

Two days later, Carlson got his interview. I sat in with Assistant U.S. Attorney Sullivan, Special Agent Goodwin and Special Assistant Attorney General Neronha when they questioned the detainee. Carlson explained that he had been in the Segregation Unit (SEG) of the facility for four months, during which time Anderson and Burdick had also been placed there. Since the SEG was small, only eight cells, Anderson and Burdick were able to communicate freely. The murder suspects, according to Carlson, talked often about the crime. Carlson stated that there was some friction between the two, with Anderson blaming Burdick for their situation. And while their individual accounts of the carjacking-murders were consistent, Anderson alone showed no remorse, even bragging about what he did. Carlson further stated that Anderson laughed when he told Burdick how he had been lying to get a lighter sentence, though he did not reveal exactly what it was he had lied about. Carlson admitted that this could just have been 'jail talk' by Anderson to cover up the fact that he was cooperating with authorities.

Finally, Carlson insisted that he had written the letter to the newspaper, because he was disgusted by Anderson's attitude, and he also admitted that in the past he had sent letters to other newspapers from jail when he got upset about something.

Sullivan advised Carlson that it was required that they provide a copy of the letter to the defense, and that he could be asked to testify by either side at trial. Carlson then asked Sullivan if the U.S. Attorney's Office could help him if he did testify.

"No," Sullivan replied.

On June 9, 2001, friends and family of Amy and Jason marked the first anniversary of their deaths. The Shutes quietly reviewed their memories as they observed that date of Amy's passing while Jason's immediate family honored him by spending the day together, later visiting his grave, which they found covered with flowers and other gifts.

That same week, the winners of the first annual Jason Burgeson Memorial Scholarship Awards were announced, with scholarships presented to two graduates of Apponequet Regional High School. All those qualifiers expressed interest in pursuing drama, communications or journalism, which were just a few of Jason's interests. Perry Medina and Casey Fleming were the first recipients of the award. Fleming announced plans to attend Boston University, while Medina decided on Emmanuel College, also located in Boston. Both were to study communications.

Chapter 27

Devil's Advocate

As summer arrived, the victims' families were expecting a final decision to come out of Washington, D.C. any day. However, there was still no definite time frame in place as the U.S. Attorney General Office continued to review the case to decide if they would pursue the death penalty against Floyd, Sanchez and Day, the three defendants who had not already signed plea agreements with the government.

Then, on July 17, 2001, Sanchez, who had maintained his innocence the longest, officially pled guilty to the federal charges pending against him. Like Anderson and Burdick before him, he managed to sidestep the death penalty. Sanchez, however, was not asked to cooperate. Needless to say, no one was happy with this latest development, except Sanchez himself. It was disappointing and disheartening to the friends and family of Amy and Jason, who were beginning to wonder whose side the U.S. Attorneys were working for. The Shutes and Burgesons wanted answers. They flooded every state and federal law enforcement office with phone calls, demanding to know why this deal had been made. They were categorically ignored. They also came to me, but I had no answers for them. I was as surprised as anyone.

Now, three of the murderers had entered guilty pleas which the government accepted, leaving only Day and Floyd who still faced prosecution and possible death sentences.

On August 24, Gregory Floyd dangled a guilty plea in front of federal prosecutors. Floyd informed the prosecution through his lawyer that he would be willing to plead out on all charges against him IF, AND ONLY IF, he did have to pay the ultimate price for his crimes. To the horror of the Shutes and the Burgesons, they learned that Unites States Attorney for Rhode Island, Curran, had recommended accepting that plea bargain and giving Floyd a federal discount.

Now, under regulations that the newly appointed U. S. Attorney General, John Ashcroft, recently put into place, it was entirely up to him to decide to accept or reject the deal that Floyd put on the table. With regard to the other defendant, Kenneth Day, now twenty-three, Ashcroft also had to consider whether or not to authorize Curran to pursue the death penalty against him.

Kellie and her husband were on vacation in Bar Harbor, Maine, celebrating their second wedding anniversary when word about Floyd's agreement became known. The couple spent the day hiking and taking in the natural beauty of Arcadia National Park. When they returned to the B&B where they were staying, there found a note taped to the door. It said simply; "Kellie, call your mother." There was no phone or television in their room.

Kellie's heart sank instantly and a familiar dread washed over her. She knew her mother would not have called her if it wasn't an emergency. With a heavy heart, she called home, expecting the worst. She couldn't even allow herself to be relieved when she learned of Floyd's offer and Curran's recommendation to accept it. She was thoroughly disgusted and saddened by the news. More so than any of the others, Floyd was the one she wanted to see put to death. He had pulled the trigger, ending the lives of her brother and Amy Shute.

When Kellie got off the phone with her family, she cried and cried. She could not help but recall the video which her brother had made on her wedding day exactly two years before. When the camera found him, he lifted the sunglasses he was wearing to the top of his head and peered into the lens. His eyes seemed to be looking directly at his sister and her new husband as he said, "Kellie and Nick, I wish you a lifetime of happiness."

A little while later, Kellie turned to her husband and said, "Nick, we've been putting our whole life on hold, not starting a family, because I did not want to be pregnant during the trials. But if they make a deal with him, they'll make deals with everyone. So when we get back, why don't we try to start a family?"

Unbeknownst to them, she was already pregnant when they got home from the trip.

Already outraged by Sanchez's plea a couple weeks prior, the Burgesons and the Shutes used their current media celebrity to amplify their displeasure with the judicial system. They had seen enough plea agreements, and demanded that the federal government reject Floyd's proposal and put the alleged shooter to death instead.

Kellie Surdis told news reporters, "Jason and Amy begged for their lives, and they were killed anyway. It's not like these are innocent people here. They are pleading GUILTY and getting lesser sentences for that."

"My son pleaded for his life," Nadine Burgeson said, "and he got a bullet. My son's dead. Amy Shute is dead. This is just insane. The whole justice system doesn't make sense to me."

"Gregory Floyd's a coward," Kellie added. "Why, when he's faced with the same fate (as Jason and Amy) should we even listen to what he has to say? He should be willing to face the same fate."

It was easy to understand the families' frustration and anger, and in anticipation of Ashcroft's backing of U.S. Attorney Curran, it was a tense time for everyone.

Nadine Burgeson said she did not agree with prosecutors accepting the first two plea offers, but added, "You have to start somewhere. The plea with Sanchez, I don't think ever should have happened. They don't tell us what they're going to do. I've sent letters to Ashcroft; I've sent letters to the President of the United States. I don't know what more I can do."

"We wanted zero agreements," Kellie said. "We're in a powerless position. By law, they have to listen, but I don't think they heard us."

Amy's grandmother said her granddaughter never had the same chance to negotiate her life. "I would have liked to see all five of them get the death penalty," she said. "It just isn't fair."

Jim Colvin felt that federal prosecutors were botching the case. "We've been quiet for too long," he said. "We're definitely dissatisfied."

Floyd's attorney, who earlier in the week confirmed that the offer was made, tried to pacify the discontented by perpetuating the harshness of the proposed judgment. Unlike the same verdict when handed down by the state court, he said, "a federal sentence of life without parole really means life without parole." But nobody was buying any of it. The families didn't want to see these last two young men in prison at all. They wanted them put to death for what they did.

Just as Sanchez had encouraged Floyd to pull the trigger at about 2:30 AM on June 9, 2000, the families of the victims encouraged the government to pull the trigger on Floyd. To paraphrase some of Sanchez's own words which he used that morning, the Burgesons and Shutes may certainly have been thinking, *What's taking so long? Give me the intravenous mixture of compounds designed to induce rapid unconsciousness followed by death through paralysis of respiratory muscles and/or by inducing cardiac hyperpolarization, and I'll administer it.*

Just when things could not seem to get any worse, the United States became the victim of a terrorist attack that shocked the world. Thousands of innocent people were killed on 9/11, while the murderers of Jason and Amy remained alive. For the Burgesons and Shutes, the national tragedy stretched their anguish to the limit.

Then, on September 26, the inevitable happened and the United States Attorney General, John Ashcroft, accepted Floyd's offer. The admitted double murderer agreed to plead guilty to all charges against him and the Federal Government agreed to imprison him for the rest of his life with no possibility of parole. He would not be put to death, but he would die in prison, most likely of natural causes. No other promises were made to Floyd or asked of him, and at that time he had made no indication that he would be interesting in testifying against Day, now the only one of the five double-murderers who had not pled guilty.

Day, it seemed, was content to take his chances in court before a jury of his peers, electing to go to trial for no other reason just as he had nothing to lose. He would be tried for conspiracy as well as aiding and abetting a car-jacking - death resulting, the latter of which is statutorily punishable by up to life imprisonment or by death. However, because of the plea agreements with the other four co-conspirators, the U.S. was not authorized to seek the death penalty against Day. Therefore, life imprisonment became the maximum allowable sentence Day could receive. That's just the way it was. And Day seemed to revel in this. He enjoyed putting the families through hell, because he's the devil, as far as I'm concerned. But Ashcroft was blamed by the Shutes and the Burgesons for the government's inability to put any of the five defendants to death for the murders of their children.

The following week, former Rhode Island Attorney General, Jeffrey Pine, publicly expressed his discouragement over the plea agreement that U.S. Attorneys made with Gregory Floyd. Pine, now in private practice with a law firm in Providence, perceived it to be a serious oversight that no rationale explanation was ever offered in support of the decision not to recommend the death penalty against the double murderer. He also faulted the government for not providing adequate notice to the families and for not permitting their input to have more of an influence in the decision-making process. However, his sharpest criticism was reserved for the Department of Justice for their decision not to comment on the developments in the case, especially after the news of the plea became public. The Justice Department refused to even say whether U.S. Attorney Margaret Curran had sought the death penalty and her bid was rejected, or if she had even argued in favor of prosecuting the case in that manner. Pine could not fathom why the public would not have been made privy to that information. The families, he said, had a right to be outraged.

While there was no federal Victims Rights Amendment at the time that would provide victims with absolute rights in federal court cases such as this one, Pine had testified in Washington during Congressional hearings of just such a measure and supported the initiation of one wholeheartedly. However, Congress, as Pine pointed out, had yet to act on the issue. "In the meantime," he said, "the victims of violent crime in the federal court system do not have the same rights and privileges that they enjoy in state court." Rhode Island has had a Victims Rights Amendment since the mid 1980's, and it reads, in part; "A victim of crime shall, as a matter of right, be treated by agents of the state with dignity, respect and sensitivity during all phases of the criminal justice process."

The lack of explanation by the U.S. Attorney's Office was so troubling to the former Rhode Island Attorney General that he lashed out at Curran on behalf of the exasperated families. "Although U.S. Attorneys are not elected," he said, "there is a responsibility to be accountable to the public on high profile cases coming out of that office, and the stonewall of silence and limited comment by both Ms. Curran and her spokesman was not a good reflection on that office. Don't we have a right to know her position on such a serious case?"

Beyond that, Pine offered, continuing his diatribe, it was unfortunate that such a cold-blooded, brutal, execution-style killing would not be put before a jury as a possible death penalty case.

"Ultimately," he said, "a jury, judge and appellate courts would have to approve such a sentence before it could be imposed, but I believe the federal prosecutors should have pushed hard for it in this case. The families had wanted to see justice done by a jury after a strong prosecution, and they were prepared to accept the result. Now, they will never know what that result would have been."

On November 8, 2001, the U.S. Government sat down with Floyd for the first time to talk about the possibility of him testifying in the upcoming trial of Kenneth Day, approximately two months away. Floyd had recently spoken to his attorney, James McCormick, whom he advised that he was considering testifying against Day. The news of Floyd voluntarily consenting to speak to prosecutors about the June 2000 carjacking-murders was more than a little surprising to both sides.

McCormick immediately contacted Assistant U.S. Attorney Sullivan, and a meeting was arranged. Floyd was interviewed at the Adult Correctional Institution Intake Services Center in Cranston, where he was being held. Besides McCormick and Sullivan, Special Agent Goodwin and I were also present.

Sullivan asked Floyd if he was willing to discuss the events of June 8 - 9, 2000, and the convicted double murderer affirmed this to be his intention.

The Assistant U.S. Attorney cautioned him that he would receive no benefit for any information he provided. Floyd acknowledged that he understood, and the first question he was asked was why he was offering the prosecution his unsolicited cooperation at that time. The triggerman in Amy and Jason's murders stated that he began thinking about "coming clean" soon after he offered to plead guilty in September, and he provided two primary motivations for wanting to go on the stand now to talk about it. The first reason, he said, was for self-respect. What he may have meant by this was confessing for the purpose of atonement, a need compelling him to do what he thought was right. The second purpose he mentioned was providing relief to the families from some of their pain, which he thought could be achieved by telling them what really happened on June 9, 2000.

Floyd reiterated that the gun used in the killings belonged to him. He insisted that he did not steal the gun, but bought it from Ira Nasberg. Then, he recounted the events of that night and early morning. His statement concluded with his account of his looking for someone inside Traveler's Aid while Burdick waited outside in the SUV around 4:00 AM.

At this point, Floyd's attorney announced that he had to leave for a court appearance on another matter. Floyd advised that he would be able to provide additional details at a later date.

During this time, I took on another professional task, which in hindsight, I should have put off for the time being. As if my life wasn't complicated enough, I enrolled in a master's program at Bryant University. I don't know if it was ambition or just another diversion I needed to keep me from focusing on problems in my personal life.

Day's trial, which was expected to begin by mid-January, 2002, was postponed about a month. Jury selection finally began on Thursday, February 11, and concluded on Valentine's Day. The following morning, what would have been Jason's 22nd birthday, the federal trial against Kenneth Day in the carjacking/murders of Amy Shute and Jason Burgeson got underway.

The charges against Day included Conspiracy to Carjack, Carjacking - Death Resulting and as Aiding and Abetting to each of the preceding offenses.

From the beginning, Day's attorney made no objection to the admissibility and accuracy of the forensic testing or the results, due to the fact that a vast majority of it also implicated Floyd, Burdick, Anderson and Sanchez, all of whom had pled guilty to the same crimes, and that all this evidence was only relevant to establish their roles and participation in this conspiracy. As a result, Day's counsel agreed that this evidence could be admitted through the hearsay testimony of FBI agents without formal legal foundation or chain of custody testimony.

I can say this, we were all confident, the prosecutors included, that this was practically a slam dunk. With all the evidence and corroborative witness testimony, including the four other pleas and convictions, if it wasn't a slam dunk, it was the closest thing you could get to one.

We weren't anticipating any surprises. Day's trial attorney had informed the government that he did not intend to rely on any insanity or diminished capacity defenses. That would have been the only wild card, because you never know how a jury is going to respond to testimony from psychiatric and other medical professionals.

Disregarding Count II of the Redacted Indictment, Carjacking - Death Resulting, for the moment, Day was charged in Count I with conspiracy to commit carjacking. To prove conspiracy, the government needs to first prove that the agreement specified in the indictment existed between at least two people. Such an agreement can be spoken or unspoken. The United States must then prove that Day shared a general understanding of the crime, although not all the details. These facts must also establish that Day willfully joined in the conspiracy. Willfully, meaning that he did so voluntarily and intelligently. That is to say, with a bad purpose, either to disobey or in disregard of the law and not through ignorance, accident or mistake. Mere presence at a crime scene is not sufficient. The United States, then, must show two types of intent: an intent to agree and an intent to commit the underlying crime of carjacking, though not necessarily the two deaths. It was only necessary to show that the deaths resulted from the carjacking.

The United States must furthermore show that one of the co-conspirators committed at least one overt act in furtherance of the conspiracy. The government did not need to prove that Day personally committed the act or even knew that the act had been committed.

On the aiding and abetting charge, the United States needed to show that Day intentionally helped someone else commit the crime. To do this, the government had to first prove that Floyd committed all of the elements of carjacking which resulted in the deaths of the victims. The prosecution must then demonstrate that Day willfully associated himself in some way with the carjacking and participated in it as something he wished to bring about. They did not need to show that Day performed the underlying criminal acts, or was even present when they were performed, or that he was even aware of all of the detail. However, mere presence was not enough, either.

This was a claim that prosecutors anticipated being made by Day's attorney in his defense; that he was "merely present." The other legal and evidentiary issues the defense was likely to challenge were all considered. Even if the defense argued that Day generally conspired to commit the robbery, but lacked the specific intent to steal a car or cause death or serious bodily injury, it could still be proven that Day was liable for these crimes. The defense was likely to claim that at the time Jason's vehicle was taken by Floyd and Burdick, Day was waiting in Sanchez's car, expecting that the couple would only be robbed. Of the events that ensued, he was merely present.

Notwithstanding that it was Floyd who actually stole the SUV and shot the victims, Day could still be convicted of carjacking, and would be equally responsible for the deaths that resulted. The prosecution was set to advance two alternative theories to show Day's liability as a co-conspirator. To convict Day of carjacking under the aiding and abetting theory may have been the most applicable. Accordingly, the Unites States had to prove that Floyd, as the principal, committed the act of carjacking, and secondly, that Day became "associated with Floyd's endeavor and took part in it, intending to ensure its success." The First Circuit Court has held that the second element requires a specific showing of knowledge and intent that "the defendant consciously shared that principal's knowledge of the underlying criminal act, and intended to help the principal." The first element was easily satisfied, since Floyd had already pled guilty to carjacking - death resulting. The confession of Burdick and Anderson could all be used to further establish Floyd's role as the principle in the crime.

With regard to the second element, there was ample evidence available to show Day's awareness that Floyd, as the principal, committed all the elements of the crime of carjacking and had the requisite intent. There was also sufficient evidence to support a claim that even before Floyd took the SUV,

Day had knowingly associated himself with a criminal conspiracy and actively participated in it. Floyd's testimony that Day was the first person that night who suggested that they rob someone, the drug buyer, and that Day encouraged Floyd to bring the gun, would go a long way to show Day's liability. The defendant's own videotaped confession in which he admitted that he and his co-conspirators were out that night looking "to get somebody," was in itself damning. The government had other evidence prepared to show that Day was aware that an attempt to steal the van was going to be made and that he was part of a group that was waiting nearby to provide a means of escape or to further assist in a criminal activity undertaken by Floyd and Burdick.

Even if Day was somehow able to convince a jury that he had no knowledge of Floyd's intent to carjack the victims until after Floyd had stolen the SUV, prosecutors could, nonetheless, establish Day's knowing participation because the carjacking was not complete when Floyd took the vehicle. Carjacking is a continuous offense. It begins at the time the motor vehicle is taken from the control of the victims with the requisite intent, and is not complete until the victims have been separated from it physically. The carjacking, in this case, thus began in Providence when Floyd took control of the van at gunpoint, and ended in Johnston when the victims were executed and thereby separated from their motor vehicle, which was subsequently driven away by Floyd. It would be argued that even if Day had only initially intended to commit a garden variety robbery, and was not a participant in the carjacking plot until he saw Floyd driving the SUV with the victims inside, he certainly was, thereafter, joining in the conspiracy and assisting Floyd with full knowledge in an on-going carjacking. Testimony from the co-conspirators was available to show that Day was a non-protesting passenger in Sanchez's car and later as a member of the group that participated with them in discussions about raping Amy and murdering Amy and Jason. The testimony of Floyd, Burdick and Anderson would also show that Day acted of his own free will, remaining an non-protesting member of the murderous group by his actions, which included searching the SUV for valuables and riding on the vehicle's bumper while it was transporting the victims from one section of the golf course to another, where the victims were eventually murdered.

Even after he was dropped off at home afterward, Day never made any attempt to contact the police and tell the authorities what had happened. Not to mention, he was apprehended just a few feet from the murder weapon.

It was easy to see why we were all hopeful that Day would be handed a just sentence that so many people, not just the victims' families, felt he deserved – death.

Chapter 28

Shocking Decision

O n the very first day of testimony, jurors were shown graphic photos of the crime scene and the prosecution called several witnesses, including friends and family of Jason and Amy. Assistant U.S. Attorney Sullivan painted the picture of two college students who were home for the summer, enjoying carefree days when they were abducted and brutally murdered. Day's lawyer, in his opening statement, did not deny that his client was present that night, but asserted that Day was not involved in the actual killings. The prosecution answered by establishing that Floyd would not have taken the gun if Day had not insisted he bring it along with them that night.

When court resumed on Tuesday, February 19, 2002, several police officers, as well as the medical examiner, were called to testify. Among these was patrolman John Lough, who was one of the last people to see Amy and Jason alive. He told jurors that he had seen them standing near Jason's SUV in the early hours of June 9th, 2000, and that he later saw the same vehicle being driven by a young male. He said he did not pull the car over because the scene was not unusual, as many clubs were letting out at the time, and he did not know that Jason and Amy were in the back seat.

A forensic examiner for the FBI's crime laboratory in Washington, DC testified next. Among the facts he reported was that the bullet fragments taken from the bodies of Jason and Amy matched exactly the markings from the gun found by investigators in Day's bedroom.

Over the course of the next few days, Gregory Floyd found himself on the witness stand testifying against Day, his former roommate and "brother," whom he had not initially named in connection with the crime because he wanted to protect him. He proceeded to describe in detail how the night of June 8 progressed, from planning to play pool with his friend, to having several robbery attempts foiled, to abducting and murdering two innocent victims in the early hours of June 9. He explained how he and the others looked for targets who appeared to have money, and that they were about to give up when Day shouted, "Ooh, ooh, look!" as they drove past Amy and Jason. Floyd claimed that once they arrived at the golf course, Day told him to kill Amy and Jason, because they had seen his face.

The answers to some of the questions that followed were listened to very closely by the families of Amy and Jason. A major source of their pain stemmed from the complete lack of motive by the killers. More than anything, they wanted to know the actual reason why their loved ones had been taken from them. It could not have been for eighteen dollars, or for a joyride. These reasons did not make any sense. The pain this caused them was precisely what Floyd said he wanted to help relieve by testifying. They were all hoping that he might shed some light on this mystery for them. What they heard from him, however, was even more disconcerting and additionally tormenting.

When the federal prosecutor asked Floyd why Amy and Jason were abducted after they had surrendered all their money and the SUV, he responded, "I have no idea. Soon as he (Burdick) told Amy to get in — it was nothing planned about it. Everything just jumped off."

The spontaneous kidnapping theory was not working in the prosecution's favor either. They needed to show intent and conspiratorial action.

"No one knew what the hell they were doing," Floyd said of their drive prior to Sanchez leading them to the golf course.

To try to get the direct examination back on the right track, Sullivan asked Floyd, "When did you decide, when did you form the intent to kill Amy and Jason?"

"I can't say that I really did," Floyd responded. "It just happened."

"It wasn't an accident, was it?"

"No."

"You pulled the trigger three times, didn't you?"

"I did."

"After you pulled the trigger the first time and saw what effect that had, you pulled it two more times, did you not?

"I didn't really watch the effect. I just pulled the trigger."

Cummings asked Floyd directly, "Why did you do it?"

"I can't answer that."

"Was it to be a man in front of your friends?"

"It was — I guess you could say it was something like that, I guess. I don't know."

Upon cross-examination, Day's defense attorney, Joseph DeCaporale, posed a similar question to Floyd, and then went in for the kill, putting the witness immediately on the defensive. "What did you feel at the moment when you were standing over them and you pulled that trigger three times? Tell us what you felt."

"I can't say what I felt."

"Were you proud?"

"What's to be proud of?"

"Were you happy? Did you feel *any* emotion at all? Did you?"

"I can't say for sure."

The defense attorney asked to approach the witness and then presented Floyd with a photograph taken of the two victims at the murder scene. "Have you ever seen that picture before?"

"Yes."

"What does it represent?"

"It's the two victims."

"That's how you left those two victims in that construction site on the night of this murder, correct?"

"That's what the picture says, yes."

"And how do you feel about that?"

"I didn't stick around to see what happened."

"You didn't stick around to see what happened," DeCaporale repeated. "Didn't care, did you? Did you?"

Floyd said that he recalled feeling only numb when he shot Amy and Jason, and nothing else. No discernible explanation of why he shot the two young people could be garnered from his entire testimony.

DeCoparle attempted to further dismantle Floyd's credibility by quoting from the triggerman's earlier statements taken during various interviews with law enforcement agencies over the course of the last year and half. The line of questioning was intended to portray him as a self-serving, opportunistic liar who could not be trusted.

Floyd admitted that he gave false information at first because he did not want to be blamed for the shootings, and said he did not mention Day's participation in his original statements because he was trying to protect Day. He stated that he wanted to tell the truth now so that justice could be served and the families could begin healing.

Upon re-direct, it was further stressed by the prosecution that Floyd's testimony was entirely voluntarily, and that he had nothing to gain by testifying. Sullivan reiterated that Floyd had already pled guilty and had received life imprisonment without the possibility of parole, a sentence that he would serve whether or not he appeared as a witness in the criminal trial of Kenneth Day. Floyd confirmed that prosecutors made no promises or otherwise alluded that his sentence would be reduced or commuted to any degree.

"And nobody's going to do anything for you, right?" Sullivan asked.

"Correct."

"So why are you testifying now?"

"Well, I hope to get some kind of self-respect out of this. Possibly if it helps the family heal."

On re-cross, DeCaporale confronted Floyd about his admission of guilt, which could have cost him his life if he had not entered into an plea agreement with the government.

"You weren't afraid to die, were you?" the defense attorney asked.

"Was I afraid to die?" Floyd responded. "What kind of a question is that?"

"It's a question. Answer it. Were you afraid to die?"

"Of course I was."

"Do you think Amy was afraid to die?"

"Yes."

"Do you think Jason was afraid to die?"

"Yes."

"But you weren't afraid to blow their brains out, were you? Were you?"

Montgomery's challenge of Floyd's integrity as a witness was an effective one, but the prosecution wasn't hinging its whole case against Day on Floyd's testimony. There was plenty of evidence to support the charges and win the verdict that everyone wanted.

We thought.

On Friday, February 22, 2002, Raymond Anderson, who had been promised by federal prosecutors that he would be given consideration if he testified, unexpectedly refused to be sworn in when he was put on the witness stand. This sudden turn of events prompted the judge to call for a recess. Anderson was taken down to a holding cell inside the courthouse, and a short time later he was visited by Assistant U.S. Attorney Sullivan, Agent Goodwin and me. Anderson's attorney, Robert Mann, was also present. Anderson was asked why he suddenly decided not to cooperate. He did not provide a reason, but stated that he had intended to testify up until two days ago. When asked if this was because he had not told the truth in his interviews with the government, Anderson replied that he had not lied, and that everything he said was true. He confided that he had not been threatened or coerced by anyone, and that it had nothing to do with Kenneth Day, for whom he felt no loyalty. Anderson simply stated that he was no longer sure testifying was the right thing to do.

The impact of this decision on his plea agreement was discussed, and Anderson stated he understood that he would receive no benefit from the government if he did not testify. No additional promises were made to Anderson to solicit his testimony. Sullivan advised Anderson that he would be treated fairly regardless of his decision.

At that time, Robert Mann asked to speak with his client alone. Sullivan, Goodwin and I exited the room to accommodate the attorney's request.

When it was just the two of them, Mann laid it on the line, informing Anderson that if he did not testify he would not be given credit, and since he had already pled guilty, he would be sentenced to life without parole like the others. It took several minutes, but Mann finally convinced Anderson and we were all asked to return.

Anderson told us that he would testify, after all, and that he had acted the way he did because he was scared. Anderson further stated that he had never testified before, and when he got to court that day he was just not sure if he was doing the right thing. However, when he was placed back on the stand that Friday afternoon, he did cooperate, his testimony continuing the following Monday. He told the court everything he knew. He claimed that Day had invited him out on the night of June 8th with the understanding that they were going to rob someone.

Day's lawyer used similar tactics against Anderson as he did with Floyd, pointing out inconsistencies in Anderson's previous statements to paint him as a man who was simply trying to avoid the death penalty by saying anything.

The following day, February 26, 2002, Judge Ronald Lageux shocked the entire courtroom.

With the jury not present, Lageux turned to Day's lawyer and asked, "Mr. DeCaporale, do you have a motion to dismiss?"

The defense counselor was taken by complete surprise, and he hesitated initially, prompting the judge to ask him the question a second time. When DeCaporale realized that he was being baited, he quickly stood up and addressed the bench.

DeCaporale had just dropped a fat worm on a hook in front of a hungry fish. DeCaporale began throwing out every possible motion for dismissal that he could think of. When Lageux heard what he was looking for, he made his ruling. In a nutshell, he scolded the state for its attempt to use the federal government to prosecute its case. He explained that in state court, this crime would meet murder, kidnapping and robbery, but because this was federal court, prosecutors needed to show intent by the suspect to commit these crimes. Citing the recent judgment made by the 1st Circuit Court of Appeals in Boston involving drug dealers who killed a woman during a carjacking, Judge Lageux ruled that the prosecution did not prove intent on Kenneth Day's part at the time of the carjacking to kill or impose severe bodily harm upon Amy and Jason. Because of this, it was Pearson's decision to dismiss all federal charges against Day outright.

When he made this announcement, everyone's jaw just dropped to the floor at once. There was no sound at all for a moment or two, but as the implication of the judgment sank in deeper, muffled sobs began to grow.

I couldn't believe it.

Day was free.

We were in trouble.

The judge gave no indication that he was considering dismissal. Looking at Sullivan, I saw the same amazed look on everyone's face.

Day had an altogether different look in his eyes as he grinned in triumph. He figured he beat the rap. I thought I saw him laughing. I had to turn away.

When the jurors were called back in, they saw all the sad faces, heard the weeping and waited for the judge to inform them of his decision, which stunned them, as well. Lageux left observers shaking their heads when he said it was his hope that Day would be prosecuted for the murders of Amy Shute and Jason Burgeson in state court.

Family members were overwhelmed with a broad-range of emotions, from numb to furious. Carol Shute was so upset she barely made it out of the courtroom before she became sick to her stomach, vomiting into a waste basket in the hall. The devastation was complete and total.

What made it even more startling for me, as well as the other investigators and prosecutors, was that we were all so confident that the necessary intent *had* been established. The conviction was just supposed to be a matter of going through the proper procedure. We had been riding high up until that point. The four other accomplices had pled out already, and we were looking at the trial as a formality, with Day simply taking everyone with him on one final joyride. State court or federal court, sooner or later, he would be going away for a long time. Either way, we expected Day to be sentenced to life imprisonment, with the only difference being that federal guidelines stipulated no possibility of parole. Day really did have nothing to lose, and no chance of wiggling out of this.

At least, that's what we thought.

Afterward, we all went back to Sullivan's office. Everyone was downcast. Some sat quietly brooding while others cried or fumed, unleashing angry, profanity-laced tirades. I felt like I had let the families down, and I'm sure the others felt the same way. But we really couldn't afford to sit around too long feeling sorry for ourselves. We had to pick ourselves up and move forward. So we gathered to lick our wounds and come up with a new game plan.

The state immediately vowed to charge Day as soon as possible for a variety of crimes related to, and including, the murders of Amy Shute and Jason Burgeson. That trial, however, would not likely start for at least two years, during which time the families will have to relive the horror all over again. It would be the same trial, as well, except now state instead of federal statutes would apply. Another change would be the addition of U.S. Attorney, Laura Pisaturo, to the prosecution team. She would take the place of Mary Rogers, and work alongside Gerard Sullivan, both of whom would stay on to assist state attorneys in the prosecution of Kenneth Day for murder by the state of Rhode Island.

The problem was this: because we never indicted Day on the state murder charges, instead dismissing them without prejudice so that we could pursue them in a federal venue, we would first have to reinstate those charges. In the mean time, we were fortunate that Day had been convicted on unrelated robbery charges, so he would remain in jail until we had time to regroup and indict him on the state murder charges. It's not double jeopardy, because two separate courts were involved.

What may not be fully understood by some people is that the federal system does not prosecute murder cases, per se. The individual state where a homicide occurs will most likely prosecute the crime. There is no federal murder statute, at least not murder of civilians who are not government employees. Only homicides that involve some kind of national interest or specific circumstances are considered. Car jacking - death resulting was the federal charge for which Day had been tried. It was a chance and we took it. Unfortunately, we lost. But we still had Plan B.

While the family and friends of Amy and Jason were decrying the inequities of our justice system, what was even more frightening to consider is that the same judicial finding might also have freed some or all of the other defendants. Had Burdick, Anderson, Sanchez and Floyd not pled guilty, and opted instead to challenge the charges against them in federal court, as Day had, they could have gotten away with murder. What might have been the consequence if the federal charges against them had been pursued and dismissed, and we were subsequently not able to hold them on unrelated charges, as we were with Day? It was a sobering thought, but thankfully it was nothing more than that.

In the end, the harsh reality was that the previous four plea bargains accepted by government prosecutors may have been the best way to go, after all. The heart, however, makes this acknowledgment difficult, if not impossible, for many people, especially those losing loved ones in such a brutal manner, to accept.

By contrast, at the same time that most people around the state were up in arms over the dismissal of federal charges against Day, the reaction was much different at the prison in Cranston, where Day was incarcerated. There, the inmates were celebrating. Once word of Pearson's decision reached ACI officials, it spread quickly through the prison population. Criminals of every sort were hooting and hollering and clanging objects against the bars of their cells. Day returned a conquering hero, and it took some time for the guards to restore order. The reason for the outburst may have been explained as a simple expression of unity for something in which they could all relate; a hatred for the system. But it was still a vulgar, animalistic reaction, and it's the reason they were in cages.

The dismissal of the federal charges against Kenneth Day, while shocking to so many of us, was not so surprising to some others. David Bruck, a veteran death penalty lawyer, was one who had anticipated such a revealing decision. Bruck, who worked with the Federal Death Penalty Resource Project, a federally financed program that provides assistance to court-appointed lawyers in federal capital trials, recognized the significance of the case being entirely local, with no federal interest.

More than anything, Bruck said, the case illustrated a clash of Bush administration principles. While both President Bush and Ashcroft were supporters of the death penalty, he noted, they are also strong supporters of state's rights.

"This case reflects the federalization of the death penalty," he stated, "which would seem to contradict the Bush administration's respect for states' rights in other areas."

He said that carjacking was a crime which was rarely prosecuted in the federal court system to begin with, and in the Shute-Burgeson case there was virtually no federal aspect beyond the fact that the crime occurred in Rhode Island while the victim's vehicle was registered in Massachusetts.

"If respect for states' rights were paramount," Bruck said, "then in this case, it would seem Mr. Ashcroft should not proceed to seek the death penalty."

He further noted that the plea agreements of Day, Floyd and Sanchez were accepted by Ashcroft, while the other two defendants pleaded guilty during the Clinton administration, when the regulations did not require the United States Attorney General's approval. Ashcroft had adopted this regulation in response to the criticism that white defendants were more often allowed to enter into plea bargains than defendants who were members of minorities. In the Shute-Burgeson case, under Janet Reno, one of the first two defendants to plead was white, Burdick, while the other, Anderson, was black. Ashcroft accepted plea deals from Sanchez, who is Hispanic and Floyd and Day who are both black.

In his first six months since taking office in January 2001, Ashcroft rejected plea bargains in at least three capital cases in which the Unites States "Attorney General had recommended accepting the agreement," said Bruck, whose project monitors the federal death penalty.

While the Justice Department would not comment specifically on the Rhode Island case, it did provide numbers on how the death penalty was administered under Ashcroft. Of the twenty-eight cases he had reviewed from February 1 to June 1, 2001, he rejected the death penalty for twenty defendants and authorized it for just eight, a department spokesman reported. The Justice Department would not, however, provide a breakdown by race or state. They also declined to say what the United States attorneys in those twenty-eight cases had recommended.

Bruck is not the only federal death penalty lawyer to proscribe that the Rhode Island case should never have been prosecuted under federal law.

An underlying tenet of American federalism has long held that law enforcement is generally a matter for the states. Since the birth of the nation, capital punishment was authorized for only a small number of national offenses, including espionage, homicide committed on federal property and murder in the course of a bank robbery. This list of condemnable crimes has certainly grown through the years. After the 1932 Lindbergh baby kidnapping, for instance, interstate kidnapping was added to the list. Assassinating the president did not become a federal crime until after the assassination of John F. Kennedy. During the late 1980's, while America was in the middle of the War On Drugs, Congress enacted laws that made certain drug-related murders subject to the death penalty.

By 1994, the number of federal capital offenses increased dramatically when Congress, as part of an omnibus crime bill, adding more than forty crimes for which Unites States prosecutors could seek the death penalty, just one of which was carjacking that resulted in death. That crime was included in the aftermath of a case involving a thirty-four year old Maryland mother who was dragged to her death while trying to rescue her daughter during a carjacking. The enactment of that law and its impact upon convictions that actually lead to an execution, like other federal death-eligible offenses, was tragically misleading.

By and large, the message that the national government has been sending all along is that it's up to the individual nation-states to kill their own. The Feds would only step forward to pull the switch for certain crimes, where there is a clear federal connection. The understanding of this do-it-yourself approach to condemning criminals, if nothing else, was a clear indication to Bruck and others that convicting Day was an improbability, at best, from the get go.

Additionally, under Reno, a United States Attorney in a non-death penalty state could not take into account the absence of the death penalty in deciding whether there was substantial federal interest. When both the state and federal government have jurisdiction to prosecute a crime, Justice Department guidelines suggest that the federal government should take the case only when there is a "substantial federal interest." From 1995 to 2000, Bruck reported that there were twenty-one federal carjacking/murder cases. Figures, he pointed out, which do not include Puerto Rico, where there is a special arrangement with the island's government for the United States attorney to assume jurisdiction of carjacking cases. During the same time frame mentioned, Reno authorized seeking the death penalty against 285 defendants, according to a Justice Department study, only seventeen of which were from the dozen states without the death penalty. Several of those were included in a 1996 case in which Reno decided to seek the death penalty against four reputed members of the Latin Kings street gang, all of whom were tried in Rhode Island federal court on racketeering and murder charges. She had also recently approved taking a case in neighboring Massachusetts, where there also was no state death penalty on the books. That case involved a serial killer nurse, who was accused of murdering four patients and attempting to murder three others at a Northampton veteran hospital. A much larger number of patients who were in her care, some 350 in all, died mysteriously during the seven years she was employed there. In that time, the death rate at the hospital soared, and in one three year period it spiked, when the average number of deaths more than tripled. She later received a life sentence for the deaths of which she had been convicted.

When Ashcroft took over, he changed the guidelines so that the absence of the death penalty in a state could now be a determining factor in deciding whether the federal government would take the case. Even so, in Rhode Island, before the Shute-Burgeson carjacking case, there had been only one other federal prosecution in which the death penalty was an option, and the U.S. Attorney had recommended against it.

Considering all these reasons, when Judge Laguex dismissed the federal charges against Kenneth Day on February 26, 2002, it could not have been completely unexpected. However, the fact remains, the Shutes, the Burgesons, federal prosecutors and David Bruck, all had the same knowledge and had access to this information prior to the trial. The difference being that the families did not have a choice. They had to fight back, to gain justice for Amy and Jason, regardless of the odds. If they had it to do all over again, I'm sure they would have made the same choice.

As it stood, they would be doing just that, only this time in state court.

Chapter 29

If at First You Don't Succeed

The state trial of Kenneth Day was such a long way off, and seemed so completely out of the control of everyone except state prosecutors, that it was difficult to keep it on the front burner. With all that the families had been through, they must have felt the same way. The investigation was complete. There was nothing new to become involved with. It was simply a matter of waiting for a court date to be announced. Life went on. It certainly went on for Burdick, Anderson, Sanchez, Floyd and Day, but not for Amy and Jason.

On April 5, 2002, Jeff Harper suffered a brain aneurysm and died, after nearly two years of blaming himself for Amy's death by not being there to protect her when she needed him most. His family and friends, including the Shutes, had done all that they could to help him get past the guilt and get on with his life, but no one could get through to him.

He spent a lot of time with the Shutes after Amy was killed, just as he had when she was alive. He thought of Erin and Elizabeth as his own sisters, and he didn't want to lose this family as well. For Carol and her two daughters, Harper's presence was difficult for them at times, making the transition into living without Amy more challenging.

In the end, he could not live without Amy. He was interred just three plots away from where she was buried.

Jeff Harper was twenty-six.

Kellie and Nick Surdis were expecting their first child around this time. When her obstetrician originally calculated the date of birth, Kellie knew what the doctor was going to say before she said it: June 9. She felt agonized when she thought about her child being born on the same date that Jason was killed. Fortunately, their daughter came a little earlier. On May 31, Kellie gave birth to a healthy baby girl. The child, however, was born with a large red birthmark on the back of her head, and Kellie couldn't help but notice that it was located in the same exact spot as the mortal wounds Jason suffered almost two years prior.

On July 16, 2002, the Shute and Burgeson families attended Day's trial on robbery charges unrelated to the carjacking/murders. Family and friends of Jason and Amy outnumbered those of the actual victims of the two robbery incidences. Their presence did not go unnoticed by Day, who sought to agitate them and beat them at their own game. In a brazen and vulgar display, he frequently turned toward female family members during the court proceeding and winked or blew kisses at them, particularly Amy's youngest sister, Elizabeth. It would become so frequent and distracting that deputy sheriffs were called upon to position themselves between Day and the courtroom benches where the Shutes and Burgesons were seated.

During closing arguments, Day's lawyer tried to show that his client's accusers were unfairly prejudiced against him, claiming that Day had only been "fingered" in these two incidences *after* he had been arrested for the murders of Amy and Jason, when his picture appeared in the newspaper. He also argued that there were too many discrepancies between the witness testimony of the robbery victims, therefore increasing the chances that they were wrong in identifying Day as their attacker. The prosecution replied that there are photographs of criminals in the news all of the time, and that the victims did not finger Day merely "for the sake of pointing," but because Kenneth Day was the man who had robbed them. Additionally, the prosecution informed the jury that discrepancies between the testimony of witnesses is not unusual, especially when the victims are beaten with baseball bats or have guns to their heads, as the victims in these cases did. But these victims all agreed on one important fact; Kenneth Day attacked them. And the jury agreed, as well.

When the first guilty verdict came in, there were plenty of tears mixed with smiles, which might best be summed up by something Nadine Burgeson told the media afterward; "It was good to see him found guilty of something."

There were seven charges in total, including conspiracy, robbery and assault. Day grinned and clapped sarcastically as the jury's decisions were read.

A motion for a new trial was denied, and on September 5, 2002, Day was sentenced. He received a total of eighty years, forty-five to serve because some of the sentences ran concurrently. Day was technically eligible for parole after fifteen years, but because of the severity of the crime he would most likely not be considered for parole until he served at least two-thirds of his sentence. Therefore, for these robbery charges alone, he would be locked up anywhere from thirty to forty-five years. Whatever time he would be given to serve for his participation in Jason's and Amy's death would be added to this, and Kenneth Day, like three of his four other accomplices, would likely never be a free man again. With that trial still pending, the nightmare for the Shute and Burgeson families was still far from over.

Five days later, September 10, was sentencing day for Gregory Floyd. He was given life, the remainder of which would be spent in federal prison, with no possibility of parole. Judge Lageux made the comment that he would have sentenced Floyd to death had he been given that authority.

Floyd did exhibit remorse for his actions, and when he was given the opportunity to speak he stated that he, himself, believes he deserved the death penalty, a statement that seemed more than a little disingenuous because he was the architect of a plea agreement which specified that he would only waive his right to a trial if his punishment precluded being put to death.

Carol Shute and Nadine Burgeson both gave tearful and emotional vic-tim-impact statements, addressing the killer of their children to let him know how he had torn their families apart.

From past experience, listening to these statements are always very painful, usually dominated by grief or anger, but Nadine Burgeson gave one of the most chilling statements I've ever heard.

I was stunned by her words, which conveyed the only thing she had to look forward to waking up each day, she said, was that it meant she was one step closer to dying and being with Jason again.

I looked around the courtroom seeing the same reaction on the faces of other people who were in the courtroom that day.

The following month, on October 8, 2002, Harry Burdick was sentenced to life in federal prison for his part in the carjacking-murders. Burdick's lawyer attempted to gain clemency from the court by mentioning that his client was a father of two small children. Carol Shute later responded to this sympathy tactic by saying, "He should have thought about his two kids that night."

Burdick, like Gregory Floyd, showed remorse for his actions. He told the court that he did not belong on the streets and that he did not know how to say sorry to the victims' families.

One month later, two more defendants were sentenced for their complicity in murders of Amy Shute and Jason Burgeson. On November 7, Samuel Sanchez became the third defendant sentenced to life in federal prison. But first, the court was subjected to several hours of testimony from a forensic psychiatrist who introduced evidence attempting to depict Sanchez as a victim himself, suffering from a series of mental and emotional disorders that affected his judgment and behavior. Judge Lageux announced that it was "hogwash," and once again stated that he would have given this defendant death, instead of life, if it were in his power to do so.

On November 13, Raymond Anderson received thirty years for his part in the June 2000 murders. Judge Lageux told the courtroom he was sorry, but the sentence had to reflect the fact that Anderson was the least culpable of the five men and that he had cooperated substantially with authorities. Up to fifty-four months could be shaved off his sentence, depending on good behavior.

Family and friends reacted with unanimous dissatisfaction. "Judge Lageux did what he thought was right," Carol Shute told reporters. "But thirty years is not enough. It's not enough."

As 2002 ended and a new year rolled in, there was no news about when Day's state carjacking-murder trial would begin. It was hard to believe when the third anniversary of Amy and Jason's death came and went. And still there was no official word on the trial.

The Burgesons busied themselves that summer organizing a benefit to raise money for the student scholarship fund that they had established in Jason's name. On Sunday, August 17, 2003, a memorial golf tournament was held at Lakeville Country Club. The event raised more than $11,000, which would be awarded to future graduates of Apponequet Regional High School who wanted continue their education in the field of the arts, which Jason so loved.

At the end of the month, on August 29, 2003, it began. Kenneth Day was indicted by the state of Rhode Island on nine charges, including carjacking, robbery, conspiracy and the murder in the deaths of Amy Shute and Jason Burgeson, charges which had been dismissed in federal court the year before.

The families were pleased that the case was finally proceeding. "The longer it drags on, the more painful it is," Mr. Burgeson said. "It's really taking a toll on us, dragging on, and on, and on." Amy's grandmother expressed similar sentiment, saying, "It will be a relief to get all of this over with because every day that they bring something up, it is like going back to day one."

The following month, on September 17, 2003, Day was arraigned in Superior Court. The trial date was not scheduled at that time, but it was expected to get underway by the middle of the following year.

It was nearly four years to the day that Jason and Amy were killed, when the state murder trial against Kenneth Day finally began. On the first day of the pretrial hearing, June 1, 2004, Gregory Floyd was called to the stand. However, the convicted murderer refused to testify or even raise his right hand to be sworn in. The presiding Superior Court Justice, Joseph Rodgers, ruled immediately that the prosecution could introduce Floyd's prior testimony as evidence instead. About his decision not to testify, Floyd commented, "It doesn't matter at this point."

He was wrong. It mattered to everyone, but him. The families were all in attendance, hoping this trial might bring them complete closure, something that had eluded them since June 9, 2000.

In his opening statement, Assistant U.S. Attorney, Gerard Sullivan, gave a riveting twenty-five minute speech which he began by reconstructing the night of the abduction. He beautifully described June 8, 2000, which for Jason and Amy started out as, "one of those endless summer days perhaps enjoyed best by the young." He paralleled Jason and Amy's plans for a night out on the town with what Floyd and Day had on their minds. "While Jason Burgeson told others to bring their friends," Sullivan said. "Kenneth Day told Gregory Floyd to bring his gun."

When his narrative reached the golf course and the murder scene, he pointedly detailed Day's role in the crimes. "After robbery attempts at which Day was present and participated in," Sullivan began, "after Day helped search the SUV, after Day suggested rape, after Day urged Floyd to commit murder, Floyd killed the victims in cold blood with a gun that Day encouraged him to bring. On a day filled with promise, on a day filled with fun, friends and family for Jason and Amy."

Before prosecutors showed a police videotape of the crime scene, several members of the victims' families got up out of their seats and left the courtroom.

It was a moving presentation of facts that certainly left an impression on the jurors.

By comparison, Day's defense lawyer offered only a brief opening statement. In Joseph DeCaporale's five minute dialogue, he focused almost entirely on the testimony given previously by Floyd. "The government in this case will call thirty-eight or so witnesses," DeCaporale said. "I tell you now: You should believe thirty-seven of them because, you see, the government's case is based solely on the testimony of Gregory Floyd. I will argue that his testimony it totally unworthy of belief. His testimony will show he lied on three of four prior occasions."

DeCaporale stated that there was little disagreement about who committed the crimes or what the forensic evidence will show. But, he added, "in order to convict Kenneth Day you need to believe Gregory Floyd beyond a reasonable doubt." He was quick to add that Floyd would not be appearing in court for this trial, just as he had refused to testify earlier that week at the pretrial hearing.

On June 10, 2004, four years and one day after the couple had been murdered, the final defendant in the case was found guilty on all nine charges filed against him relating to the horrific crime. Jurors deliberated for less than five hours over two days before finding Kenneth Day criminally liable in the deaths of Amy and Jason, whose families and friends rejoiced, knowing that he would be given the harshest sentence that the state allows.

Two months later, on August 16, 2004, he was given four consecutive life terms. Unlike a life sentence in federal court, he would be eligible for parole. However, with four life sentences, to be served consecutively, not concurrently, Day would never rob, rape or participate in a murder ever again - at least not outside prison walls.

"The crime committed defies description," said Superior Court Judge Joseph Rodgers at Kenneth Day's sentencing. "These are the most barbaric, senseless, merciless, horrific, dehumanizing crimes that this court has been exposed to in my thirty-plus years as a judge."

When Day was led out of court, the families watched and smiled, knowing it would be the last time any of them would have to look at his face, appeals notwithstanding. The pain of losing a child, an anguish that not even the death penalty for all five defendants would have quelled, would be with them for the rest of their lives, but the four-year courtroom ordeal, at least, was finally over. Perhaps now, they could begin healing, knowing that those responsible were safely behind bars, where they could not cause any other parent the terrible heartache of losing a child.

Whenever someone talks about the murders of Amy and Jason, the reaction is always the same. Invariably, the person nods in painful acknowledgment and let out deep sigh of empathy. From there, some people become instantly emotional. Others just shake their head, refusing to even think about the case because it is too upsetting. Parents usually get angry, appalled by the very thought that someone so precious to them, whom they would give their own lives to protect, could fall prey to homicidal predators. They all recognize that it could just as easily have happened to them, and everyone who is familiar with the circumstances of these murders is moved in some way. Then, at some point, they all say the same thing, describing the crime as the most awful thing they ever heard. This is usually followed by the term, heinous.

People may have their own definition of heinous, and most of these are probably very similar. Being in law enforcement, I have a slightly different perspective on such things, which is shaped by personal experience as well as the theories of others in law enforcement and related fields who have much more experience. Lonnie A. Athens is a respected criminologist who has studied the nature of violent crime exclusively, and in my search to understand what drove these five individuals to kill two innocent people, I turned to his work on the subject. Athens spent more than two decades interviewing violent felons while serving as a consultant on capital murder cases. He has taught criminology at Georgetown University Law Center, and is now an associate professor in the criminal justice department at Seton Hall University. Athens himself survived a childhood of deprivation and brutalization at the hands of his father and other individuals in the surrounding communities. Accepted wisdom would predict that, given his experiences, he'd end up turning to violence himself. He did not, and I was curious to know how he'd beaten the odds, and how Gregory Floyd, Kenneth Day and others like them become killers.

Jason Burgeson's sister Kellie Surdis's victim impact statement shows the pain the family suffered.

"The Johnston police called again; they had a confession and five men in custody. The police called with the answer to the question of "Why?" The answer was a very unsettling one; "Because they felt like it." They robbed Jason and Amy of a combined eighteen dollars, and then they carjacked them and kidnapped them, and killed them for something to do. They didn't know Jason and Amy; they picked them out of nowhere, just two innocent kids. The five felt they needed to get some sick sense of excitement. They were bored with just doing plain old robberies. They needed to spice it up. They had so much time to change their minds. The fifteen minute or so ride from Providence to that golf course, any one of them could have had an ounce of sympathy, to think the game had gone far enough, that there was no need to continue. But they did not. Not one of the five said, 'Hey, we do not have to do this.'"

If anybody knows what makes these people tick, it would be Lonnie Athens. In his seminal 1989 book, *The Creation of Dangerous Violent Criminals*, he defines a heinous violent crime as one in which "people are not only severely injured or killed, but one which involves a secondary factor whereby the provocation is grossly disproportional to the injuries inflicted upon a victim," as was clearly the case in the Shute-Burgeson murders. While there are qualitatively distinct degrees of provocation in the commission of all violent crimes, the ones considered heinous are those that occur with the most minimum provocation.

Athens has stated that, "Most people dread becoming the victim of a heinous violent crime more than any other crime because they fear that without any real provocation on their part, someone could gravely harm them." He said this is justifiable fear in today's society, even for those people who are "most heavily shielded from the vagaries of social life."

Amy and Jason were not high risk individuals for this kind of victimization. When they were abducted, they did not put up a fight; they did what they were told; they believed their kidnappers who told them that they would not be harmed. But they were murdered, anyway, and it is difficult for anyone to understand why it had to happen.

More times than you may think, just as it appears to be the case with Floyd, the perpetrator of such a crime does not have a conscious understanding of what drove him to murder. However, that is not to say that it was an impulse murder. To the contrary, the roots of violence are deep-seeded, and often misunderstood.

Athens believes that many criminologists falsely label all violent criminals as equally violent, or with the same potential for violence. His own studies suggest just the opposite. In other words, there are violent criminals, and then there are dangerously violent criminals. The difference, he says, lies in a particular subject's current stage of criminal development. Like a minor league ball player, a violent criminal has to pass through several different levels, developing further in each before moving on and reaching the Majors. Not very many, actually, get that far.

"Those select few criminals who will commit grievous violent acts with the least amount of provocation are the most violent ones."

This, Athens agrees, invariably raises the question: how does a human being in our supposedly highly civilized society become the type of person who would commit these violent crimes without any apparent moral qualms or reservations?

What makes a person become a dangerous violent criminal is the question with which his life's work has enabled him to answer.

While Athens believes, as do other noted criminology theorists, that these individuals are created, or shaped by the people and experiences who misshaped their lives and perception in perverse and profound ways, the difference is that in Athens' model, the individuals are not spurred to kill because of a singular, even if highly traumatic and life-changing experience. Rather, it is a process, an experiential one, which he refers to as "violentization," and it involves passing through four separate stages, like levels of a complex video game. Each stage is based upon distinct social experiences, the culmination of which is the most dangerous of violent criminals in our society. What makes his theory further unique is the idea that the process can be halted anywhere along the way, before a criminal is transformed into the worst of the worst. However, once the highest level is achieved, it cannot be reversed. Essentially, a killer is made, and will continue on this path until stopped, killed or incarcerated for life.

Athens' theory is the one that makes the most sense to me, and in and of itself is not especially difficult to understand. What is more challenging, and important, is determining where a criminal fits into the Athens model at any given time. Did Gregory Floyd go through the entire process of violentization to become a dangerous violent criminal? What about the others? Were they on their way? For many, including the victims' families, does it really matter? Probably not. But what about others in society who might have fallen prey to Floyd or become victims to other predators?

The real benefit in the pursuit of understanding the criminal mind is using that knowledge to the benefit of society by taking a preemptive action and preventing homicides before they occur. Some people don't think this is feasible, or even possible. Others believe something can be done, including criminologists such as Lonnie Athens. Giving these researches the benefit of the doubt, an extended problem would be what to do if we actually were able to identify an individual who is on the way to becoming one of the dangerous violent criminals we most fear and detest. Can we actually help them, and help ourselves at the same time, by altering their future and preventing the homicides that they are all too likely to commit at some point? And just how far can we go with that knowledge? You want to get these people off the streets at all costs, but how can society contain, or detain, them in our world today? And whose responsibility would it be to act on this knowledge?

In the Philip K. Dick short story *Minority Report* (and the Tom Cruise movie of the same name), the futuristic plot centers around technology that gives certain individuals the ability to see murders before they happen. In a city that has gone six years without a homicide, its Department of Pre-Crime detectives are empowered to act on their foreknowledge, arresting people who are about to commit a murder and imprisoning them.

In that kind of future, motive might have little or no relevance upon a murder investigation, but today it remains essential. Even if Floyd himself honestly did not know why he pulled the trigger of his gun - three times, in fact - there is a reason. It's probably quite complex, and certainly not as simple as saying that Floyd is evil, or blaming an upbringing of poverty, or not knowing his father or even a chemical imbalance, because plenty of people with such disadvantages and afflictions do not evolve into killers.

Richard Rhodes, who has written more than twenty books and has won numerous awards, including a Pulitzer Prize for *The Making of the Atomic Bomb*, wrote his book, *Why They Kill*, which was based largely on Lonnie Athens' studies of violent criminal behavior. "Athens' work," Rhodes observed, "discredits protestations that violence persists because of poverty, race, culture or genetic inheritance....Criminal violence emerges from social experience, most commonly brutal social experience visited upon vulnerable children, who suffer for our neglect of their welfare and return in vengeful wrath to plague us."

This should not be misinterpreted as a shifting of blame onto society for our problems with violent crime. That cannot be done anymore than you can blame society for a disease such as cancer. However, Rhodes believes, an effort to understand and conquer these afflictions has to be made. Since a Pre-Crime Unit to contain murderers does not exist, Athens has come up with what Rhodes and others have deemed to be an effective way to prevent homicide, instead of just picking up the pieces after a murder, as we generally do. Athens contends that this can be accomplished by looking closely at the individuals who commit these horrific acts.

I did not want to delve into the personal background and social experiences of Floyd and the others. However, a general understanding of what makes someone dangerously violent will help us figure out what precipitates unprovoked criminal homicides such as this one.

Athens understands that most people harbor strong feelings of hostility towards these violent criminals who plague our communities, and that they want them caught swiftly and severely punished for burdening them with anxiety and fear over their own and their family's personal safety. What law-abiding citizens are rallying against, according to Athens, is a finished product, the most violent offenders. But where do they come from? How do they evolve?

"Discovering the significant social experiences," Athens said, "which a small number of people have undergone over their lives is a much more difficult task than it may appear. Human social experiences can provide a murky and nebulous domain through which one can quickly and easily lose one's way."

And Athens has worked out a system in that regard.

He believes that people are who they are as a result of the social experiences, in particular the most significant ones, which they have undergone in their lives. This is a factor that other criminologists neglect in their study of criminal behavior. Most studies focus on either internal biology, such as hormonal, chromosomal or brain chemistry, or on external influences from outside their bodies, such as socio-economical and cultural factors. Another school of thought, focusing entirely upon the human mind, links psychopathic or sociopathic considerations as the sole means to a criminally violent end.

"Extreme cultural determinism is as absurd as its biological bedfellow," Athens said. "Of course, neither biological nor cultural determinists ever wish *entirely* to exclude the significance of the other...Both sides, however, seem to share in a type of arithmetical fallacy which argues that causes of events in the life of an organism can be partitioned out into a biological proportion and a cultural proportion, so that biology and culture together add up to 100 percent."

This, of course, is the basis behind the Nature vs. Nurture debate.

The solution to this problem of dualism, according to Athens, "lies not in taking a multidisciplinary approach which would very likely compound the problem, but rather in taking a *holistic* approach which would eliminate this problem altogether." In doing so, if a holistic approach were taken, "violent criminals could be studied in a way which does not wrench their organic bodies apart from their social environments, thereby making it possible for the first time to construct a non-dualistic theory of their creation," and essentially becoming a bridging concept, fusing together the study of the bodies of criminals with the study of their social environments. Both multidisciplinary and conventional approaches, by contrast, keep these torn asunder.

The basic tenet behind Athens' theory is a four-stage process, made up of levels of their own. The first stage, he calls "*Brutalization.*" Here, usually very early in life, a person is subjected to "violent subjugation," such as very strict or harsh discipline. "Personal horrification," is needed to proceed through this stage, and this is something that Athens exemplifies as a child watching his mother get routinely abused, physically or mentally. Finally, "violent coaching" is when someone takes an active interest in teaching a child that violence is the way, often the only way, to solve personal problems.

Graduation to the next stage of violentization leaves the subject in what Athens calls "*Belligerency.*" This is where a dangerous and violent attitude develops in the subject. Typically, fantasies of revenge are formed, in which the subject realizes that he must do something so as not be further brutalized, and that something is to utilize violence, which he was trained to do, if it becomes necessary. When this resolution to use violence in his future relations with people is made by the subject, they pass onto the next stage of the process of violentization; *Violent Performance.* The subject, now belligerent, acts on this new-found understanding and uses violence at will. The final stage, *Virulency*, is marked by brashness, confidence or cockiness. The successes of previous violent performances have also affected other people, who fear and perhaps admire the subject for his behavior. The subject, in turn, is further emboldened by the adulation, believing he is invincible. The subject enjoys the notoriety and power and does not believe he will be caught, for which Athens uses the terms "violent notoriety" and "social trepidation." Finally, the culminating experience of *malevolency* completes the process of "violentization," and what emerges is a dangerous violent criminal who is capable of heinous and atrocious crimes, such as the one Floyd was responsible for committing.

Chapter 30

Why They Killed

When looking at criminologist Lonnie Athens' model of how a criminal evolves into one that is dangerously violent, some very interesting comparisons can be made with regard to Gregory Floyd. In killing Amy and Jason, it is apparent that Floyd passed into the fourth and final stage of "Violentization," which Athens calls *Virulency*. According to Athens' theory, however, Floyd cannot be considered one of society's most dangerously violent criminals because he was caught before he could undergo further experiences that would have permitted him to complete this stage.

I feel through a better way of understanding violent behavior, we can identify potentially violent criminals and prevent individuals like Gregory Floyd from wreaking havoc on entire families; its worthiness would be indisputable. The always elusive "ounce of prevention" approach is not easily realized, especially in the criminal justice environment whose cure has long been the building of more prisons. Athens' theories seem quite sound, and deserving of a closer look.

In my opinion, when Johnston police first caught up with Floyd in May 2000 he had completed the second stage of *Belligerency*, as evident in his need to own a gun, which he insisted was for personal protection. This 'strike first' attitude is a key element to the advancement through this stage of Athens' "*Violentization*" paradigm. His progression through the third stage, *Violent Performance*, can probably best be illustrated by his arrest sheet. After these defeats (convictions), the violent feat on Buttonhole Golf Course catapulted him into the last stage of "*Violentization*", as exemplified by the sense of power and invincibility that Floyd seemed to feel was observed by at least one of the other accomplices. Raymond Anderson provided sworn testimony in which he described Floyd's behavior in the first few moments after the shootings just that way. "He looked like," Anderson said of Floyd, "I swear he looked like he felt - like he was untouchable. He looked just like he was try-ing to act like Superman or something. You know what I mean? Just pacing, enjoying everything, every little moment of the whole time, just enjoying it and that was it. There was nothing more. He didn't say anything. Sometimes he'd smile. Sometimes he'd just be straight. He didn't - he didn't care."

Burdick, in his initial interview, told us that Floyd confronted him at the gas station after the shootings and said, "I'm a cold-blooded fuckin' killer and proud of it." However, this was not corroborated or presented in court testi-mony.

Floyd's arrogance was displayed in his further actions, which included brazenly riding around the streets of Providence, which he typically frequented, in the car belonging to one of the murder victims. He even left the Massachu-setts plates on the vehicle, as if he did not think that he would get caught.

Richard Rhodes, in his book, *Why They Kill*, about Lonnie Athens and his work, considered this kind of 'seemingly self-defeating behavior' in crim-inals. Athens' theories helped him understand why violent criminals brag about their crimes. "Athens' work," he wrote, "revealed that individuals who decide to use violence need the fearsome respect of their intimates and seek it even at the risk of being caught."

What, then, should be done with dangerous violent criminals and those who are still developing their violent natures when they are apprehended? According to Athens, these are two entirely different questions, which require two very different approaches. For those who have already completed the *Virulency* stage, Athens' research has found that the damage is done, and that these full-fledged dangerously violent criminals already in existence cannot successfully be reformed. The death penalty debate aside for the moment, all that can be done for society, with regard to these individuals, is to lock them up and throw away the key. Or in Athens' words, "The nature of their past experiences makes them more unamenable to any currently devisable rehabilitation efforts."

On the other hand, criminals who have not progressed to the level of the dangerously violent, but are somewhere within Athens' model of "Violentization," remain viable candidates for rehabilitation. Intercession at the earliest possible stage, Athens believes, would pay the highest dividends, with the most effective means of preventing the development of new violent criminals depending heavily upon stopping the experience of "brutalization" from being passed on from one generation to the next. Measures, such as educational campaigns and psychological counseling, include programs that would provide people with alternative and more appropriate, non-violent, means of resolving conflict. Brutalization, however, must to be halted permanently, not just interrupted, in order for any program to effectively prevent an offender from developing further in the process that is "Violentization."

According to Athens, it is easier to stop someone from becoming a violent criminal who preys on people than to convict and imprison him for a long period afterward. He goes on to say, "Similarly, it makes more sense to take steps to rehabilitate a nascent violent criminal than it does later to insure his lengthy imprisonment.."

Violentization is transmitted experientially across generations, Athens observed, as the brutalized evolve into brutalizers, "ensuring that we always have a plentiful supply of new candidates to replace those who lose their lives, are sent to prison or possibly undergo maturational reform." He emphasizes, however, that such violent progression is neither inevitable nor gradual, and that the process from start to finish can take many years or run its course in a matter of months. It also may be interrupted, sometimes for long periods, while women who become dangerously violent generally complete the process much later than men.

With regard to the heinous actions of Gregory Floyd, Athens' studies demonstrate that males typically enter the belligerency stage just prior to their teens, with at least some completing violentization before their mid or late teens. Floyd was nineteen. Athens' work also demonstrates that there is no such thing as an impulsive murder, that they are all consciously considered at some point prior to the lethal action.

Richard Rhodes has said that Athens' model of "Violentization" has stripped away superficialities and exposed the gears and levers of the very apparatus of evil.

Athens' work, he wrote, "discredits protestations that violence persists because of poverty, race, culture or genetic inheritance" He feels that social experiences, especially on children who are neglected, breeds violent criminal behavior.

In that sense, a person like Gregory Floyd could be viewed as a cancer, at least in a metaphoric sense, a plague on society, even evil, if you will, and hated by others for his actions. However, only when he is hated the way Jonas Salk hated polio might something wholly beneficial be derived from such an emotion.

None of this, to reiterate an earlier point, should be construed as an attempt to excuse or exonerate Gregory Floyd for the murders of Amy Shute and Jason Burgeson. Nor am I suggesting that any blame be shifted from any murderer, Floyd and his accomplices included, to ourselves as a society. Rather, to break this cycle of violence, or any cyclical behavior that is detrimental to ourselves and abhorrent to society, it is incumbent upon individuals to recognize that they are at risk, not only of committing serious violent acts, but passing that behavioral trait on to others close to them. Only when this peril is identified and understood can corrective action be undertaken to stop it in its tracks.

As for Harry Burdick, Kenneth Day, Sammie Sanchez and Raymond Anderson, their roles cannot be minimized. They were Floyd's intimates, whose fearsome respect he needed to gain with the use of violence. These young men were all well on their way to following in Floyd's footsteps through the violentization process. Had one or more of them not been sent to jail for life, but instead continued on and completed Athens' fourth stage, there is no telling how many more lives might have been lost along the way.

The true survivors of this tragedy, the families of Amy Shute and Jason Burgeson, continue to grapple with the reason for their loss. The understanding of theories such as *violentization* may tell us more about criminal behavior, but does not explain this. It does not lessen the pain, afford forgiveness or grant peace of mind.

The date June 9, 2000 is forever burnt into the families' memories, much the same way that other dates marking tragedies come so easily to mind, such as December 7, 1941, November 22, 1963 and September 11, 2001.

In the first few months after her brother Jason was killed, whenever Kellie had to write down the present date, she would found herself writing, June 9, 2000. For a long time afterward, the events of that day affected all aspects of her life, not just her emotional state. She started to see the world very differently, and is not proud to admit that when she looked at strangers she felt anger towards them, especially men that had a resemblance to one of her brother's killers. It became a real challenge for her to trust anyone, and just going outside the house created a high level of anxiety.

When people from around Lakeville saw the Burgesons together, they all seemed to recognize them instantly and look at them with pity or just stare at them like they were freaks. That's how Kellie saw it, anyway, and this enraged her. Nadine Burgeson told her daughter that she shouldn't get angry, explaining that people just don't know what to say, and that it wasn't their fault. In her heart, Kellie knew her mother was right, but she could not help how she felt, either.

For Amy's youngest sister, Elizabeth, there was no escape from the constant stares and whispers. Being in a public high school, she felt the gossip the worst, and Carol felt terrible that the girl had to be subjected to this at such an early age. But while it might have been most obvious at school, everywhere she went she felt much the same way Kellie did; like people were looking at her, pointing her out to others and saying things like, "There's that girl. The girl whose sister was killed." Erin was also affected by this unwanted attention, but it was easier for her to escape the scrutiny of the public. While attending Rhode Island College that fall, nobody knew who she was, and she avoided telling the other students her last name.

It got to the point for Kellie that she would avoid going out after dark, and would always carry mace in her purse. She slept with a can on the night stand by her bed. If she could have taken it into her dreams with her she would have because, quite often, when she fell asleep, she would see Greg Floyd, Harry Burdick, Sammie Sanchez, Kenneth Day and Raymond Anderson in her nightmares. Her personal Freddy Krueger, times five.

Similarly, Carol Shute struggled to find anything positive or good in anything or anybody, including herself. The first time she attended a celebratory event, it was a friend's fortieth birthday party. When Carol found herself actually having a good time and laughing, the floor seemed to fall out from underneath her feet all at once. Guilt and grief overwhelmed her and she had to be taken home. She even felt ashamed, despite being among her closest friends. She still could not help but think that they were passing judgment on her, staring at her and condemning her for enjoying herself so soon after her daughter had been killed.

With the help of counseling, she came to understand why she felt that way, and in time she began to recognize that there were plenty of good people in the world, people who really cared. People such as the Rhode Island Victims' Advocacy & Support Center, as well as her employer and co-workers, who supported her and her family in many ways, including allowing her to take multiple leaves of absence to cope with her depression and to attend the numerous trials. All these people, and many others, would renew her faith in humanity. Carol now believes that there is more good in this world than bad, even though you don't hear about the positive as much as the negative.

Kellie found that wisdom is harder still to come by. Earlier in her life, she prayed on a daily basis and attended Church on Sunday with her husband, but Jason's death shook her faith in God, as well. She could not find it within herself at that time to attend services and be thankful. She felt abandoned and angry that there had been no deliverance from evil for Jason. Every time she saw a white SUV on the road (and the more she looked, the more of them she saw) her heart sank and an overwhelming sadness engulfed her. Whenever she went out somewhere and saw a young man wearing a baseball cap backwards, like Jason used to do, and walking with friends or a couple holding hands, she felt the same melancholy and began to cry.

She saw people all the time that looked like her brother, and for a split second she would think that maybe it was him. She thought she must have been losing her mind that this was how it begins, and even the understanding that it was not unusual for people who had experienced traumatic loss to have such dark thoughts and self-delusions, this insight did not make it any easier.

Sometimes, as Kellie drove to her parents' house, she caught herself wondering if her brother was home, and then she was sharply reminded, like the deep, clean slice of a razor, that it was only her mind playing another trick on her. For that brief moment, however, while she was in this pretend world, where things were the way they used to be, she was happy again. It was not a fantasy in which she could indulge frequently, because the cemetery where Jason is buried is on a direct route to her parent's home. She goes there often to visit him. It hurts her to think that she will never again be able to give her brother advice about girls or tell him how proud she is of him or how much she envies the way he just lived life. Never be able to give him a big bear hug and tease him and say, "You may be six feet tall, but I will always be your big sister." Never hear him tease her back and say, "No, I am bigger than you. You are my *little* sister now."

For the Shutes, particularly Carol, the visits to the cemetery are still quite frequent. At every holiday or other special day of the year that Amy had been fond of, Carol places a seasonal knick knack at her daughter's grave to mark the occasion. For Halloween, which Amy so loved, Carol always carves out a jack-o'-lantern for her. So do Amy's friends, and come October, there are many pumpkins and jack-o'-lanterns all around her marker.

But it never gets any easier, Carol has found. There's not a day that goes by that she doesn't think about Amy. She is the first thing on her mind when she wakes up in the morning and the last thing she thinks about before she goes to bed. The tears still come easy and often. Today, when people approach her and praise her for the strength she exhibits in dealing with her pain, she sometimes does not feel deserving, because she knows she is pretending. Inside she still is torn up, no matter what her outward appearance may be. She wore her heart on her sleeve for more than four years, because she could not even begin to heal until the trials were over. The wound has closed somewhat, but it is still open. She discovered in counseling that the pain doesn't go away, you just learn to live with it, and you have to leave the anger behind. Once she came to terms with the fact that she could not change what happened, she understood how important it was to remember all the good memories and to hang on to them dearly. She credits her family and therapy for where she is today. Carol came to realize that her energy would be better spent on Erin and Elizabeth, who deserve a good life and to not be constantly haunted by the memory of their sister. It should not consume the rest of their lives. Recovery and acquiring the ability to move on, however, did not come without Carol making a serious effort to get well. It was a commitment. Every week, for more than three years. And still she struggles at times to hold on to the good memories and to continue moving forward. Recovery, she found out, like life, is a journey, not a destination.

Jason's mother, Nadine, learned the same difficult lesson at a meeting on healing that she attended with her daughter, Kellie. The speaker explained to her that when something happens in our life that is so painful, we sometimes think we are moving forward but we are not. The woman said it was like riding a horse, but you're sitting on it backwards. When she said that, it struck Nadine that this was exactly what she had been doing. She had been going along in her life believing she was moving forward and accepting the things that she could not change, but all the while she had been looking backward in her mind. She realized that of all the things that had happened in Jason's short life, she was dwelling on only the negative. This understanding prompted a desire in Nadine to change.

Unresolved anger was the biggest obstacle that Carol Shute has had to overcome. She knew something had to be done to channel this anger, because it was eating away at her soul. When her counselor first suggested that she place the names or images of Amy's murderers on glass jars and smash them in order to help release some of her pent-up rage, Carol just laughed. However, after she tried it, she didn't laugh anymore. The act of heaving the jars and watching the glass shatter, envisioning that they were Floyd, Day, Burdick, Sanchez and Anderson themselves disintegrating into tiny pieces, was extremely liberating. And it felt damn good. She realized that her neighbors at the time must have thought she had gone completely off the deep end, crying and screaming as she threw glass into the stone fire pit in her backyard. Carol ran out of jars long before all the anger could be released, but it was a helpful exercise.

Carol's counselor has also encouraged her to look for the good in everything that happens, but she would be the first to tell you that there is no good in this. However, she insists that in many ways her relationships with Erin and Elizabeth have benefited from this tragedy. It has brought them all closer together than they otherwise might have been. Carol and her youngest daughters developed an unbreakable adult relationship at a very early age, something that was only just beginning to develop between her and Amy, who was twenty-one when she was killed, and her mother. Carol treasures this closeness with her daughters now, the openness and the honesty, and believes that this is Amy's everlasting gift to them.

It's impossible to say if Amy and Jason might have remained together as a couple had they not been murdered, but they will forever be linked in life, not in death.

Amy and Jason, this book is for you. You are not forgotten.

We are all travelers
Along a path,
How we choose to react to events along
the way,
Is ultimately up to us,
And will determine the final outcome.
There is nothing more to be said, only
done.
So step forth...and
Dance like nobody's watching.

(A poem written by Amy Shute)

THE END

Afterword

Most people, in the end, are judged by the lives they have led, the cumulative sum of their actions and attitudes. Even in a life cut tragically short, the impact each of us has on those around us is personal and indelible. How we treat not only the people that we care about but everyone we come in contact with is the truest litmus upon which we can be judged. In the hearts and minds of those we leave behind, how we are remembered is our only lasting legacy. How unfair then, would it be, to be remembered solely for the circumstances surrounding how we had died?

For Amy Shute and Jason Burgeson, this has been a burden on their mortal memories. Family and close friends knew them for their special individualities. To so many others, however, who know them only from the news coverage following the tragedy of June 9, 2000, they remain mostly unknown or only as one-dimensional victims of a violent crime. This book was written to tell the story of the events leading to their untimely deaths, and to effectively humanize Amy and Jason, showing them for the people they were in life.

I chose only to delve into the killers' very public actions, which caused such egregious harm to so many people that are chronicled in this book. That notwithstanding, in the frustrating attempt to make sense of such a senseless act, various theories into the causality of violent criminal behavior needed to be explored. For me, it was the results of studies made by criminologist Lonnie Athens which shed the most insightful light on the mechanism behind what prompts someone like Gregory Floyd to perpetrate the most heinous of crimes against other human beings. Athens' shows how individual violence is the result of learned behavior, and that society's worst offenders all go through several stages of an experiential process that Athens calls "Violentization." Most appropriate, the criminologist's findings summarily disprove his field's prescriptive reliance on socio-economic factors as the seed of cultural violence. Athens' theories were explored in this book because of the relevance they lend toward the understanding of the violence perpetrated against Amy Shute and Jason Burgeson.

I chose not to probe into the individual and social experiences of Amy's and Jason's killers, because I do not want to lend merit to any of the personal hardships, environmental or biological deficiencies which remotely might be construed as a justification for what they did. The unconscionable action of these murders, and the particular manner in which they carried out this crime, was completely unjustified. Moreover, I feel it would be an insult to the families if any blame at all were to be placed on something other than the lack of humanity and depravity shared by the five men who were responsible for deaths of Amy Shute and Jason Burgeson.

When Amy Shute and Jason Burgeson were held up at gunpoint and kidnapped in the early morning hours of June 9, 2000, their abductors were satisfied with robbery and car theft, crimes with which all five suspects were very familiar. However, this was the first time that any one of the young criminals were known to have participated in a murder. In the aftermath of the double homicide, the police and investigators, along with the families and friends of the victims, began to ask why. Among the many answers that were uncovered, this was one that would never be resolved with any degree of satisfaction.

Just ten days after the arrest of the five murder suspects, the Chief of

Police in Johnston, Rhode Island, told the local media, "When everything is said and done, no one is going to know why they did what they did." Unfortunately, the chief was right. "There's no sense to it," he said emphatically. "There's no reason. It will never make any sense." He went on to say that it was the most bizarre case he has ever been a part of. "This was a hideous crime. It was a really brutal murder."

Violent crime was not something that was new to the chief. Before becoming the top cop in Johnston in 1995, he was a member of the neighboring capital city department for more than thirty years, retiring as a Commander and Deputy Chief in Providence.

Today, the families remain no closer to understanding why Amy and Jason were killed that night. A true explanation has long confounded everyone involved or affected by the case. Some experts believe that, in certain instances, killing can be a team sport, with the decision to take human life fostered within the group dynamic itself, and the only reward seemingly being the approval of their peers. As twisted a rationale as this may be, had any of the suspects acted alone in the robbery and carjacking, murder would not likely have resulted. What precisely induced someone in this group to commit such a heinous crime is what is most difficult to comprehend, but it has been described as a 'wolf pack' mentality, a sanguinary response that left authorities to inaccurately conclude that the senseless taking of the two young lives was nothing more than a robbery and carjacking incident that got out of hand. This summation, though arguable, doesn't begin to resolve the cause and effect conundrum of lesser crime that suddenly turns deadly. When murder is committed without any clear motive, these offenders are sometimes called thrill killers. This may be most accurate because the rush of excitement derived by the killers seemed to occur in the complete absence of any true motivation.

It is further thought that the selection of random victims is a contrivance by which the group's most brutal member asserts his authority. The others play a pivotal role as well, not only supporting the violent action without question, but enjoying their own involvement in the predatory hunt. In the case of Amy and Jason, it can reasonably be asserted that all five of their killers accepted or otherwise arrived at a decision, even if it was not directly discussed, that they were going to kill someone that night. All the ingredients were there. First and foremost, there was a gun. It mattered little who owned the weapon or who was in possession of it up to, and including, the moment it was fired three times. It was *their* gun. And just as all of them were aware of the lethal firepower at their disposal, they understood that 'going to get somebody' in Day's parlance meant more than just robbing someone, at least on that particular day. Otherwise, they would have simply taken Jason's SUV and left the couple behind, alive, content with a brief joyride and whatever money they scored. However, when Amy and Jason were ordered into the back of the stolen vehicle and driven to a secluded golf course in an adjoining town, it was a fulfillment of the suspects' unspoken desire to murder someone, in my assessment. None of them were willing to back down from that charge when it seemed imminent that the lives of the two young strangers in their company would be taken. Maybe each did not want to appear weak to the others, trying to impart some street ideal of machismo.

For little else, what to most people, in a gross understatement, is considered no good reason to harm anyone, the lives of Amy Shute and Jason Burgeson were tragically taken. For their families as well as the team of investigators, including myself, it was only the beginning of a long fight for justice, even after the swift capture of the defendants.

Typically, such a case would be handled by state prosecutors. However, because Rhode Island was one of only a dozen states that did not have the death penalty, the families of the victims and my department together waged a battle to have the case prosecuted by United States Attorneys. A federal carjacking statute had been enacted in 1992 after a Maryland mother was killed during a carjacking. The statute, while allowing a penalty of capital punishment if the crime results in bodily injury or death, also permits sentencing of life imprisonment at the recommendation of federal prosecutors. Our goal was to have the suspects tried at the federal level because it was the only way that a conviction might possibly invoke the sanction of death. However, with no federal inmate executed in the U.S. since 1963, we knew the quest for justice against Amy's and Jason's killers would be a hard-fought one. Also working against us was a dichotomous clash of Bush Administration principles. While President Bush and U.S. Attorney General John Ashcroft are both proponents of the death penalty, they are also strong supporters of states' rights. The U.S. Government did not want to become the official executioner for states who were themselves against condemning an individual to death.

Some semblance of solace, however, was levied upon the recent news in regards to Kenneth Day, who on July 2 was given four consecutive life sentences for his role in the carjacking/murder, upheld by the State Supreme Court of Rhode Island based on a decision by presiding Superior Court Justice Joseph F. Rodgers Jr.

"It is our opinion that the manner in which the subject crimes of carjacking and murder were committed - cruel, heartless, inhumane, malicious, savage and vicious being just a few of the applicable adjectives - alone justifies the imposition of this sentence upon defendant," wrote State Supreme Court Justice William P. Robinson III. "There is nothing in the record indicating tthat defendant has, to this day, shown any real remorse for what he has done, and we note that he apologized to the victims' families only after extensive prodding by the trial justice during the presentence hearing."

Rhode Island Attorney General Patrick C. Lynch, who publicly hailed the ruling, stated in the Providence Journal article announcing the verdict he had spoke to both Amy and Jason's mothers to thank them for "being so strong and perservering" throughout the lengthy legal process that took way too long to come down through the state and federal courts.

There were many other factors working against us, yet despite these challenges, together with the Shutes and Burgesons and a host of local and federal investigators, I entered this legal and moral battle fully confident that good would triumph over evil. Within the context of this struggle, I wanted to be sure that Amy Shute and Jason Burgeson were remembered, and kept in our memories.

This is that story.

Detective Raymond Pingitore

Bibliography

Athens, Lonnie A. *The Creation of Dangerous Violent Criminals*. Illinois: University of Illinois Press, 1992.

Rhodes, Richard. *Why They Kill*. New York: Vintage Books, 1999.

Feb. 2008